MW01679821

Study Guide

Criminal Justice Essentials

STUDY GUIDE

BY SHANNON BARTON-BELLESSA

SUE REID

CRIMINAL JUSTICE ESSENTIALS

NINTH EDITION

WILEY-BLACKWELL

A John Wiley & Sons, Ltd., Publication

This edition first published 2012

Wiley-Blackwell is an imprint of John Wiley & Sons, formed by the merger of Wiley's global Scientific, Technical and Medical business with Blackwell Publishing.

Registered Office
John Wiley & Sons Ltd, The Atrium, Southern Gate, Chichester, West Sussex, PO19 8SQ, UK

Editorial Offices
350 Main Street, Malden, MA 02148-5020, USA
9600 Garsington Road, Oxford, OX4 2DQ, UK
The Atrium, Southern Gate, Chichester, West Sussex, PO19 8SQ, UK

For details of our global editorial offices, for customer services, and for information about how to apply for permission to reuse the copyright material in this book please see our website at www.wiley.com/wiley-blackwell.

A catalogue record for this book is available from the British Library.
ISBN 978-0-470-67121-4 (paperback)

This book is published in the following electronic formats: Wiley Online Library [ISBN 9781118112441]

Set in 11/13 pt Dante by Toppan Best-set Premedia Limited

Printed and bound in Singapore by Markono Print Media Pte Ltd

1 2012

ONTENTS

RODUCTION

The role of crime and justice in the community cannot be overemphasized. The criminal justice system touches every facet of our lives, ranging from the most basic laws that govern the right to freedom and liberties to the right and duty to punishment. In Sue Titus Reid's ninth edition of *Criminal Justice Essentials*, she continues to provide information setting the foundation for a broader study and understanding of the criminal justice system. This *Student Study Guide* (SSG) is the first in the series and is designed both to assist the student with grasping concepts and as a guide in preparing for examinations. As a student, you will take a course in the Introduction of Criminal Justice for a variety of reasons, including as part of your major or minor, to complete general education/foundation studies requirements, or just for curiosity. Regardless of your reason, there are a few things you must keep in mind in preparing for examinations and mastering the material, such as how to study and prepare for classes.

The text is organized into five distinct sections: (1) Introduction to Criminal Justice Systems (Chapters 1 and 2); (2) Entry into Criminal Justice Systems: Policing (Chapters 3, 4, and 5); (3) Processing a Criminal Case: Criminal Court Systems (Chapters 6, 7, and 8); (4) Confinement and Corrections (Chapters 9, 10, and 11); and (5) Juvenile Justice: A Special Case (Chapter 12). Each of these sections will be summarized below.

Chapter 1, Criminal Justice: An Overview, provides an overview of the entire criminal justice system and the processing of a case. This chapter has been fully updated from the eighth edition. New topics in this chapter include a section on physician assisted suicide. **Chapter 2, Crime, Offenders, and Victims**, includes an overview of data collection efforts. The most recent crime statistics available at the time of publication are included in the text. Information has also been added on mentally and physically challenged victims as well as other victim characteristics. More attention is given to specific crimes, with a section now being included on crimes such as child abuse, elder abuse, stalking, cybercrime, white-collar crime, terrorism, animal cruelty, and gun control. **Chapter 3, The Emergence and Structure of Police Systems**, begins the discussion of detection and investigation of crimes. More specifically, this chapter provides a discussion of the historical development and evolution of law enforcement. With this chapter not only have special focus or topic sections been added, but it has also been reorganized, with the section on

International policing being moved toward the end of the chapter. More specifically a section on the evolution of U.S. Customs and Border Protection (CBP) has been added and a special focus on policing on campuses and in other areas, such as shopping malls and high schools, has been included. **Chapter 4, Policing in a Modern Society**, includes an overview of the constitutional issues confronted by law enforcement. The most recent and up-to-date constitutional and case law is included. Special attention has been given to training of law enforcement officers on terrorism and terrorist activities and an enhanced focus on ending racial profiling. **Chapter 5, Problems and Issues in Policing**, includes statistics on problems in policing. Special attention has been given to the issues of domestic violence and affirmative action. **Chapter 6, Criminal Court Systems,** emphasizes the historical development of the court systems. This chapter has been expanded to include a discussion on diversity and the judicial system. **Chapter 7, Prosecution, Defense, and Pretrial Procedures**, provides an overview of the roles and functions of the prosecution, defense, and pretrial procedures in the court process. In addition, the ninth edition now includes sections on the public defender system, assigned counsel systems, and contract attorneys. In **Chapter 8, Trial, Sentencing, and Appeal**, issues surrounding the trial process continue to be of the utmost concern in terms of ensuring the proper disposition of cases throughout the system and the role of the victim in the process. This chapter has been expanded to include a discussion on the role of victims' participation in sentencing, as well as issues of race, gender, and the efforts to control disparity in sentencing. A section on the impact of wrongful convictions has also been added. **Chapter 9, The History and Structure of Confinement**, includes information on the historical development and evolution of the current correctional system. The most recent statistics on the prison and jail populations at the time of going to press have been included. The specific sections on boot camps, the work ethic of prisons, and prison and jail overcrowding have been removed and incorporated into the chapter. **Chapter 10, Life in Prison**, includes an overview of the issues the offender confronts while incarcerated. The ninth edition also includes updated case law and an expanded discussion of rights versus privileges while incarcerated. In addition, special focus has been given to Eighth Amendment prohibitions against cruel and unusual punishment and First Amendment rights to free speech. **Chapter 11, Community Corrections, Probation, and Parole**, covers information on alternatives to incarceration. These include probation, which is an alternative used either as a direct sentence or in lieu of incarceration, and parole, a sentence administered after some term of confinement has been served. Additionally, this section has been updated to include a discussion on the issue of decriminalizing minor drug offenses. Special attention has been given to the passage of legislation such as the Second Chance Act; the use of medical parole; sex offender registration laws; the Adam Walsh Child Protection and Safety Act; and Jessica's Laws. This chapter has further been fully updated to include a discussion on the effectiveness of correctional programming and alternatives as well as the various constitutional issues confronting inmates and administrators. **Chapter 12, Juvenile Justice Systems,** presents a brief overview of the entire juvenile justice system, including the historical development and evolution of handling juveniles separately from the adult system. Data on juvenile delinquency have been updated. The chapter also now includes a specific focus on the increased use of waivers, sending juveniles to the adult court system and into jails and prisons. Other issues such as the increased use of drug courts to address substance abuse issues; institutional types for juveniles; capital punishment; and the deinstitutionalization movement are added.

The purpose of this *Student Study Guide* (SSG) is to provide a variety of different tools to begin to reinforce the material from the text. This book is in no way designed to be all-inclusive but rather acts as a mechanism to assist with comprehending some of the more important concepts. Information in the SSG includes the following:

1. *Learning Objectives:* The learning objectives from the text are reiterated in the *Student Study Guide*. The purpose of including this material again is to reinforce to the student the importance of what should be gained following the review of the chapter.

2. *Summary:* A summary of the chapter is provided. Although many of the important concepts are reviewed in the summary, it is not meant to be the only material you should study for the exam. This is a cursory overview that should be used to guide your understanding but again is not meant to be all-inclusive and should not be substituted for reading your chapter.

3. *Key Terms:* The key concepts are designed as essentially a vocabulary list. All of these terms are included within the chapter and may be found in the Glossary. The key terms will also be used to answer the crossword puzzles and the word searches.

4. *Study Questions:* The study questions are reiterated from the end of the identified chapter. Your instructor may wish to revisit these or assign them for points. These questions are a good way to integrate the material and to generate your own perspectives during class.

5. *Activities:* The activity section of the SSG is designed to help the student think about how to apply the concepts learned in the chapter. These activities may be completed by you on your own or they are designed to be used as assignment material by your instructor. Most of the chapters include questions that require students to peruse their state criminal justice webpage. These activities are designed for the student to gain a better understanding of general information put into practice.

6. *Student Study Guide Practice Questions:* A total of 10 true/false; 10 multiple-choice; and 10 fill-in-the-blank questions are provided for each chapter. Students should strive to answer these questions without referring back to the text. These questions provide a general format that your instructor may wish to use on the exam.

As previously mentioned, this study guide is designed to assist you with better understanding the material. No material, however, can replace the process of time management, reading the material for major concepts, and reinforcement of terminology. As in any introductory course, there is a lot of, normally new, material presented in a short amount of time (ordinarily 10 or 16 weeks). Be sure to read and review the material on a daily basis. Not only does this reinforce what you have already learned, but you will be better prepared for your examination(s). Many students choose to read all of the chapters and begin studying one or two days before the exam. Although there may be isolated exceptions where this may work, this method for comprehension is certainly not recommended or typically manageable. Be sure to take good notes from class and supplement them with the text. Use the SSG to ensure that you understand the concepts. Be prepared to ask your instructor questions if you do not understand the material. Overall, it is the hope of the author that this supplemental material will assist the student in comprehending the primary text and in succeeding in better understanding and appreciating the criminal justice system.

TRODUCTION TO IMINAL JUSTICE TEMS

MINAL JUSTICE: A OVERVIEW

LEARNING OBJECTIVES

After reading this chapter, you should be able to do the following:

- **List, define, and illustrate the major punishment philosophies**
- **Discuss the importance and impact of discretion in criminal justice systems**
- **List and describe briefly the major components of criminal justice systems**
- **Explain the difference between *civil law* and *criminal law***
- **Contrast the *inquisitory* and the *adversary* systems**
- **Explain what is meant by constitutional limits on criminal law**
- **List and analyze the sources of criminal law**
- **Define *crime*, explain how crimes are classified, and discuss the general elements of a crime**
- **Explain criminal *defenses***
- **Comment on the meaning and current legal status of physician assisted suicide (PAS)**
- **Explain the pros and cons of including sexual behavior, child pornography, and the use of marijuana for medicinal purposes within the criminal law**

Criminal Justice Essentials: Study Guide, Ninth Edition. Shannon Barton-Bellessa.

CHAPTER OUTLINE

KEY TERMS

administrative law
adversary system
AIDS (acquired immune deficiency syndrome)
attempt
attendant circumstances
case law
causation
civil law
common law
crime
criminal
criminal justice system
criminal law
cruel and unusual punishment
defenses
deterrence
discretion
due process
equal protection
euthanasia
felony
general deterrence
incapacitation
individual deterrence
injunction
inquisitory system
jurisdiction
just deserts
legal duty
mala in se
mala prohibita
mens rea
misdemeanor
Model Penal Code (MPC)
negligence
physician assisted suicide (PAS)
rehabilitation
retribution
sanction
statutory law

CHAPTER SUMMARY

This chapter is the first of two overviewing the criminal justice system and criminal law. The chapter begins with a discussion of the philosophies of punishment that underlie the creation of laws, and that also influence enforcement of those laws and responses to violations: for example, sentencing and incarceration or their alternatives. The punishment philosophies guiding the criminal justice system include: **incapacitation**, **retribution**, **rehabilitation**, **deterrence** (**both specific and general**), and **reparation or restitution**. The philosophical concept of retribution underlies all others. Without the need for punishment in its truest connotation there would be no need to create a separate system designed to respond to behaviors deemed outside of acceptable societal limits. Since the 1970s in the United States, the **"Get Tough on Crime"** movement, which includes the philosophies of deterrence and retribution, often combined in the **just deserts approach**, has dominated the field of criminal justice. The underlying assumptions of getting tough on crime presume that individuals are thinkers with the capacity for free will and therefore rational in their decision-making processes and should be punished accordingly. This ideological approach to the creation of criminal justice policy emphasizes the need to punish the offense (just deserts, deterrence, and incapacitation) rather than the offender (rehabilitation). Despite the focus of the criminal justice system on holding individual offenders accountable for their actions, however, rehabilitative approaches to prevent and respond to criminal behavior are increasingly being used. Although one approach to crime is at the forefront in policy, systematic punishment-oriented responses to criminal behavior co-occur.

The second section of the chapter begins by discussing the role of **discretion** in administering punishment. The concept of discretion permeates the entire criminal justice system process, beginning with a law enforcement officer's decision on how to respond to behavior, the prosecutor's decision to charge, the courtroom workgroup's involvement in plea bargaining, the judge's decision to sentence, and ultimately the correctional system representative's decisions on where to detain and ultimately when to release offenders. Discretion is impossible to eliminate from the criminal justice system; however, there are mechanisms to control its use and/or limits, such as law enforcement policies on arrest and detention and the issuing of sentencing guidelines. If left unchecked, discretion can result in abuses in the system that may ultimately lead to wrongful convictions or unfair disparities in the treatment of defendants and victims.

The next section of the chapter provides an overview of the various components of the criminal justice system (**police**, **prosecution**, **courts**, and **corrections**) that will be discussed in more detail in the remaining chapters. This section is presented for illustrative purposes and to establish the framework for a system based upon reciprocity and cooperation between all actors in the criminal justice system. As discussed in the chapter, one must keep in mind that a case may enter the system when a crime is reported to police or when police observe the behavior. However, not all persons arrested proceed to the end of the criminal justice system.

There follows an overview of **criminal law**, which is the crucial basis for all criminal justice systems. The legal system distinguishes between criminal and civil law. These distinctions exist not only in legal responsibility but also in the burden of proof required to determine guilt. A criminal justice system is based on a society's willingness to grant legal authority to some individuals to impose punishment. Criminal law provides that foundation in modern societies and has existed for centuries, predating and forming the basis for much of our civil law.

Criminal justice systems may be based on either the **adversary** or the **inquisitory model**. U.S. systems follow the **adversary model**, in which all accused persons are presumed innocent and the state must prove their guilt beyond a reasonable doubt. The creation of the adversarial system presumes essentially a winner and a loser. Therefore, legal mechanisms are established in a manner that requires the prosecutor to "fight" (advocate) on behalf of the state (the victim serves as a witness to the crime) and the defense to "fight" (advocate) on behalf of the accused (whether that is with or without representation). In contrast is the **inquisitory system**, in which the accused are presumed guilty and must prove their innocence. Although not defined within the modern legal realm, the inquisitory system can in fact manifest itself through law enforcement practices best illustrated by the style of policing to be discussed in later chapters. The adversary system is characterized by **due process** and **equal protection**. These concepts define the basic rights outlined by the U.S. Constitution providing protections for individuals processed through the U.S. criminal justice systems. Other constitutional limitations include the prohibition of statutes that are vague or too broad and the outlawing of cruel and unusual punishment.

Criminal law emerges from statutes enacted by the legislative branches of government, administrative rules and regulations, constitutions, and court decisions. All of these are important sources of law. Further, the equal protection clause of the **Fourteenth Amendment** means that, in general, the government may not infringe on the rights of persons solely because of characteristics such as race, age, national origin, ethnicity, religion, or gender. Likewise, other constitutional protections include the **Eighth Amendment** protections against cruel and unusual punishment; the **Fourth Amendment** protection against unreasonable search and seizure; and the **Sixth Amendment** providing the accused the right to have the assistance of counsel in all criminal prosecutions.

The next section of the chapter includes a discussion of the various sources of criminal law. **Statutory law** applies only to the **jurisdiction** in which it is passed. Statutes define the procedures that are appropriate for law enforcement (**procedural law**), and define the elements necessary for an act to constitute a violation for the civil or criminal law (**substantive law**). Further sources of law include that which comes from court decisions (**case law**) and law that is derived from or influenced by customs, tradition, or judicial decisions (**common law**). Another form of law, **administrative law**, is delegated by state legislature and Congress to all rule-making by state and federal agencies.

The chapter then proceeds with a discussion of the concept of **crime**. Defined as an "act or omission prohibited by law for the protection of the public, the violation of which is prosecuted by the state in its own name and punishable by incarceration," crime sets the foundation for the creation of criminal law and the behaviors that legally fall within criminal justice systems. Crimes are classified as serious (**felonies**) or less serious (**misdemeanors**). Crimes may be classified as ***mala prohibita***, criminal because they are so designated by society (e.g., drug offenses, prostitution, etc.), or ***mala in se***, criminal *per se* (e.g., murder, theft, etc). Within this framework certain elements of a crime must exist and be proven before a person is convicted. Those elements include an illegal act that concurs with a guilty mind, **causation**, and, for some crimes, **attendant circumstances**. Some acts that fit these elements may not be considered criminal because the accused has an acceptable defense. The intent requirement is further outlined in the **Model Penal Code (MPC)**.

Finally, the chapter ends with a discussion of some of the more controversial acts or violations of law that have been debated by scholars, politicians, and the general public alike: for example, behaviors or acts such as the legality of **physician assisted suicide**. The debate surrounding the ability of a person to die with dignity and the morality of a physician providing mechanisms for the taking of life continue. The issues surrounding other behaviors where morality is the overarching concern, such as sexual activity between consenting adults, child pornography, and medical marijuana, are reviewed. The ultimate reach of the criminal law is briefly reviewed and concludes this chapter, setting the foundation for the remainder of the text.

KEY TERMS

administrative law Rules and regulations made by agencies to which power has been delegated by a state legislature or by the U.S. Congress. Administrative agencies investigate and decide cases concerning potential violations of these rules.

adversary system One of two primary systems for settling disputes in court. In a criminal case, the accused is presumed to be innocent. A defense attorney and a prosecuting attorney attempt to convince a judge or a jury of their versions of the case. *See also* **inquisitory system.**

AIDS (acquired immune deficiency syndrome) A serious disease that attacks the immune system; it is communicated through exchange of body fluids, especially during sexual activity and blood transfusions, but it can also be transmitted in other ways. The disease can be treated, but there is no cure.

attempt In criminal law, refers to a crime that may be defined as involving a *substantial* step toward the commission of a crime, combined with the *intent* to commit that crime.

attendant circumstances Facts surrounding a crime, which are considered to be a part of that crime and that must be proved along with the elements of the crime.

case law Legally binding court interpretations of written laws or rules made by the courts. *See also* **common law.**

causation In criminal law, the requirement that the act charged be the *cause* of the harmful consequence(s).

civil law Distinguished from criminal law as the law that pertains to private rights.

common law Broadly defined, the legal theory and law that originated in England and is also common in the United States. More specifically, common law consists of the guidelines, customs, traditions, and judicial decisions that courts use in decision making. It is contrasted with *constitutions* and *written laws*.

crime An illegal act of omission or commission that is punishable by the criminal law.

criminal A person found guilty of an act that violates the criminal law.

criminal justice system The entire system of criminal prevention, detection, apprehension, trial, sentencing, punishment, and parole, probation, or other forms of supervision within the community.

criminal law Statutes defining acts so offensive that they threaten the well-being of the society and require that the accused be prosecuted by the government. Criminal laws also prescribe punishments that may be imposed on offenders.

cruel and unusual punishment The punishments prohibited by the Eighth Amendment to the U.S. Constitution, as interpreted by the courts. Some examples are torture, prison conditions that shock the conscience, excessively long sentences, and the death penalty for rape but not murder.

defenses Responses by the defendant in a criminal or civil case. They may consist only of a denial of the factual allegations of the prosecution (in a criminal case) or of the plaintiff (in a civil case). An *affirmative defense* occurs when the defense offers new factual allegations in an effort to negate the charges.

deterrence A punishment philosophy based on the assumption that the acts of potential offenders can be prevented. *Individual deterrence* refers to the prevention of additional criminal acts by the specific individual being punished; *general deterrence* refers to the presumed effect that punishing one offender will have on other potential offenders.

discretion In a criminal justice system, the authority to make decisions based on one's own judgment rather than on specified rules. The result may be inconsistent handling of offenders, as well as positive actions tailored to individual circumstances.

due process The constitutional principle that a person should not be deprived of life, liberty, or property without reasonable and lawful procedures. Due process must be provided in any adult criminal proceeding, including postconviction procedures, such as prison disciplinary hearings or parole revocations. Many aspects of due process have been extended to juvenile court proceedings.

equal protection All persons under like circumstances must receive essentially the same treatment in the criminal justice system; they may not be discriminated against because of race or ethnicity, gender, minority status, disability, nationality, religion, or sexual orientation. Not all jurisdictions recognize all of these categories.

euthanasia Painlessly ending the life of another, often at that person's request, because the individual is suffering intense pain that cannot be controlled and is near death as the result of an incurable disease. It is considered to be an act of mercy and may be referred to as *mercy killing*. The practice is illegal in most jurisdictions. *See also* **physician assisted suicide (PAS)**.

felony A serious offense, such as murder, armed robbery, or rape. Punishment ranges from execution to imprisonment in a state or federal institution but also includes probation, community work service, fines, and other less punitive sanctions, as well as a combination of these measures.

general deterrence *See* **deterrence**.

incapacitation A punishment theory usually implemented by imprisoning an offender to prevent the commission of any other crimes by that person. In some countries (and in earlier days in the United States), incapacitation involves mutilation, such as removing the hands of thieves and castrating sex offenders.

individual deterrence *See* **deterrence**.

injunction A remedy issued by a court to order a person or an agency to do something or stop doing something; based on a request by a party who petitions the court for the relief. There are several kinds of injunctions, including those that are preliminary (until a further hearing), partial, temporary, or permanent.

inquisitory system One of two primary systems for settling disputes in court, in which the defendant must prove his or her innocence, in contrast to the **adversary system**, which has a presumption of innocence, requiring the state (or federal prosecutors in federal cases) to prove the defendant's guilt beyond a reasonable doubt.

jurisdiction The lawful exercise of authority; the area within which authority may be exercised, such as the geographical area within which a particular police force has authority. Courts may have *original jurisdiction* to hear the case; if more than one court has authority to hear the same case, those courts have *concurrent jurisdiction. Exclusive jurisdiction* means that only one court may hear the case. *Appellate jurisdiction* is the power of a court to hear a case on appeal.

just deserts The belief that those who commit crimes should suffer for those crimes; also the amount or type of punishment a particular offender deserves.

legal duty An obligation to another that is imposed by law, such as the duty of a parent to go to the rescue of his or her child.

mala in se Actions that are intrinsically immoral, such as murder, forcible rape, and robbery.

mala prohibita Actions, such as the possession of small amounts of marijuana, that are wrong because legislation prohibits them, although there may not be general agreement that they are wrong in themselves.

mens rea The required criminal intent of the accused at the time an alleged criminal act was committed.

misdemeanor A less serious offense, punishable by a fine, probation, or a short jail term, in contrast to a felony, a more serious crime.

Model Penal Code (MPC) A systematized statement of criminal law by the American Law Institute. This code is often used as the model for drafting state criminal statutes.

negligence In law, an act that a reasonable person would not do, or would not fail to do under similar circumstances. Liability for negligence does not require a criminal intent.

physician assisted suicide (PAS) An act by a physician that enables a patient to take his or her own life in a relatively painless way, such as prescribing a sufficient amount of drugs to kill a person.

rehabilitation A punishment philosophy based on a belief that the offender can and will change to a law-abiding person through treatment programs and facilities. Rehabilitation may be most likely to occur in community-based programs rather than during incarceration in penal institutions. The *rehabilitative ideal* is embodied in specific treatment facilities, such as those for substance abuse offenders, as well as by use of probation, parole, the indeterminate sentence, and the juvenile court.

retribution *See* **just deserts**.

sanction A penalty or punishment that is imposed on a person in order to enforce the law.

statutory law Law that the legislature has originated and passed by written enactment and that has been signed by the state's governor (or, in the case of federal law, by the president of the United States).

STUDY QUESTIONS

These questions are found at the end of your chapter. Your instructor may wish to revisit these or assign them for points. These questions are a good way to integrate the material and to generate your own perspectives during class.

1 Briefly summarize some violent crimes that have occurred on U.S. soil.

2 Explain and distinguish among deterrence, rehabilitation, incapacitation, and retribution. Explain how these punishment and sentencing philosophies relate to the justice model of punishment.

3 Discuss the punishment implications of the examples discussed in Criminal Justice Systems Dilemma 1.1.

4 How do you think discretion should be regulated in criminal justice systems? Discuss the process in terms of specific personnel, such as police, prosecutors, judges, and juries. Consider your answer at the end of the course to determine whether your personal views have changed.

5 Contrast civil and criminal law.

6 Distinguish between the adversary and the inquisitory systems of criminal justice.

7 Explain the meaning of due process and equal protection. What other constitutional limitations are placed on criminal law and included in this chapter?

8 Do you think capital punishment is cruel and unusual punishment? How about a life sentence without parole for drug possession? For drug sales? Would your answer to the last two questions depend on the amount of drugs?

9 List and discuss the sources of criminal law.

10 How are crimes classified?

11 Discuss the basic elements of a crime.

12 What are criminal defenses?

13 Explain what is meant by physician assisted suicide (PAS) and the current legal status of this practice.

14 Should the criminal law be used to control any or all of the following: premarital sex, extramarital sex, same gender sex, driving while intoxicated, use of seat belts?

15 Analyze the U.S. Supreme Court decision concerning the sexual behavior of gay men.

16 What position should criminal law take on the use of marijuana for medicinal purposes?

LEARNING ACTIVITIES

1.1 The importance of the role that crime plays in everyday life cannot be overemphasized. One way to ascertain the level of interest within your community is to review the local newspaper to determine how much attention is given to crime in your local community. Pick one newspaper publication that has a daily distribution cycle. Review the first section of that paper for five days in a row. Chart the following: (1) Identify the newspaper and the dates explored; (2) How many crime stories appeared in the first section of this newspaper by day and total for the five-day period?; (3) Given the attention to crime in this newspaper, in the space provided below discuss the significance of crime in your community; (4) Based on the information provided in these stories, which philosophy of punishment do you believe is followed in the identified community and why?

1.2. The differentiation between felonies and misdemeanors is often misunderstood by the general public. Using the criminal codes for your state, list the levels of seriousness for each offenses category, e.g., Felony A, B, C, etc. Using the same newspaper articles identified in question 1.1, how many of those crimes constituted misdemeanors? How many crimes constituted felonies? Did the level of seriousness impact where the crime stories occurred in the newspaper? Explain your answer.

1.3 One of the most widely misunderstood concepts in the criminal justice system is that of the legal duty to act. Using the following scenarios, identify whether the person(s) had a legal or moral duty to respond. Explain your answer and be prepared to discuss your responses in class.

1.3a You are a trained off-duty volunteer emergency medical technician (EMT). You are driving home one night from a basketball game and you approach a two-vehicle accident. The road is blocked so you cannot proceed through. Upon recognizing an accident has occurred, you get out of your vehicle and approach the scene. You notice that the female driver in vehicle one is badly injured and gasping for breath. You look to vehicle two and notice that the male driver there has a gash on his forehead but does not appear to be in imminent danger. You make the choice to call for emergency assistance and treat the driver in vehicle two. While assisting the male driver and waiting for the response, the driver of vehicle number one dies. Did you have a legal duty to respond to driver one? Why or why not? Explain your answer.

1.3b You are a trained on-duty nurse. You are driving to the pharmacy to pick up a batch of flu shots. While driving you approach a two-vehicle accident. The road is blocked so you cannot proceed through. Upon recognizing an accident has occurred, you get out of your vehicle and approach the scene. You notice that the female driver in vehicle one is badly injured and gasping for breath. You look to vehicle two and notice that the male driver there has a gash on his forehead but does not appear to be in imminent danger. You make the choice to call for emergency assistance and treat the driver in vehicle two. While assisting the male driver and waiting for the response, the driver of vehicle number one dies. Did you have a legal duty to respond to driver one? Why or why not? Explain your answer.

1.4 Pick a crime story from a reputable news media outlet, e.g., newspaper (in print or online) or magazine (e.g., *Time*, *U.S. News & World Report*, etc.). Make/print a copy of the story. Based upon your reading of the event, did the various actors in the criminal justice system (police, prosecutors, and judges) follow either the adversarial model or the inquisitory model to process the case? In the space below, provide evidence to support your response.

STUDENT STUDY GUIDE PRACTICE QUESTIONS

True or False

1.1 The criminal justice system was designed to prevent people from violating its rules and to sanction, or impose legal punishment on, those who do.

1.2 The concept of general deterrence assumes that the individual should be punished to prevent society from committing a future crime.

1.3 The concept of individual deterrence assumes that the individual should be punished less harshly to prevent him or her from committing future crime.

1.4 A case may enter the criminal justice system after it has been reported to the police or when police observe behavior that appears to be criminal.

1.5 Suspects only proceed to trial upon pleading innocent to a charge.

1.6 An act is not considered a crime if the attempted activity/behavior is not completed.

1.7 The Communications Decency Act of 1990 was one attempt by Congress to regulate and prevent children from viewing pornography online.

1.8 Due process rights are found in the Eighth Amendment to the U.S. Constitution.

1.9 The equal protection clause of the Fourteenth Amendment means that, in general, the government may not infringe on the rights of persons solely because of characteristics such as race, age, national origin, ethnicity, religion, or gender.

1.10 Substantive laws define the procedures that are appropriate for law enforcement.

Multiple Choice

1.11 Which philosophy of punishment is based on the premise that human behavior is the result of antecedent causes that may be known by objective analysis and that permit scientific control?

a Rehabilitation
b Deterrence
c Incapacitation
d Retribution

1.12 The assumption that an individual who commits a burglary fully comprehends and has the ability to weigh the costs of the offense (potential for punishment) over the benefits of the crime (monetary gain) describes which philosophy of punishment?

a Rehabilitation
b Deterrence
c Incapacitation
d Retribution

1.13 The process of using your own judgment to make decisions describes the use of:
- a Purposeful reasoning
- b Discretion
- c Malice
- d Acumen

1.14 Which of the following statements best describes the ability to control discretion in the criminal justice system?
- a The use of discretion may never fully be eliminated in the criminal justice system
- b The use of discretion may be controlled through policy development
- c Discretion occurs at all levels of the criminal justice system
- d All of the above

1.15 Criminal law is best described as:
- a A vehicle for legal redress for those who have been harmed by others
- b A legal process used to regulate marriage and divorce or dissolution
- c A legal process that provides the basis for the actions that take place in the criminal justice systems
- d A legal process used to regulate the handling of dependent and neglected children, and the inheritance of property

1.16 A law enforcement officer stops an individual for driving 50 mph in a 35 mph zone. Upon approaching the vehicle, she notices a plume of sweet-smelling smoke wafting from the vehicle. Suspecting that the passengers may be smoking marijuana, she asks the passengers to step out of the vehicle and she proceeds to search the car. This type of stop and search of a vehicle is governed by which type of law:
- a Procedural law
- b Substantive law
- c Case law
- d Common law

1.17 Laws governing crimes of morality such as sex between consenting adults are known as:
- a *Mala in se*
- b *Mala prohibita*
- c *Voir dire*
- d Attendant circumstances

1.18 Which approach to the criminal justice system presumes that the accused are innocent?
- a Inquisitory
- b Disciplinary
- c Adversary
- d None of the above

1.19 Which approach to the criminal justice system places a greater emphasis on conviction than on the process by which that conviction is secured?
- a Inquisitory
- b Disciplinary
- c Adversary
- d None of the above

1.20 Failure to act may also constitute a crime but only when a person has a(n) _____ to act.

a obligation
b legal duty
c moral code
d None of the above

Fill-in-the-Blank

1.21 _____ may be defined as an "act or omission prohibited by law for the protection of the public, the violation of which is prosecuted by the state in its own name and punishable by incarceration."

1.22 _____ are classified as less serious offenses and are generally punishable by a short jail term, fine, probation, or a combination of these or other penalties that do not involve incarceration in a secure facility.

1.23 _____ are classified as more serious offenses and are normally punishable by more than one year in jail, incarceration in a prison, or capital punishment.

1.24 _____ refers to acts that are considered criminal in nature.

1.25 _____ refers to acts that are not universally regarded as criminal; they are criminal because the legislature has designated them as crimes.

1.26 The term _____ refers to the mercy killing of individuals.

1.27 The _____ model of punishment is based on deterrence and retribution, and constitutes a reaction against the perceived ineffectiveness of rehabilitation.

1.28 For some crimes the prosecution must prove the existence of _____ which are facts surrounding an act.

1.29 In the crime of conspiracy, which involves an agreement between two or more people to commit an illegal (or, in some jurisdictions, an unlawful) act, the _____ constitutes the act.

1.30 For an act to be a crime, the _____ and the _____ must occur together.

CROSSWORD

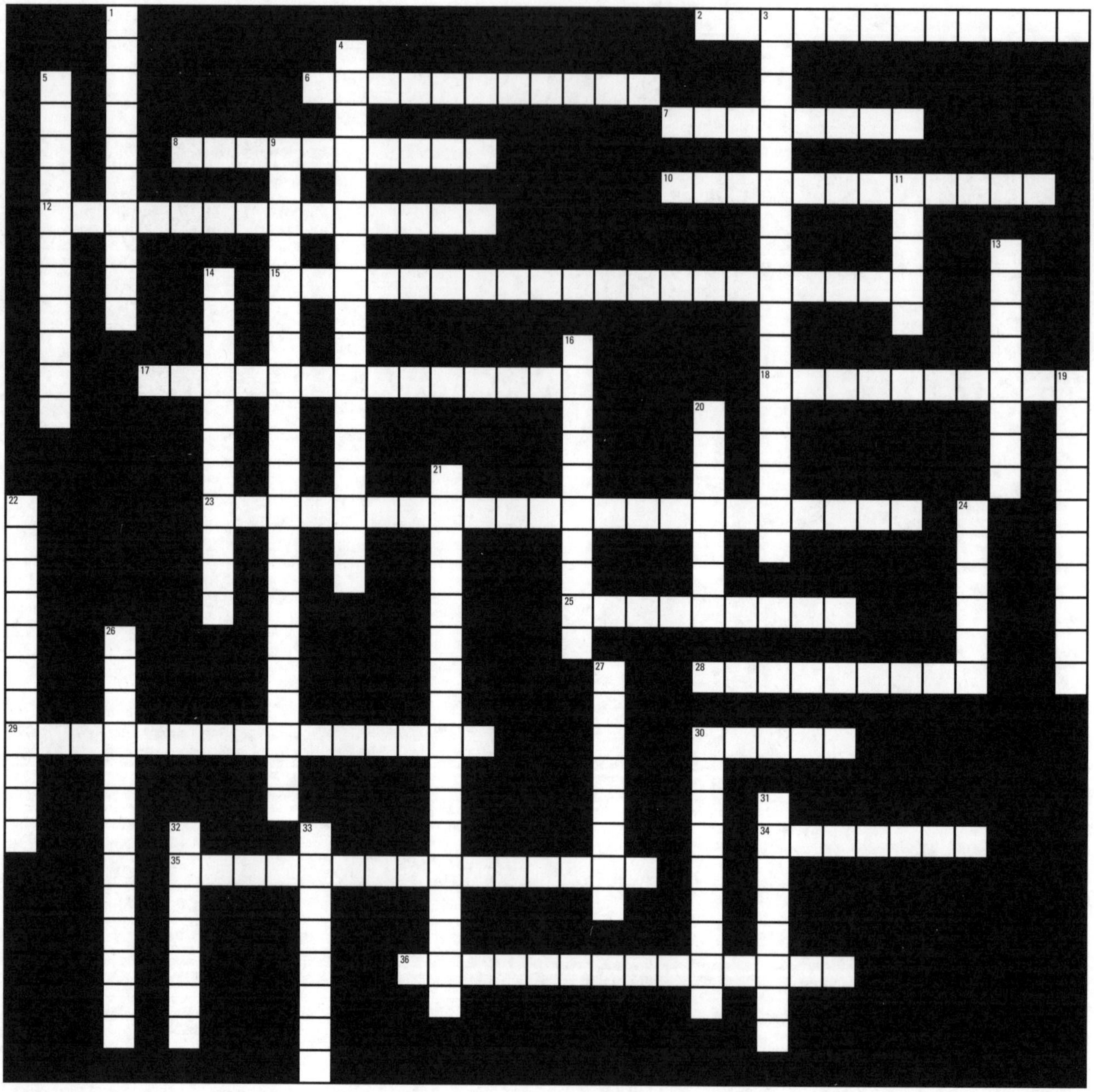

ACROSS

2 Law that the legislature has originated and passed by a written enactment. (2 words, no spaces)

6 The belief that those who commit crimes should suffer for those crimes; also the amount or type of punishment a particular offender deserves to receive.

7 Distinguished from criminal law as that law pertaining to private rights. (2 words, no spaces)

8 In the criminal justice system, authority to make decisions based on one's own judgment rather than on specified rules.

10 The lawful exercise of authority; the area within which authority may be exercised, such as the geographical area within which a particular police force has authority.

12 A punishment theory usually implemented by imprisoning an offender to prevent the commission of any other crimes by that person.

15 A form of the deterrence punishment philosophy referring to the prevention of additional criminal acts by the specific individual being punished. (2 words, no spaces)

17 Model proposals developed by legal scholars of the American Law Institute covering issues such as kinds of culpability and intent. (3 words, no spaces)

18 A court order prohibiting a person or persons from acting in a certain manner.

23 Facts surrounding a crime, which are considered to be a part of that crime and which must be proved along with the elements of the crime. (2 words, no spaces)

25 In criminal law, the requirement that the act must be the cause of the harmful consequence.

28 An element of a crime. The alleged offender's lack of action may be a crime only if he or she was required by law to act in a certain manner. (2 words, no spaces)

29 All persons under like circumstances must receive essentially the same treatment in the criminal justice system; they may not be discriminated against because of race, gender, minority status, ethnicity, disability, or religion. (2 words, no spaces)

30 An illegal act of omission or commission that is punishable by the criminal law.

34 A factor in an element of a crime, an act.

35 One of two primary systems for settling disputes in court. The accused is presumed to be innocent. A defense attorney and a prosecuting attorney attempt to convince a judge or a jury of their versions of the case. (2 words, no spaces)

36 A punishment philosophy based on a belief that the offender can and will change to a law-abiding citizen through treatment programs and facilities.

DOWN

1 The constitutional principle that a person should not be deprived of life, liberty, or property without reasonable and lawful procedures that must be made available in any criminal action, including post-conviction procedures such as prison disciplinary hearings or parole revocations. (2 words, no spaces)

3 Rules and regulations made by agencies to which power has been delegated by a state legislature or by the U.S. Congress. Administrative agencies investigate and decide cases concerning potential violations of these rules. (2 words, no spaces)

4 A form of the deterrence punishment philosophy referring to the presumed effect that punishing one offender will have on other potential offenders. (2 words, no spaces)

5 Statutes defining acts so offensive that they threaten the well-being of the society and require that the accused be prosecuted by the government. (2 words, no spaces)

9 The entire system of criminal prevention, detection, apprehension, trial, and punishment. (3 words, no spaces)

11 _____ and unusual punishments are prohibited by the Eighth Amendment to the U.S. Constitution, as interpreted by the courts. (1 word)

13 Actions that are intrinsically immoral, such as murder, forcible rape, and robbery. (3 words, no spaces)

14 A less serious offense, punishable by a fine, probation, or a short jail term, in contrast to a felony, a more serious crime.

16 A punishment philosophy based on the assumption that the acts of potential offenders can be prevented.

19 Acts that may be harmful to others but for which the actor had no immoral or wrongful purpose.

20 The criminal intent of the accused at the time the criminal act is committed. (2 words, no spaces)

21 A system in which the defendant must prove his or her innocence, in contrast to the adversary system, which has a presumption of innocence, requiring the state (or federal prosecutors in federal cases) to prove the defendant's guilt. (2 words, no spaces)

22 The belief that those who commit crimes should suffer for those crimes; also the amount or type of punishment a particular offender deserves to receive. (2 words, no spaces)

24 A serious offense, such as murder, armed robbery, or rape.

26 Actions that are wrong because legislation prohibits them, although there may not be general agreement that they are wrong in themselves. (2 words, no spaces)

27 Responses by the defendant in a criminal or civil case.

30 Broadly defined, the legal theory and law that originated in England and are common in the United States as well. (2 words, no spaces)

31 A penalty or punishment that is imposed on a person in order to enforce the law.

32 Legally binding court interpretations of written laws or rules made by the courts. (2 words, no spaces)

33 A person found guilty of an act that violates the criminal law.

WORD SEARCH

s i r u i l t i a r g o p i s n c t p o o w s v t
e t u n e g l i g e n c e a a o y r e r s n e l l
c o m m o n l a w t i e a f e h t b q t s a e m i
n o i t c i d s i r u j a t t e m p t n t r m n n
a a m f i m n l a i e e d o c l a n e p l e d o m
t g e a e a a e n b r e h a b i l i t a t i o n w
s t e m l l n d q u d r w o i d e c a s v m e a c
m r i n l a o i m t e c e a c r r t y i e s l n l
u r m o e p i n n i b m s i l c o s d t e y e i b
c a e i g r t n y o n n v t a l e u s s r p e m r
r d t t a o a i s n i i t u a c a y a o a d w l c
i i s c l h t l n e l t s s i l s n t a l e a t n
c s y n d i i l d l e a c t d y a u i t a t l s e
t c s a u b c t a e t s s e r u t l r m n e e t s
n r y s t i a w a i t u t o t a e e a a i r s t i
a e r i y t p n o u j e t r t o t p m i m r a i n
d t a s t a a n m l r i r s e n r i r m i e c r j
n i s m r t c e a r s v l r i s e p v o r n n e u
e o r n f d n n e i s e s n e f e d l e c c i b n
t n e m h s i n u p l a u s u n u d n a l e u r c
t i v u r m c q j o m d s o e e c r t a u a s s t
a i d e i e n a t d e t t o i n l e n s t q w s i
p o a r m i s d e m e a n o r i e e i t u m e d o
o e c i a i d s t a e u t h a n a s i a t j e t n
a e d i c i u s d e t s i s s a n a i c i s y h p

administrative law
attempt
causation
crime
criminal law
deterrence
equal protection
general deterrence
injunction
just deserts
mala prohibita
Model Penal Code
rehabilitation
statutory law

adversary system
attendant circumstances
civil law
criminal
cruel and unusual punishment
discretion
euthanasia
incapacitation
inquisitory system
legal duty
mens rea
negligence
retribution

AIDS
case law
common law
criminal justice system
defenses
due process
felony
individual deterrence
jurisdiction
mala in se
misdemeanor
physician assisted suicide
sanction

ANSWERS TO CROSSWORD

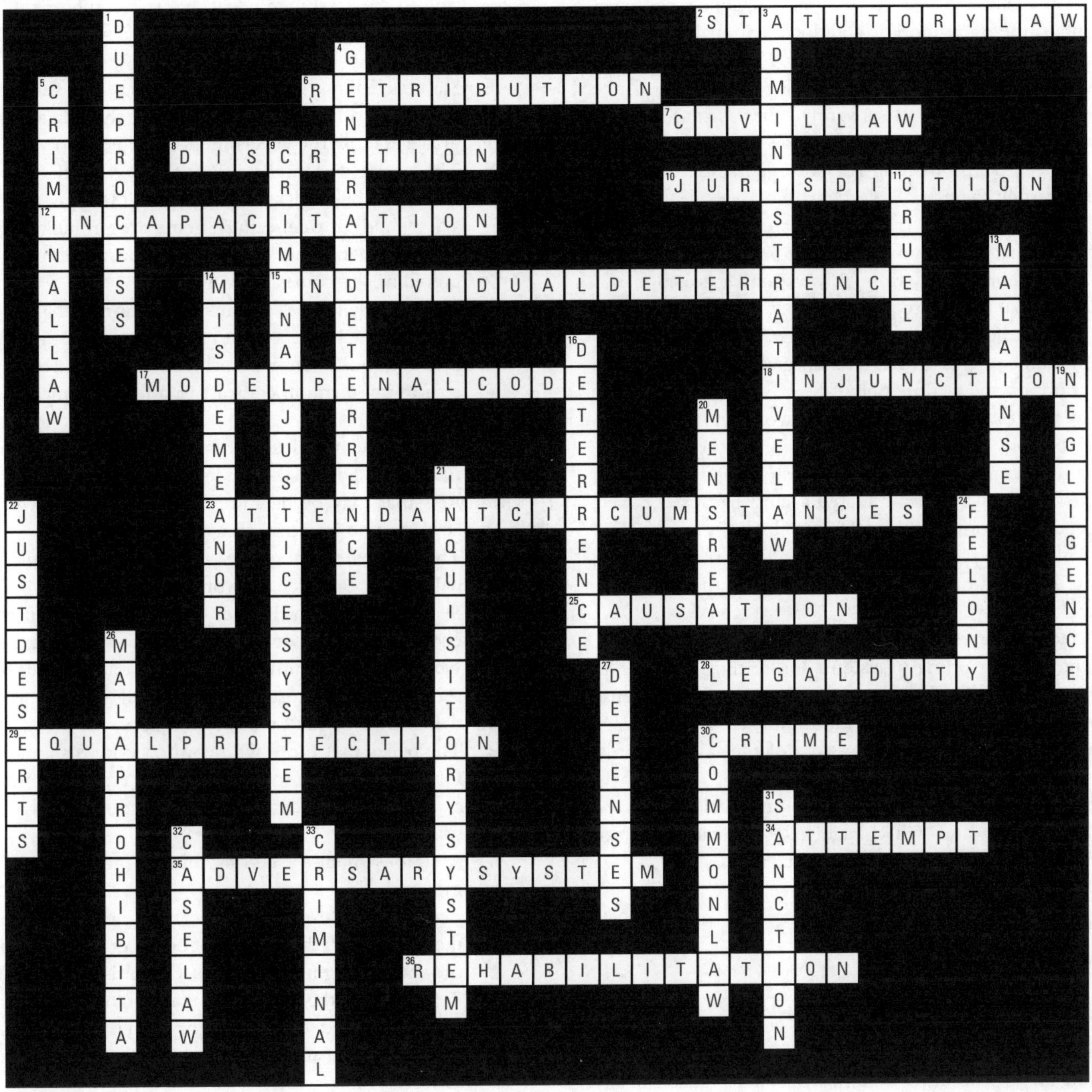

ACROSS

2 Law that the legislature has originated and passed by a written enactment. (2 words, no spaces)

6 The belief that those who commit crimes should suffer for those crimes; also the amount or type of punishment a particular offender deserves to receive.

7 Distinguished from criminal law as that law pertaining to private rights. (2 words, no spaces)

8 In the criminal justice system, authority to make decisions based on one's own judgment rather than on specified rules.

10 The lawful exercise of authority; the area within which authority may be exercised, such as the geographical area within which a particular police force has authority.

12 A punishment theory usually implemented by imprisoning an offender to prevent the commission of any other crimes by that person.

15 A form of the deterrence punishment philosophy referring to the prevention of additional criminal acts by the specific individual being punished. (2 words, no spaces)

17 Model proposals developed by legal scholars of the American Law Institute covering issues such as kinds of culpability and intent. (3 words, no spaces)

18 A court order prohibiting a person or persons from acting in a certain manner.

23 Facts surrounding a crime, which are considered to be a part of that crime and which must be proved along with the elements of the crime. (2 words, no spaces)

25 In criminal law, the requirement that the act must be the cause of the harmful consequence.

28 An element of a crime. The alleged offender's lack of action may be a crime only if he or she was required by law to act in a certain manner. (2 words, no spaces)

29 All persons under like circumstances must receive essentially the same treatment in the criminal justice system; they may not be discriminated against because of race, gender, minority status, ethnicity, disability, or religion. (2 words, no spaces)

30 An illegal act of omission or commission that is punishable by the criminal law.

34 A factor in an element of a crime, an act.

35 One of two primary systems for settling disputes in court. The accused is presumed to be innocent. A defense attorney and a prosecuting attorney attempt to convince a judge or a jury of their versions of the case. (2 words, no spaces)

36 A punishment philosophy based on a belief that the offender can and will change to a law-abiding citizen through treatment programs and facilities.

DOWN

1 The constitutional principle that a person should not be deprived of life, liberty, or property without reasonable and lawful procedures that must be made available in any criminal action, including post-conviction procedures such as prison disciplinary hearings or parole revocations. (2 words, no spaces)

3 Rules and regulations made by agencies to which power has been delegated by a state legislature or by the U.S. Congress. Administrative agencies investigate and decide cases concerning potential violations of these rules. (2 words, no spaces)

4 A form of the deterrence punishment philosophy referring to the presumed effect that punishing one offender will have on other potential offenders. (2 words, no spaces)

5 Statutes defining acts so offensive that they threaten the well-being of the society and require that the accused be prosecuted by the government. (2 words, no spaces)

9 The entire system of criminal prevention, detection, apprehension, trial, and punishment. (3 words, no spaces)

11 _____ and unusual punishments are prohibited by the Eighth Amendment to the U.S. Constitution, as interpreted by the courts. (1 word)

13 Actions that are intrinsically immoral, such as murder, forcible rape, and robbery. (3 words, no spaces)

14 A less serious offense, punishable by a fine, probation, or a short jail term, in contrast to a felony, a more serious crime.

16 A punishment philosophy based on the assumption that the acts of potential offenders can be prevented.

19 Acts that may be harmful to others but for which the actor had no immoral or wrongful purpose.

20 The criminal intent of the accused at the time the criminal act is committed. (2 words, no spaces)

21 A system in which the defendant must prove his or her innocence, in contrast to the adversary system, which has a presumption of innocence, requiring the state (or federal prosecutors in federal cases) to prove the defendant's guilt. (2 words, no spaces)

22 The belief that those who commit crimes should suffer for those crimes; also the amount or type of punishment a particular offender deserves to receive. (2 words, no spaces)

24 A serious offense, such as murder, armed robbery, or rape.

26 Actions that are wrong because legislation prohibits them, although there may not be general agreement that they are wrong in themselves. (2 words, no spaces)

27 Responses by the defendant in a criminal or civil case.

30 Broadly defined, the legal theory and law that originated in England and are common in the United States as well. (2 words, no spaces)

31 A penalty or punishment that is imposed on a person in order to enforce the law.

32 Legally binding court interpretations of written laws or rules made by the courts. (2 words, no spaces)

33 A person found guilty of an act that violates the criminal law.

ANSWERS TO WORD SEARCH

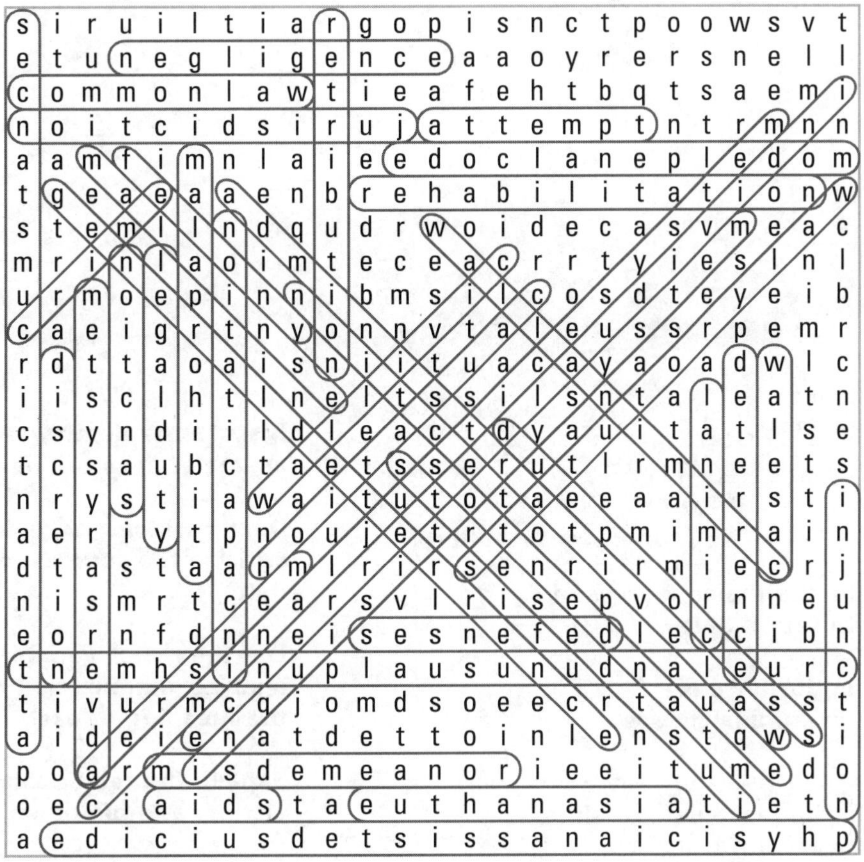

administrative law
attempt
causation
crime
criminal law
deterrence
equal protection
general deterrence
injunction
just deserts
mala prohibita
Model Penal Code
rehabilitation
statutory law

adversary system
attendant circumstances
civil law
criminal
cruel and unusual punishment
discretion
euthanasia
incapacitation
inquisitory system
legal duty
mens rea
negligence
retribution

AIDS
case law
common law
criminal justice system
defenses
due process
felony
individual deterrence
jurisdiction
mala in se
misdemeanor
physician assisted suicide
sanction

...ME, OFFENDERS, ...D VICTIMS

LEARNING OBJECTIVES

After reading this chapter, you should be able to do the following:

- **List and evaluate the major sources of crime and victimization data**
- **Recognize the importance of misdemeanors in criminal justice systems**
- **List and explain the reasons that crime data may not be accurate**
- **Discuss reasons for the nonreporting of crime by victims**
- **List and define the eight serious crimes as categorized by the Federal Bureau of Investigation**
- **Analyze and summarize recent crime data, noting changes in the rates of violent and property crimes**
- **Explain the meaning of *hate crime*, and analyze the U.S. Supreme Court decision regarding cross burning**
- **Discuss the demographic characteristics of offenders and victims**
- **Define *victimology* and describe and criticize the sources of victimization data**
- **List the major variables used to analyze victimization data and explain the meaning of each**
- **Explain the relationship between victims and offenders**
- **Discuss ways in which criminal justice systems have attempted to respond to the needs of victims and evaluate each**
- **Evaluate your own fear of crime and assess whether you alter your lifestyle as a result**
- **Discuss at least five types of crimes beyond those included among the eight serious crimes as recorded by the FBI**

Criminal Justice Essentials: Study Guide, Ninth Edition. Shannon Barton-Bellessa.

CHAPTER OUTLINE

KEY TERMS

aggravated assault
arson
Baby Moses laws
Bureau of Justice Statistics (BJS)
burglary
child abuse
crime rate
crimes known to the police
cybercrime
cyberstalking
date rape
elder abuse
fetal abuse
forcible rape
hate crime
index offenses
kidnapping
larceny-theft
lesser included offense
manslaughter
marital rape
motor vehicle theft
murder
National Crime Victimization Survey (NCVS)
National Incident-Based Reporting System (NIBRS)
parental kidnapping
prima facie evidence
property crimes
rape
restitution
robbery
self-report data (SRD)
stalking
statutory rape
Uniform Crime Reports (*UCR*)
victim compensation programs
victimology
victim precipitation
violent crimes
white-collar crime

CHAPTER SUMMARY

Chapter 2 provides an overview of crime measurement, including a summary of the extent of crime, and sections on offenders and the victims. Although there are multiple techniques for collecting crime data, the three basic methods used are: *Uniform Crime Reports* (*UCR*), the National Crime Victimization Survey (NCVS), and self-report studies. Each of these, along with the National Incident-Based Reporting System (NIBRS, an expanded version of the *UCR*), is described and analyzed in the chapter.

The ***Uniform Crime Reports*** (*UCR*) is the most frequently cited and used method for gathering data. Conceived in 1929 by the International Association of Chiefs of Police in an effort to have a standardized reporting system, the *UCR* was put into practice the following year by the FBI. Today, nearly 17,000 law enforcement agencies voluntarily participate in reporting these official data to the FBI annually. These data include both crimes reported to the police and crimes cleared by arrest. Data are divided into two indices: Part I **index offenses** and Part II index offenses. Part I index offenses consist of eight crimes considered to be the most serious (**violent crimes**: **murder and nonnegligent manslaughter**, **forcible rape, aggravated assault** and **robbery; property crimes: burglary, larceny-theft, motor vehicle theft,** and **arson**). The Part II index offense list consists of 21 other less serious offenses such as driving under the influence and simple assault. The major shortcoming of this data collection effort is that not all crimes are reported to the police. This phenomenon is known as the **dark figure of crime.**

Recognizing the limitations and lack of flexibility of this method for gathering data, the FBI has recently revised its method of collecting and recording official crime statistics. Its most significant change, the **National Incident-Based Reporting System** (NIBRS), is in operation in many states. The NIBRS program was piloted in 1987 in South Carolina and enacted in 1988. Since that time the use of this technique as an alternative to gathering official statistics has grown. The NIBRS views crime as an incident that involves many elements, including alcohol and drug abuse; the types of victims, weapons, and criminal activity; the victim's and arrestee's residency; the relationship between victims and offenders; and a description of property and property values. The collection of these additional elements of criminal acts will significantly enhance our ability to analyze crime. One limitation of this data-gathering technique, however, is it requires more resources and time to implement in a law enforcement agency. Because of this, it has not been widely implemented; therefore, the ability to generalize the data does not currently exist.

The **National Crime Victimization Survey** (NCVS) is the second form of data collection. Unlike the *UCR*, this method of data gathering seeks to tap into the dark figure of crime, or those crimes that go unreported to the police from the victims' point of view. This interview process seeks to reveal not only the amount of crime that is occurring but also why victims choose not to report their crimes and the impact of the victimizations. Beginning in 1973, this self-reporting method uses a nationally representative stratified, multi-stage cluster sample of 76,000 households comprising approximately135,300 persons in the United States. Direct interviews are conducted with persons over the age of 12 regarding their victimization(s) and experience with the criminal justice system. Proxy interviews may be conducted with those individuals aged 12 or 13 when a knowledgeable household member insists upon them not being interviewed or for those who are incapacitated. Households are interviewed every six months for three years. Shortcomings of the results arise, however, because data do not give any information on arrests; direct interviews are conducted only with those over the age of 12; and results are dependent on the accuracy of perception and reporting of crime victims.

The third major source of crime data – **self-report data** (SRD) – provides information not secured by either of the official methods on characteristics of people who say they have committed crimes. Many of the original versions of self-report studies relied on juveniles in school systems to report their delinquency. More recent studies have included adult populations. SRD provide valuable data for social scientists who study why crimes are committed, as well as for officials who must make decisions concerning the use of resources aimed at crime control and prevention. SRD allow the study of repeat offenders. The major problem with this approach is that respondents may underreport or overreport crimes, and they may tap into less serious forms of delinquent and criminal activity.

As the chapter further notes, data sources can be used to analyze the nature and extent of crime, but it is important to analyze carefully the time periods and the definitions of crimes being measured before comparing data from the various sources. As previously noted and further expanded upon in the chapter, the *UCR* divides crime types into violent and property crimes. Each of these crime types was reviewed for not only the standard definitions but the rates of these offenses as well. It is important to keep in mind that state statutes will differ in their exact definitions of these offense types. The *UCR* includes standard definitions that require police agencies to decide which offense categories crimes fit and report accordingly. From the *UCR* data, the FBI further divides the reports into hate crime statistics and law enforcement officers killed in the line of duty. The majority of data used to make decisions regarding resource allocation through the criminal justice system are derived from the *UCR* for offenders and the NCVS for victims. Three main variables are typically used for offender and victim analysis: age, race, and gender. Results from these data sets indicate that the majority of crimes are committed by persons age 18 and over; adults accounted for approximately 85.1 percent of violent offenses; and adults were arrested for drug abuse violations more than any other category of arrest. The majority of all persons arrested were white (69.2 percent) and were male (74.7 percent). Persons between the ages of 12 and 19 were more likely to be victimized than persons ages 25 and over. African Americans were more likely to be victims of violent and household crimes, while men were more likely to be victimized than women.

Next the chapter presents information on the recently developed and rapidly expanding study of **victimology**. Characteristics of crime victims, along with the problems those victims face in criminal justice systems, are discussed. The first federal legislation recognizing the plight of victims was passed in 1982 and known as the **Victim and Witness Protection Act**. This act created a system for the treatment of victims and witnesses in the criminal justice process, victim notification of court proceedings, and restitution. Since the creation of this Act, other legislative responses have expanded **victim compensation programs** as well as other support mechanisms throughout the process at both the state and federal level. The chapter further explores the notion of who is most likely to be victimized. Although they are the most frequently studied, women, the elderly, and children are not the most frequent crime victims. Most violent crimes are committed against African American men, and men are more frequent crime victims than women. Brief mention is made of the smallest victims – newborns who are abandoned by their parents – and the **Baby Moses laws** designed to encourage parents to give those infants a chance at life and adoption. The recent addition of data on mentally and physically challenged persons is discussed.

Crime victims face a number of problems within the criminal justice system, including fear of being blamed for the offense (**victim precipitation**), fear that officers will not be sympathetic to the offense, and fear of retaliation by the perpetrator. The chapter further reviews efforts to assist crime victims, mentioning such measures as revised court procedures and the passage of the **Victims of Crime Act** (VOCA) in 1984, which authorized that federal funds be distributed by the Office of Justice Programs through its Office for Victims of Crime and the Bureau of Justice for state **victim compensation** and assistance programs. This money was specifically designed for hiring counselors to work with victims, to compensate victims, and even for technology such as computers used to assist victims.

Like most changes in the system, recognizing the rights of victims creates other needs, such as training programs for professionals within the system and financial backing for those programs as well as for victim compensation plans. Furthermore, victims' rights and defendants' rights may come into conflict. Nevertheless, changes made in the system to help victims may produce positive results, such as increased crime reporting and more arrests and convictions. But what appear to be positive results could create problems for the system and society because of the increased need for jails and prisons. Thus, a study of crime victims provides another example of the need to assess the effect that changes in one aspect of the system have on the rest of the system and on society.

Finally, the chapter explores a few other offenses that generate a great deal of concern within the criminal justice community but are not included in official crime statistics or victimization reports. Those crimes are: **child abuse, elder abuse, stalking, cybercrime, white-collar crime, terrorism, animal cruelty,** and **gun control.** As reported, child abuse includes neglect, psychological, and physical abuse of children. It may also include kidnapping or parental kidnapping. In 2009, there were an estimated 702,000 children reported abused or neglected. This concern over abusing family members is not exclusive to the needs of children. A growing area of attention has been given to elder abuse. Although this area is more difficult to measure because of the lack of reporting, legislation has been enacted to protect the rights of the elderly against fraudulent acts and other forms of abuse. Similarly, the recognition of stalking and cybercrimes has come to the forefront of many state legislatures. Antistalking statutes and the creation of a cybercrime division point to the increased awareness and focus on the prevention of these crime types. Other offenses such as white-collar crimes have gained increased recognition for the serious level of economic hardships they can cause when not policed. Terrorists' activities, meanwhile, continue to be policed heavily, with the focus being placed not only on the importance of protecting both the U.S. and the world, but also on the costs to freedoms and liberties of those residing in the United States in doing so. The chapter concludes with a discussion of gun control legislation and the significance of legislation limiting gun ownership and availability.

KEY TERMS

aggravated assault technically, an assault is a threat to commit a battery, but often the term is used to refer to a battery. Aggravated assault generally involves a battery inflicted by use of a deadly weapon.

arson The willful and malicious burning of the structure of another with or without the intent to defraud. Burning of one's own property with the intent to defraud is included in some definitions. Many modern statutes carry a more severe penalty for the burning of a dwelling than of other real property.

Baby Moses laws Provisions for protecting from prosecution persons who abandon newborn babies in ways that will protect those infants, such as leaving them in designated *safe places*.

Bureau of Justice Statistics (BJS) A federal agency mandated by Congress to collect, analyze, and publish crime data based on surveys of the general population, who are questioned about crime victimizations.

burglary The illegal or forcible entering of any enclosed structure with the intent to commit a crime, usually theft. Some jurisdictions require that the intent be to commit a felony rather than a less serious crime.

child abuse The emotional, psychological, or physical abuse of a child by parents, other relatives, acquaintances, or strangers. The use of actual children (in contrast to virtual children) in pornography is included.

crime rate The number of crimes per 100,000 population.

crimes known to the police All serious criminal offenses that have been reported to the police for which the police have sufficient evidence to believe the crimes were committed.

cybercrime Crimes that are committed by use of the Internet.

cyberstalking Stalking someone by use of the Internet. *See also* **stalking.**

date rape Forced sexual acts that occur during a social occasion. The alleged victim may have agreed to some intimacy but not to the activities defined in that jurisdiction as constituting the elements of rape.

elder abuse Violent, psychological, financial, negligent, and other types of abuse of elderly persons. The crime is frequently committed by family members and involves such acts as stealing social security checks, withholding food stamps, committing assault and battery, neglecting to provide food and medications, and so on. Fraud against the elderly committed by strangers appears to be an increasing type of elder abuse.

fetal abuse The abusing of a fetus, which may or may not lead to its death. In some jurisdictions a resulting death of the fetus may lead to legal culpability, such as a murder or a manslaughter charge.

forcible rape *See* **rape.**

hate crime As defined in the federal criminal code, a crime "that manifests evidence of prejudice based on race, religion, disability, sexual orientation, or ethnicity, including where appropriate the crimes of murder, nonnegligent manslaughter, forcible rape, aggravated assault, simple assault, intimidation, arson, and destruction, damage or vandalism of property." Penalties may be enhanced when a crime is designated as a hate crime.

index offenses The FBI's *Uniform Crime Reports* of the occurrences of the eight crimes considered most serious: murder and nonnegligent manslaughter, forcible rape, robbery, aggravated assault, burglary, larceny-theft, motor vehicle theft, and arson. In June 2004, the FBI discontinued publishing data according to index offenses because of the misrepresentation of crime in an area that can be caused by a very high (or low) volume or rate of crime of only one of these serious crimes in that area.

kidnapping Restricting the freedom of a victim against his or her will and removing that victim from one place to another.

larceny-theft The unlawful removal and taking away of someone else's property with the intention of keeping it permanently. Historically, small thefts were categorized as *petit larceny* and large thefts as *grand larceny*. Some modern theft laws do not distinguish between these two types of larceny-theft.

lesser included offense An offense that is less serious than the crime thought to have been committed by the suspect. It has some but not all of the elements of the suspected crime. For example, second-degree murder is a lesser included offense within murder, but premeditation, required for first-degree murder, is not an element of second-degree murder. Manslaughter is also a lesser included offense within murder.

manslaughter The unlawful killing of a human being by a person who lacks malice. Manslaughter may be *involuntary* (or *negligent*), the result of recklessness while committing an unlawful act (such as driving while intoxicated), or *voluntary*, an intentional killing committed in the heat of passion.

marital rape Rape of one spouse by another. Not all jurisdictions recognize this act as a crime although the number that do so is increasing.

motor vehicle theft The stealing of a motor vehicle, in contrast to the stealing of a part or larceny-theft *from* a motor vehicle.

murder The unlawful killing of another person with either express or implied malice aforethought. Some jurisdictions also include a fetus as a victim.

National Crime Victimization Survey (NCVS) Crime data collected by the Bureau of Justice Statistics (BJS) and based on surveys of people to determine who has been victimized by crime and the nature of that victimization.

National Incident-Based Reporting System (NIBRS) A reporting system used by the FBI in collecting crime data. In this system, a crime is viewed along with all of its components, including the type of victim, type of weapon, location of the crime, alcohol/drug influence, type of criminal activity, relationship of victim to offender, and residence of victims and arrestees, as well as a description of the property and its value.

parental kidnapping The crime of kidnapping a child, committed by a parent who does not have the legal authority to take the child or who has not been granted permission to do so by the parent (or other person) who has legal custody or by the court. *See also* **kidnapping**.

***prima facie* evidence** Evidence that, on its face, is sufficient to constitute a fact unless it is sufficiently refuted.

property crimes Crimes aimed at property. Serious property crimes include larceny-theft, burglary, motor vehicle theft, and arson.

rape Historically, unlawful vaginal intercourse with a woman; it is called *forcible rape* if engaged in against the will of the woman by the use of threat or force; it is called *statutory rape* if the sexual intercourse was consensual but the alleged victim is under the age to which one may legally consent to sex. More recently some rape statutes have been rewritten to include male victims and female perpetrators, as well as penetration of any body opening by any instrument (called *rape by instrumentation*), including but not limited to the male sexual organ.

restitution Punishment that requires an offender to repay the victim with services or money. This punishment may be imposed instead of or in addition to other punishment or fines and may be a requirement of parole.

robbery The use of force or fear to take personal property belonging to another against that person's will.

self-report data (SRD) Crime data collected by asking people to report about their criminal activity; usually conducted by use of anonymous questionnaires.

stalking Defined by the National Violence Against Women Survey as "a course of conduct directed at a specific person that involves repeated visual or physical proximity, nonconsensual communication, or verbal, written or implied threats, or a combination thereof, that would cause a reasonable person fear." The word *repeated* means two or more times. Jurisdictional statutes may vary from this definition. *See also* **cyberstalking**.

statutory rape *See* **rape.**

***Uniform Crime Reports* (*UCR*)** Official crime data, collected and published by the Federal Bureau of Investigation (FBI) and based on *crimes known to the police* – crimes that are reported to or observed by the police and that the police have reason to believe were committed.

victim compensation programs: Plans for assisting crime victims in making social, emotional, and economic adjustments.

victimology The discipline that studies the nature and causes of victimization, as well as programs for aiding victims and preventing victimization.

victim precipitation Concept that a criminal act may have been brought on by the alleged victim's behavior.

violent crimes Crimes defined by the FBI's *Uniform Crime Reports* as serious crimes against a person. They include murder and nonnegligent manslaughter, robbery, forcible rape, and aggravated assault.

white-collar crime The illegal actions of corporations or individuals, committed while pursuing their legitimate occupations. Examples are consumer fraud, bribery, and embezzlement

STUDY QUESTIONS

These questions are found at the end of your chapter. Your instructor may wish to revisit these or assign them for points. These questions are a good way to integrate the material and to generate your own perspectives during class.

1 Describe and contrast the major sources of crime data.

2 Why should attention be paid to misdemeanors?

3 What are the limitations of the *UCR*?

4 Explain and evaluate the FBI's NIBRS system of data reporting.

5 Why are some crimes not reported by victims? If you were a crime victim, would you call the police? Would it depend on the nature of the crime?

6 What are the advantages and disadvantages of self-report studies?

7 What have been the major changes in the amount of crime in the United States in the past decade?

8 What are the major differences between serious violent and property crimes? List and define the four crimes in each of these categories.

9 What is *hate crime*? Discuss. How does the recent U.S. Supreme Court case on cross burning relate to hate crimes?

10 Discuss the relationship between crime and each of the following: age, race, and gender.

11 Define *fetal abuse* and *Baby Moses laws*.

12 What progress has been made recently in the study of victims?

13 Discuss the characteristics of crime victims.

14 What lifestyle changes might you consider because of the risk of crime?

15 Is the fear of crime realistic?

16 What changes have been made in recent legislation to improve the plight of crime victims?

17 Select three of the specific crimes on which the chapter's last section focused and explain their importance.

LEARNING ACTIVITIES

2.1 In the text, the author uses 2009 as the most recent *Uniform Crime Report* statistics provided. Using the Federal Bureau of Investigation (FBI) Uniform Crime Reporting system, have these trends continued? Given what we know about crime in the United States, what factors may be contributing to these overall trends? Provide some examples from your local community to support your response.

2.2 Over the past 20 years, advocates for victims' rights have sought to increase their level of both participation in and compensation from the system. Using your state, what rights do victims have during the court process? What type of program(s) is/are supported at the state level to assist with compensating victims of crime? Do you believe that these programs have been effective? Why or why not?

2.3 Historically self-report studies of crime have only been able to capture minor, less serious offenses. Given what we know about potential limitations of these studies, how might a researcher create an approach to studying self-reported crime that would increase our understanding of the dark figure of crime?

2.4 The focus of terrorism in the United States continues to be an overarching concern at the local, state, national, and international level. What changes in law enforcement, travel, or other areas of your life have you personally experienced as a result of the "War on Terror"? In your opinion, do you feel citizens of the United States are safer because of these efforts? Explain your response.

STUDENT STUDY GUIDE PRACTICE QUESTIONS

True or False

2.1 In 2010, the Federal Bureau of Investigation released its data for 2009 and revealed that both violent and property crimes had decreased from 2008 figures.

2.2 The two major sources of crime data in the United States are the *Uniform Crime Reports* and the National Crime Victimization Survey (NCVS).

2.3 *Uniform Crime Reports* consists of data collected by the state police.

2.4 Property crimes are more likely to be cleared by arrest than violent crimes.

2.5 In 2009, according to the *Uniform Crime Reports*, the majority of persons arrested for any offense were white, male, and over the age of 18.

2.6 In October 2010, the Bureau of Justice Statistics reported that in 2009 there were 4.3 million violent and 15.6 million property crime victimizations.

2.7 In June 2010, the Indiana Supreme Court held that it was unconstitutional under that state's law to prosecute a pregnant woman for wanton endangerment in the first degree because she ingested drugs during her pregnancy.

2.8 Persons from higher-income households suffer more property crimes than those in lower-income households.

2.9 Research suggests that young women on college campuses may fear personal violence, especially rape, more frequently than women in the general population.

2.10 The Oklahoma City bombing on 19 April 1995 constituted the worst act of terrorism on U.S. soil to that date by U.S. terrorists, killing 168 people.

Multiple Choice

2.11 Which of the following responses does *not* reflect why offenses are not recorded in the *Uniform Crime Reports* (*UCR*):

- a Law enforcement officers or the police department may want to downplay the seriousness of the offense.
- b Not all crimes are reported to the police.
- c A delay in reporting offenses may occur because of the inability of the victim to decide whether an offense occurred or fear of retaliation.
- d The FBI requires that only senior officer arrests can be included in the *UCR* data.

2.12 The last offense added to the *Uniform Crime Reports* was:

- a Automobile theft
- b Arson
- c Aggravated assault
- d Larceny-theft

2.13 The National Incident-Based Reporting (NIBRS) system was created in 1988 in an effort to expand the Uniform Crime Reporting system. The NIBRS expanded the index offense reporting system to include how many offenses?

- a 10
- b 22
- c 38
- d 46

2.14 Which of the following is not counted as a Part I violent crime index offense?
- a Murder
- b Forcible rape
- c Burglary
- d Robbery

2.15 The National Crime Victimization Survey (NCVS) was created to tap into crimes that go unreported to the police also known as:
- a The dark figure of crime
- b Unsolved criminal resolution figures
- c The dark area of victimization
- d The National Incident-Based Reporting System

2.16 Which of the following is a criticism of self-report studies?
- a There is a potential problem with accuracy of reports.
- b Offenses included in self-report studies are deemed too trivial for inclusion.
- c Self-report studies often include too few minorities.
- d All are criticisms of self-report studies.

2.17 According to 2009 crime data, which age group is most likely to be victims of crime?
- a Age 11 and under
- b 12- to 19-year-olds
- c 20- to 49-year-olds
- d Age 50 and older

2.18 _____ is the only state to enact a statute that, in effect, provides for a charge of homicide by child abuse against a pregnant woman whose act or omission causes the death of a fetus.
- a California
- b West Virginia
- c South Carolina
- d Georgia

2.19 In 1981 the U.S. Supreme Court Justice Warren E. Burger referred to _____ as the "reign of terror in American cities":
- a fear of terrorist activities
- b fear of violent crime by strangers
- c fear of Nicaraguan Contra insurgents
- d the war on drugs

2.20 Which of the following offenses has not been targeted in the last few years by the FBI as white-collar crimes?
- a Larceny-theft
- b Bank fraud
- c Copyright violations
- d Financial fraud

Fill-in-the-Blank

2.21 _____ refers to the number of crimes solved, expressed as a percentage of the total number of crimes reported to the police.

2.22 ______ refers to crime that goes unreported to the police.

2.23 ______ refers to a growing area of concern in which the Internet is used to facilitate criminal activity.

2.24 ______ involves a course of conduct directed at a specified person that would cause a reasonable person to feel fear.

2.25 Blaming the victim for their role in the crime, particularly in the case of sexual assault, is known as ______.

2.26 In 1984 Congress passed the ______, which authorizes that federal funds be distributed by the Office of Justice Programs through its Office for Victims of Crime and Bureau of Justice for state victim compensation and assistance programs.

2.27 ______ are programs designed to alleviate some of the financial and emotional burdens suffered by victims of crime.

2.28 ______ may involve physical abuse, but in some cases it results in the death of an infant born to parents who are unwilling to care for the infant.

2.29 ______ laws make provisions for protecting mothers (or fathers) who abandon their newborn children in ways that will protect those infants.

2.30 For years, criminologists have suggested that ______crimes should be given more attention by social scientists as well as by the government.

CROSSWORD

ACROSS

1 Crimes defined by the FBI's *Uniform Crime Reports* as serious crimes against a person. (2 words, 1 space)

5 "A course of conduct directed at a specified person that would cause a reasonable person to feel fear."

7 A broad term that applies to neglect, psychological and physical abuse of a minor. (2 words, 1 space)

8 The use of force or fear to take personal property belonging to another against that person's will.

9 The discipline that studies the nature and causes of victimization, as well as programs for aiding victims and preventing victimization.

11 The abusing of a fetus, which may or may not lead to its death. (2 words, 1 space)

12 Charged crimes that are related to the major crime but are less serious. (3 words, 2 spaces)
18 A form of stalking that involves the Internet, email, or some other form of electronic communication to harass or otherwise threaten another.
21 The willful and malicious burning of the structure of another with or without the intent to defraud.
22 The stealing of an automobile, in contrast to the stealing of an automobile part or larceny-theft from an automobile. (3 words, 2 spaces)
24 The use of the Internet to facilitate crimes such as online pornography, stalking and bullying and other forms of criminal activity.
25 The unlawful killing of a human being by a person who lacks malice.
26 The illegal actions of corporations or individuals, committed while pursuing their legitimate occupations. (3 words, 1 hyphen, 1 space)
27 Forced sexual acts that occur during a social occasion. (2 words, 1 space)
28 The FBI's *Uniform Crime Reports* of the occurrences of the eight crimes considered most serious. (2 words, 1 space)

DOWN

2 All serious criminal offenses that have been reported to the police for which the police have sufficient evidence to believe the crimes were committed. (5 words, 4 spaces)
3 Provisions for protecting mothers (or fathers) who abandon their newborn children in ways that will protect those infants; these laws are becoming more common in the United States as well as some other countries. (3 words, 2 spaces)
4 Defined by the *UCR* as "the carnal knowledge of a female forcibly and against her will." (2 words, 1 space)
6 Concept that a criminal act may have been brought on by the alleged victim's actions. (2 words, 1 space)
10 A type of remedy that requires the defendant to pay the victim back for the harm caused.
13 The number of crimes per 100,000 population. (2 words, 1 space)
14 An assault that generally involves a battery inflicted by use of a deadly weapon. (2 words, 1 space).
15 The unlawful removal of someone else's property with the intention of keeping it permanently. (2 words, 1 hyphen)
16 Unlawfully seizing or carrying away of a person against their will or through fraud.
17 The illegal or forcible entering of any enclosed structure in order to commit a crime, usually theft.
19 The unlawful killing of another person with either express or implied malice aforethought.
20 Crimes aimed at the property of another person rather than at the person. (2 words, 1 space)
23 As defined in the federal criminal code, a crime that manifests evidence of prejudice based on race, religion, disability, sexual orientation, or ethnicity, including where appropriate the crimes of murder, nonnegligent manslaughter, forcible rape, aggravated assault, simple assault, intimidation, arson, and destruction, damage or vandalism of property." (2 words, 1 space)

WORD SEARCH

```
y i d m t p o n k s a g b i t g e p w n g o i i e s i i r t h e e h a e
e m i r c r a l l o c - e t i h w s e d i n n r i e n r a c c a o p i l
v s f y f i p o a m e p c n l i c n g a i l o w l a e e s e y a f e e p
r y u h g m r r l p a f v r n n r n l t i v i f a s i n d o b r a r e p
u d s r m a t f a r u s i n g s i d v f t i o l t l c e e a e p k e o b
s c f t r f l o l p t v o c a p m n t n i r v i o n r t h m r p n i b n
n e r s u a s a t e u y l n p r e m i r c e t a h n c r e p s k o m d p
o p l i c c t r d e t o e a s t r s i i a u c h d e a v i n t o t s e a
i o n f m i r a h e t y n t r t a t b n t f n e t c g m s e a l e l o o
t c p c r e t f t f i d t e x c t l t i d c e p e s n o e r l e a t r a
a n h a l e s s e r i n c l u d e d o f f e n s e l i d r e k e a f t y
z r m i r v p k i k o r r d n r t n a p r i x o l l c s r c i a t c k n
i r t a l i n o n t r s i o a i f l y l e s h o r g s o n o n o i c r o
m t p r l d t a r o a c m p h s m r n t y d o s f h r e v o g y l i n g
i e a p b e a t r t w t e o a y m e i l h m b v n f i m i o y c t u o r
t p s i s n i b l e d n s e t l e s t c s e b l i u e g l n e k t e e e
c e l r t c e c u g t a t e c g i p t i t u f b s a p n o p t n o a c y
i g y t i e n r a s m m t o c i e p a r y r o t u t a t s t r e o t g r
v i c t i m c o m p e n s a t i o n p r o g r a m s p m e e i t t o e m
e p m a c h s c i r m u o a d h t e c e e p r n n a r a p s s n l o r e
m e t s y s g n i t r o p e r d e s a b t n e d i c n i l a n o i t a n
i s a s w r o r i h a e t l a n n p u a r e t r p p e s r v m s e a f i
r n e i a a a a r a i t d o v a c p o j e h t a e v e e l i t r i e r n
c o e l m a l l e e b r i r r t i w v l f i r b l m f e t a l a b u s e
l e t n s t l s g i c p g p u v m e n e i o r r c k i c c e u t l w u t
a r r t p r o p e r t y c r i m e s d l f c u t y l i r a f a g i k p i
n f a i t m c h s s u s w n n c l h p y t o e a b v e d c e n e h s s t
o c e s v a v b a r o b b e r y e c i i e p m f e k o n n m e i i t o t
i i a t c t l i p l c m c g h a h r d c p n s c r r m a s a r r i a e y
t c e a y s s a s n o u y a e f c a p o l e y s c r u r e t p o i l a r
a k r n e l i r r i a s i b g a k m r m m e o l r d y b c s r p f k a p
n i r r s v f p e i i p e a a h g s c i i v t i i t e e t o t w i i y t
c o l d n t t m n c o u b b k b a r v s c t w h m p u a o i r w m n n m
e m r m i g v s f f y m i o a m o n t o g f c m e e r g p a y e p g g u
c m n e d d h t e f h e h n a t a p d e o v u i c f y n i l e u e s e a
u p i u y n m y l o e e z y n h o i s a g g r a v a t e d a s s a u l t
```

aggravated assault
Bureau of Justice Statistics
crime rate
cyberstalking
forcible rape
kidnapping
manslaughter
murder
parental kidnapping
rape
self-report data
Uniform Crime Reports
victim precipitation
arson
burglary
crimes known to the police
date rape
hate crime
larceny-theft
marital rape
National Crime Victimization Survey
prima facie evidence
restitution
stalking
victim compensation programs
violent crimes
Baby Moses laws
child abuse
cybercrime
fetal abuse
index offenses
lesser included offense
motor vehicle theft
National Incident-Based Reporting System
property crimes
robbery
statutory rape
victimology
white-collar crime

ANSWERS TO CROSSWORD

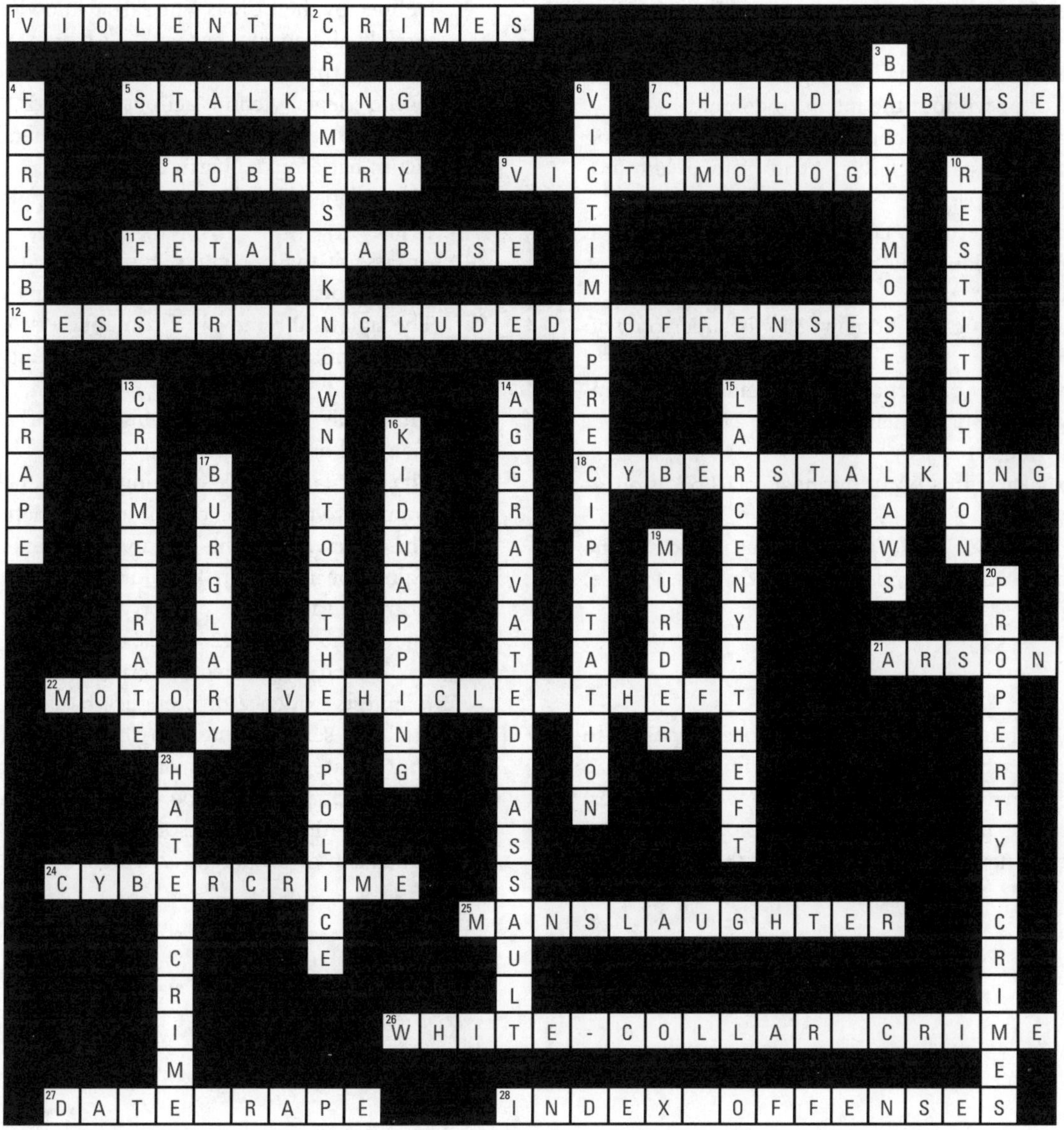

ACROSS

1 Crimes defined by the FBI's *Uniform Crime Reports* as serious crimes against a person. (2 words, 1 space)

5 "A course of conduct directed at a specified person that would cause a reasonable person to feel fear."

7 A broad term that applies to neglect, psychological and physical abuse of a minor. (2 words, 1 space)

8 The use of force or fear to take personal property belonging to another against that person's will.

9 The discipline that studies the nature and causes of victimization, as well as programs for aiding victims and preventing victimization.

11 The abusing of a fetus, which may or may not lead to its death. (2 words, 1 space)

12 Charged crimes that are related to the major crime but are less serious. (3 words, 2 spaces)

18 A form of stalking that involves the Internet, email, or some other form of electronic communication to harass or otherwise threaten another.

21 The willful and malicious burning of the structure of another with or without the intent to defraud.

22 The stealing of an automobile, in contrast to the stealing of an automobile part or larceny-theft from an automobile. (3 words, 2 spaces)

24 The use of the Internet to facilitate crimes such as online pornography, stalking and bullying and other forms of criminal activity.

25 The unlawful killing of a human being by a person who lacks malice.

26 The illegal actions of corporations or individuals, committed while pursuing their legitimate occupations. (3 words, 1 hyphen, 1 space)

27 Forced sexual acts that occur during a social occasion. (2 words, 1 space)

28 The FBI's *Uniform Crime Reports* of the occurrences of the eight crimes considered most serious. (2 words, 1 space)

DOWN

2 All serious criminal offenses that have been reported to the police for which the police have sufficient evidence to believe the crimes were committed. (5 words, 4 spaces)

3 Provisions for protecting mothers (or fathers) who abandon their newborn children in ways that will protect those infants; these laws are becoming more common in the United States as well as some other countries. (3 words, 2 spaces)

4 Defined by the *UCR* as "the carnal knowledge of a female forcibly and against her will." (2 words, 1 space)

6 Concept that a criminal act may have been brought on by the alleged victim's actions. (2 words, 1 space)

10 A type of remedy that requires the defendant to pay the victim back for the harm caused.

13 The number of crimes per 100,000 population. (2 words, 1 space)

14 An assault that generally involves a battery inflicted by use of a deadly weapon. (2 words, 1 space).

15 The unlawful removal of someone else's property with the intention of keeping it permanently. (2 words, 1 hyphen)

16 Unlawfully seizing or carrying away of a person against their will or through fraud.

17 The illegal or forcible entering of any enclosed structure in order to commit a crime, usually theft.

19 The unlawful killing of another person with either express or implied malice aforethought.

20 Crimes aimed at the property of another person rather than at the person. (2 words, 1 space).

23 As defined in the federal criminal code, a crime that manifests evidence of prejudice based on race, religion, disability, sexual orientation, or ethnicity, including where appropriate the crimes of murder, nonnegligent manslaughter, forcible rape, aggravated assault, simple assault, intimidation, arson, and destruction, damage or vandalism of property." (2 words, 1 space)

ANSWERS TO WORD SEARCH

aggravated assault
arson
Baby Moses laws
Bureau of Justice Statistics
burglary
child abuse
crime rate
crimes known to the police
cybercrime
cyberstalking
date rape
fetal abuse
forcible rape
hate crime
index offenses
kidnapping
larceny-theft
lesser included offense
manslaughter
marital rape
motor vehicle theft
murder
National Crime Victimization Survey
National Incident-Based Reporting System
parental kidnapping
prima facie evidence
property crimes
rape
restitution
robbery
self-report data
stalking
statutory rape
Uniform Crime Reports
victim compensation programs
victimology
victim precipitation
violent crimes
white-collar crime

TRY INTO CRIMINA
STICE SYSTEMS:
CING

LEARNING OBJECTIVES

After reading this chapter, you should be able to do the following:

- **Discuss the history of U.S. policing, paying special attention to the contributions of the British police**
- **Explain the meaning of decentralized policing in the United States**
- **Distinguish among local, state, and federal policing systems**
- **State and evaluate the role and function of the Federal Bureau of Investigation (FBI)**
- **Comment on recent federal legislation and the development of agencies designed to combat terrorism**
- **Discuss the nature and purpose of the Department of Homeland Security (DHS)**
- **Analyze the function and problems of the Transportation Security Administration (TSA) and the U.S. Customs and Border Protection (CBP) agencies**
- **Give an overview of campus policing**
- **Explain the difference between private and public policing, and discuss their comparative growth and importance**
- **Note early reform efforts in the organization and administration of policing systems**
- **Explain what is meant by a professional model of policing**
- **Discuss what is meant by a problem-oriented approach to policing**
- **Analyze community-oriented policing**
- **Explain and evaluate COMPSTAT**

CHAPTER OUTLINE

KEY TERMS

Bow Street Runners
COMPSTAT
constable
Department of Homeland Security (DHS)
Federal Bureau of Investigation (FBI)
frankpledge system
hundred
INTERPOL
Law Enforcement Assistance Administration (LEAA)
Law Enforcement Education Program (LEEP)
magistrate
marshal
Molly Maguires
police
posse
private security forces
proactive
reactive
sheriff
shires
tithing
Transportation Security Administration (TSA)
USA Patriot Act
vigilantism
watch system

CHAPTER SUMMARY

Chapter 3 is the first of three chapters exploring the historical development of both an informal and formal police system in England and the United States; the decentralized nature of law enforcement in the United States; and the use of private policing and security forces. In addition, information is presented on the development of international policing, the organization and administration of law enforcement agencies, and relevant legislation regarding police procedure and enforcement.

As illustrated in the chapter, initial law enforcement efforts were informal in nature and can be traced back to England and the family beginning with the use of the **frankpledge** system. In this system, families were organized into **tithings** (10 families) and a **hundred** (100 families). This informal organization was for the purposes of protecting each other, and enforcing the laws. An unpaid **constable** was responsible for overseeing that these laws and protection were enforced for the hundred. This practice continued for more than a century. Ultimately, these systems were combined into hundreds to form **shires,** which were run by an appointed **shire-reeve**, the forerunner to the **sheriff**. Eventually, as the country became more industrialized there grew a need for a more formalized system. This system (developed in England) was known as the **watch system**, which is a forerunner to the modern-day police. Under this system, watchmen were responsible for maintaining order and monitoring public behavior and manners. Many factors contributed to the need for formal policing, in both England and the United States, but crucial here was the increasing complexity of society with the coming of industrialization. The rising levels of criminal activity, public unrest, and riots that accompanied industrialization demonstrated the inability of informal methods of policing to provide adequate protection.

Modern policing can trace its roots to the work of London's **John and Henry Fielding** during the mid-18th century. Under their supervision the **Bow Street Runners** were created. These individuals were appointed constables who received training and were given a portion of the fines upon prosecution of the accused. This first attempt to formalize policing was not successful, however. In 1829, the first modern police force, known as the **Metropolitan Police,** was founded in London by **Sir Robert Peel**. Also known as **Peelers or Bobbies**, these individuals were hired to work full-time, they were given uniforms and organized by territories. This formal mechanism of policing continued throughout Europe and was transferred to the United States through immigrants. By the 19th century in the United States, most regions or territories had some form of **posse** or **vigilantism** in place. Although these rogue forms of law enforcement served the needs at the time, it was not until the mid-1880s that most American cities had developed some form of a **municipal decentralized police force**.

The second section of the chapter discusses the evolution of the formal policing system in the United States into a decentralized system having local, state, and federal levels and the resulting overlaps and gaps among levels. Agencies at each of these levels have their own jurisdictions and responsibilities. The distinctions and differences in these responsibilities illustrate the gaps in services that may be filled most effectively when agencies work in collaboration rather than as separate distinct entities. Decentralization also permits states and localities to experiment with methods that might be effective in light of the problems that distinguish their policing needs from those of the federal government. The various levels of policing cooperate in some functions, such as investigation and training. Numerous law enforcement agencies exist at the federal level, and they are available to assist states and local agencies as well. These federal agencies have undergone dramatic changes in recent years, especially since the 9/11 terrorist attacks on U.S. soil. The changes have not been without controversy, and neither has the legislation that created and empowered them. Some of the key changes in legislation include the creation of the **Department of Homeland Security** (**DHS**), which includes **the Transportation Security Administration** (**TSA**), and increased authority given to **U.S. Customs and Border Protection** (**CBP**).

The chapter continues with a discussion on the use of **private security forces** to supplement the work of public agencies. The increased use of private agencies and personnel is not without controversy. Formal, public policing systems have been the object of criticism for a long time; some citizens have reacted by employing private police or by having security devices installed in their homes or businesses. Conflict between public and private policing developed and continues, although there is some evidence of cooperation between the two. Some states have established minimum requirements for licensing private security firms.

Next, information is presented on the use of **international policing** efforts as a mechanism for countries to work in collaboration with one another. Although differences exist in the form and nature of the organizations (decentralized versus centralized), they still share a common goal of enforcing the laws internationally. One such agency, **INTERPOL**, was established in 1923 to promote cooperation among nations. Still in existence today, this group has worked to assist with preventing terrorism and tracking fugitives.

Finally, the chapter concludes with a review of the various forms of administration of law enforcement across the United States. The type of police organization and administration may have a significant effect on policing. Key reformers in professionalizing and organizing the administration of law enforcement include **August Vollmer**, who is referred to as the father of policing, and **O. W. Wilson**, an influential police chief in Wichita, Kansas, during the late 1920s who emphasized advanced training and professionalism of the officers. The chapter discusses early reform efforts in police organization and administration and then focuses on differentiating policing models: the **professional model**, **problem-oriented policing**, and **community-oriented policing**. The **professional model** of policing follows a hierarchical structure with the police chief as the central authority. This model involves many rules and regulations. During the 1960s, in an effort to focus on professionalizing law enforcement agencies, President Lyndon Johnson and Congress established the **Office of Law Enforcement Assistance** and the **Law Enforcement Assistance Administration** (**LEAA**). The LEAA office provided federal support for research, development, and evaluation of criminal justice-related programs. Money for police education was provided through the **Law Enforcement Education Program** (**LEEP**). This professional model was criticized for being too authoritarian, which led to a shift to the **problem-oriented policing model** during the late 1980s and into the early 1990s. With the problem-oriented policing approach there is less focus on an extensive division of labor, and there are fewer rules and regulations and fewer levels of authority. The emphasis is on solving problems, and the power comes from the ability of employees to succeed in that goal, not from the titles of their positions. Less attention is given to calls for service. This approach requires officers to be more **proactive** and less **reactive**. Programs such as foot patrol require officers to get back on the street and speak with the citizenry in an effort to prevent crime. The **community-oriented policing model** is an expansion of problem-oriented policing. With this model, the concept of problem-oriented policing is further expanded by placing more law enforcement officers on the street to assist with providing both service to the community and crime prevention and detection.

Finally, the chapter closes with a look at police strategies for crime reduction. These include efforts such as the development of **COMPSTAT** in New York City, whereby the NYPD used a goal-oriented strategy combined with computer technology to reduce crime. The use of foot patrols was combined with the creation of a centralized computer database to track information and be more proactive in addressing community needs through crime prevention.

KEY TERMS

Bow Street Runners The mid-18th-century system that gave the police powers of investigation and arrest to constables who were given some training and paid a portion of the fines in successfully prosecuted cases.

COMPSTAT A strategic management process acclaimed by numerous organizations as effective in crime reduction; utilizes computer technology and other modern management techniques to devise methods of fighting crime.

constable An officer of a municipal corporation who has duties similar to those of a sheriff, such as preserving the public peace, executing papers from the court, and maintaining the custody of juries.

Department of Homeland Security (DHS) The cabinet level department created after the 9/11 terrorist attacks; its creation constituted the most extensive federal government reorganization in 50 years; it combines 22 federal agencies and constitutes the third largest federal agency.

Federal Bureau of Investigation (FBI) A federal agency established in 1908 and delegated the power to investigate alleged violations of federal laws (unless they are otherwise assigned to another agency). The FBI investigates alleged civil, criminal, and securities violations. Although the agency is a federal one, it can, when requested, assist local and state law enforcement agencies with their investigations.

frankpledge system In old English law, a system whereby the members of a *tithing* had corporate responsibility for the behavior of all members over 14 years old. Ten tithings formed a *hundred*, and hundreds were later combined to form *shires*, similar to counties, over which a sheriff had jurisdiction.

hundred In English law, a combination of 10 tithings as part of the frankpledge system. *See also* **frankpledge system** and **tithing**.

INTERPOL A world police organization that was established for the purpose of cooperation among nations involved in common policing problems.

Law Enforcement Assistance Administration (LEAA) The agency, established by Congress in 1965, that provided funding for the development of police departments, police techniques, police education, and police training. It was abolished in 1982. Money for education was provided through the Law Enforcement Education Program (LEEP).

Law Enforcement Education Program (LEEP) *See* **Law Enforcement Assistance Administration** (LEAA).

magistrate A judge in the lower courts of the state or federal court system. Usually magistrates preside over arraignments, preliminary hearings, bail hearings, and minor offenses.

marshal A sworn law enforcement officer who performs the civil duties of the courts, such as the delivery of papers to begin civil proceedings. In some jurisdictions marshals serve papers for the arrest of criminal suspects and escort inmates from jail to court or into the community when they are permitted to leave the jail or prison temporarily. Marshals may also transport offenders from one jurisdiction to another; escort fugitives from their places of capture to the jurisdictions in which they will be tried; provide security for designated persons; or fly on planes as an added security measure.

Molly Maguires A powerful secret police organization in the 1870s in Pennsylvania.

police An official authorized to enforce the law, provide services, and maintain order, using physical (including deadly) force if necessary.

posse The rural police system in which the sheriff may call into action any number of citizens over a certain age if they are needed to assist in law enforcement.

private security forces Persons employed privately instead of by the government to provide security from criminal activity.

proactive In policing, preparing for, intervening in, or taking the initiative in finding criminals, rather than depending on the reports of others.

reactive In policing, depending on the reports of others to find criminal suspects, rather than working independently; it is important because police are not in a position to observe most criminal behavior.

sheriff The chief law enforcement officer in a county, usually chosen by popular election.

shires *See* **frankpledge system.**

tithing In English history, a system of 10 families who had responsibility for the behavior of members over the age of 14. Tithings were also important in protecting the group from outsiders. *See also* **frankpledge system** and **hundred**.

Transportation Security Administration (TSA) A federal agency created by the Aviation and Transportation Security Act (ATSA), enacted two months after the 9/11 terrorist attacks. The TSA was developed to take over the security screening functions for all commercial flights in the United States.

USA Patriot Act: The Uniting and Strengthening America by Providing Appropriate Tools Required to Intercept and Obstruct Terrorism Act of 2001, enacted in response to the 9/11 terrorists attacks and subsequently amended.

vigilantism Literally, *watchman*; action by a person who is alert and on guard, cautious, suspicious, ready to take action to maintain and preserve peace; actions of citizens who take the law into their own hands in an effort to catch and punish criminals.

watch system A system charged with the duties of overseeing, patrolling, or guarding an area or a person. Watchmen were prominent in the early watch system of policing.

STUDY QUESTIONS

These questions are found at the end of your chapter. Your instructor may wish to revisit these or assign them for points. These questions are a good way to integrate the material and to generate your own perspectives during class.

1. Why do we have a formal system of policing?
2. Explain the meaning of the following to the development of modern policing: Bow Street Runners, Peelers or Bobbies, posses, and Molly Maguires.
3. Define *vigilantism,* and discuss its advantages and disadvantages with regard to air travel today.
4. Compare local, state, and federal police systems. What are the advantages and disadvantages of decentralized policing?
5. What are some of the unique problems of rural law enforcement?
6. What is the role of the county sheriff in most jurisdictions?
7. What are the functions of U.S. marshals?
8. Discuss the strengths and weaknesses of the FBI, and comment on the reorganization and reputation of this agency since the 9/11 terrorist attacks. What do you think should be the FBI's role with regard to counterterrorism efforts?
9. Discuss two of the recent pieces of federal legislation designed to combat terrorism.
10. Describe the Department of Homeland Security (DHS). Comment particularly on the Transportation Security Administration (TSA) and the U.S. Customs and Border Protection (CBP) agency.
11. What developments have occurred with regard to law enforcement on college and university campuses? Do we need more security at shopping malls?
12. What is the role of private police agencies? Evaluate.
13. Explain the meaning of INTERPOL and relate its mission to eradicating the sexual abuse of children.
14. How would you describe the administration of early police systems in the United States?
15. Evaluate the traditional, authoritarian model of organizational structure of police departments.
16. Trace the development of the professional model of policing.
17. Describe and analyze the concepts of problem-oriented and community-oriented policing.
18. Explain what is meant by COMPSTAT, and discuss why it is considered, at least by some, to be effective.

LEARNING ACTIVITIES

3.1 For this activity, you should visit the U.S. Drug Enforcement Administration's webpage. Identify and briefly describe three different stories that were the focus of the DEA in the news. From these stories, what were the similarities in their operations and functions? What were the differences? How were the cases investigated? What were some of the investigative concerns that may have arisen in these cases? In what capacity did the DEA work with local or state agencies to make an arrest?

3.2 Many states are moving in the direction of centralizing their police forces both to improve police function within the community and to save costs. Search the web to find an example of a state or local law enforcement agency that has centralized its patrol efforts within the community. Identify the pros and cons of this task. How have the patrol and investigative functions within that law enforcement agency changed since the departments have merged?

3.3 In your text, the author notes that in the fall of 2001, President Bush's administration announced that it would be reorganizing the FBI to focus more on counterterrorism. A report by the General Accounting Office (GAO) and the National Academy of Public Administration indicated that one of the most notable transitions has been the transfer of 400 agents from units investigating illegal drug trafficking to units investigating terrorism. Given this information, what impact do you think this shift in focus from the "War on Drugs" to the "War on Terror" has had on drug usage and/or trafficking both nationally and internationally? How have the media portrayed this shift in focus?

3.4 With the passage of the USA Patriot Act of 2001, the shape and function of law enforcement in the United States have been altered. Visit the Electronic Privacy Information Center webpage. After reviewing the information provided here, how did the passage of this Act alter law enforcement's ability to investigate crimes and interrogate subjects? Find an example in the media of how these techniques have been applied to investigate an offense. Given the events of September 11, 2001, how do you think the law enforcement community has responded?

STUDENT STUDY GUIDE PRACTICE QUESTIONS

True or False

3.1 The shire system in England was the immediate forerunner of modern police systems.

3.2 The first modern police force was known as the Metropolitan Police.

3.3 The United States developed a decentralized form of policing, which was consistent with European countries.

3.4 The majority of police agencies in the United States are located in small towns, villages, or boroughs.

3.5 Most sheriffs are appointed officials.

3.6 The United States Constitution does provide for a central police agency.

3.7 The U.S. Marshal is the primary governmental agency charged with enforcing all federal laws not assigned to other special agencies.

3.8 The Department of Homeland Security was created after 9/11 and combines 22 former federal agencies.

3.9 During the 2004/5 school year, 100 percent of all public colleges and universities reported having sworn law enforcement officers, compared to only 75 percent of private campuses.

3.10 One form of private security is the proprietary system in which organizations or individuals have their own private investigators and security personnel.

Multiple Choice

3.11 What event during the 12th century signaled the beginning of public policing in England?
- a The appointment of a sheriff
- b The appointment of a constable
- c The creation and use of watchmen
- d The creation and use of Bow Street Runners

3.12 During the mid-18th century, London magistrates John and Henry Fielding instituted a system of law enforcement known as the Bow Street Runners. What was their primary responsibility?
- a The Bow Street Runners were constables who were given police investigation and arrest powers.
- b The Bow Street Runners were sheriffs who were given police investigation and arrest powers.
- c The Bow Street Runners were volunteers who were appointed as magistrate assistants assigned to deal with crime through investigation and arrest on the local level.
- d The Bow Street Runners were paid magistrate assistants who were assigned to deal with crime through investigation and arrest on the local level.

3.13 The first modern police force was founded by Sir Robert Peel and was organized by:
- a Tithings, and they reported to the hundreds, who then reported to the King
- b Streets, and they reported to the equivalent to a regional dispatch, who then reported to the central government
- c Territories, and they reported to a central government
- d Territories, and they reported to a decentralized government

3.14 The Texas Rangers were the:
- a First state-supported police organization in the United States
- b First international police agency assigned to deal with Mexico
- c First version of the Office of Immigration
- d First version of Drug Regulation Agency and Kidnapping Enforcement

3.15 The U.S. Department of Justice is responsible for overseeing the administration of which of these agencies?
- a U.S. Marshals
- b Bureau of Alcohol, Tobacco, Firearms and Explosives (ATF)
- c Drug Enforcement Administration (DEA)
- d All of the above

3.16 Who is considered the father of modern policing?
- a August Vollmer
- b Sir Robert Peel
- c O. W. Wilson
- d Herman Goldstein

3.17 Which model of law enforcement emphasizes a clear chain of command where subordinates in each unit report directly to their division heads?
- a Community policing model
- b Professional policing model
- c Problem-oriented policing
- d None of the above

3.18 Which model of law enforcement emphasizes solving problems, and the power comes from the ability of employees to succeed in that goal, not from the titles of their positions?
- a Community policing model
- b Professional policing model
- c Problem-oriented policing
- d None of the above

3.19 The _____ embodies the belief that minor offenders who disrupt the quality of life should be controlled, thus making neighborhoods safer, resulting in a reduction of fear and of crime.
- a social disorganization thesis
- b broken communities orientation
- c broken windows thesis
- d communities in disrepair thesis

3.20 Which form of problem-oriented policing emphasizes the sharing of information, enhancement of community safety, and the reduction in crime through the use of foot patrols?
- a Community policing model
- b Professional policing model
- c Problem-oriented policing
- d None of the above

Fill-in-the-Blank

3.21 The _____ system was one of the first informal forms of policing to organize beyond the immediate family or individual. In this form of policing, families were organized into a tithing and hundreds for the purposes of protecting each other and enforcing the laws.

3.22 The shire-reeve was the forerunner to the _____.

3.23 Under the _____ system of policing in the United States, a sheriff could call into action any number of citizens over a certain age if they were needed to assist in law enforcement.

3.24 _____ was appointed the first Director of the FBI in 1924 and served until his death in May 1972.

3.25 Founded in 1923 and reorganized in 1946, _____ was established to promote cooperation among nations involved in common police problems.

3.26 The _____ model of policing is characterized by a hierarchical structure, with the police chief as the central authority in the organization.

3.27 The professional model of policing has been criticized for being too _____.

3.28 _____ is designed to enhance the effectiveness of policing by identifying the underlying problems and attempting to solve those problems by focusing on any or all three of the traditional areas of policing: order maintenance, law enforcement, and community service.

3.29 Research suggests that _____ programs do not result in a reduction in crime but that residents feel safer within their neighborhoods and feel that crime has been reduced.

3.30 _____ is a goal-oriented strategic management process that uses computer technology, operational strategy, and managerial accountability to structure the manner in which a police department provides crime-control services.

CROSSWORD

ACROSS

2 The chief law enforcement officer in a county, usually chosen by popular election.

6 In the problem-solving approach, ______ police should be more involved, taking the initiative in preventing crime.

7 "A goal-oriented strategic management process that uses computer technology, operational strategy and managerial accountability to structure the manner in which a police department provides crime-control services."

8 The mid-18th-century London system that gave the police powers of investigation and arrest to constables who were given some training and paid a portion of the fines in successfully prosecuted cases. (3 words, no spaces)

9 In English law, a combination of 10 tithings as part of the frankpledge system.

12 A powerful secret police organization in the 1870s in Pennsylvania. (2 words, no spaces)

14 In English history, a system of 10 families who had responsibility for the behavior of members over the age of 14.

16 The rural police system in which the sheriff may call into action any number of citizens over a certain age if they are needed to assist in law enforcement.

17 A world police organization that was established for the purpose of cooperation among nations involved in common policing problems.

18 In old English law, a system whereby the members of a tithing had corporate responsibility for the behavior of all members over 14 years old. (2 words, no spaces)

DOWN

1 Persons employed by private agencies instead of governmental ones to provide security from criminal activity. (3 words, no spaces)

3 A judge from the lower courts of the state or federal court system. Usually presides over arraignments, preliminary hearings, bail hearings, and minor offenses.

4 In the problem-solving approach, ______ police wait for others to call in complaints.

5 A system charged with the duties of overseeing, patrolling, or guarding an area or a person. (2 words, no spaces)

10 Literally, "watchman"; action by a person who is alert and on guard, cautious, suspicious, ready to take action to maintain and preserve peace; actions of citizens who take the law into their own hands in an effort to catch and punish criminals.

11 An officer of a municipal corporation who has duties similar to those of a sheriff, such as preserving the public peace, executing papers from the court, and maintaining the custody of juries.

13 A sworn law enforcement officer who performs the civil duties of the courts, such as the delivery of papers to begin civil proceedings.

15 A government official authorized to enforce the law and to maintain order, using physical, including deadly, force if necessary.

WORD SEARCH

t a a s c p r m t e c o r y a n t o t s m i y c i s e a l e m i a i h s m o
r n r v r e i d e e a o a a i c r f t g n n n r t m n a a a s w e a i s l n
t s n p v p o r m a c a r t i s e h y r s i n n t i e h s p s v e a s r o o
m i o o a y s d o t m e r u t e n o e s e t n o i a t u t o m i o n i i o o
e s s a i i u r l a a e f y c f o f f e t e r d s p n m y t r p r d t i i r
d e n t s t m a e s f r y l a r c d i u r i n i s e a a t a e o a a a a t t
o p e s c c a m l m s r i r i f t e s u t m s k r s h n i s o l g u i r d r
c i n l i i u r f a o t e w s i n a t t s a f o n c e n r n o i e e r s o f
m e s o a n t h t r e e t r i r p s o a o o l t m e i r u r t c e o h a g e
l e t g v e r e a s o w o i e a y o p g t t o s s t n e c s h e r i f f o d
l m i p l i s v i g i l a n t i s m n e n m e s s i p g e i i r r i c t e t
r r e r e r i r r a e n o r e t h s r a g a n a p t t v s t u e e p m r s l
d i c n h t m b s i i r i d e a m l m c t i n s r h n f d r s n s n o n m a
e r f s e p u n f u r o w m e n e p o a a w d n l i r n n s s s a e p l r e
m a r g o r p n o i t a c u d e t n e m e c r o f n e w a l a o i v s s t a
r e m a g i s t r a t e w i o a s n s n t i f o r g s c l r n i r m r e l p
i m n e h v l a c c i t e s s t y w s t o d u h u l l p e t t s u e s c s e
t d c t i a b t h m g i o r a u s t i v e a t i e e e a m o c m t c r i e i
o e e v i t a s r u r i n b t m e t i c e v e w n a c i o c e s e e n t f r
e p v a w e y p a m o l l y m a g u i r e s s e n t l r h t e v e m o m t m
y h i i i s i m w m a e e d e r d n u h u e n i i s e l f h f r i s e n o d
n i l e t e o o a l r t l e o s e b i i i c t v p i n i o i s f n c k d e p
i s e e f c a c d a i i a t y h l i g n s n e a d d v t t r h s n r p n m t
l m m a r u a r i o m t a i i a p r n e p r i s a i e m n i a m t r a r b a
e e e a a r m o m o t i t e r l k t a a s r e n n u r t e e r t s w o b u t
i i m n m i n u r i o i i e a t n o m s e t e e a o n a m i r i e u n m i t
a e s p i t s l a p m f d e t d a o i y p i t d t r i n t i t g s l r o l w
i p r c a y t d r n a e m s e m r i p r c d r s r i a t r s e t o s b e s d
l a c a e f i c r m f c l r i s f i m s i m f w i u u n a m e i d a e h m r
l i f s t o y a t b o s e s t a i o n c m o a m n v e m p t e u t e p a a o
n o i t a r t s i n i m d a e c n a t s i s s a t n e m e c r o f n e w a l
r f e i c c m p r c l f f d d i n e l e v t d t m r o n d y o o s m f e a o
s r u e i e h a f d r i f i a y a s o a m o r t u u c v n e a s p r e a u a
s a n n n s v a o v n e l e s t s i l l v a n t l o i o o y d f f s a i a r
y s e o a s e e l m a a t r i g a u b i s g i r o n n r a c d s t s n e u h
p e l s a o u o f u s l d a c t n o o t n c s d e d e e t s e n r e r a s o
u p e m d p m t g d l r a b o c a c s a f f s r t c t e c e f f t t r s r h
n r n t t s o l r m t r s p e e t r i i t i s n r u o r n i d e s e e n s t

Bow Street Runners
Department of Homeland Security
hundred
Law Enforcement Education Program
Molly Maguires
private security forces
sheriff
Transportation Security Administration
watch system

COMPSTAT
Federal Bureau of Investigation
INTERPOL
magistrate
police
proactive
shires
USA Patriot Act

constable
frankpledge system
Law Enforcement Assistance Administration
marshal
posse
reactive
tithing
vigilantism

ANSWERS TO CROSSWORD

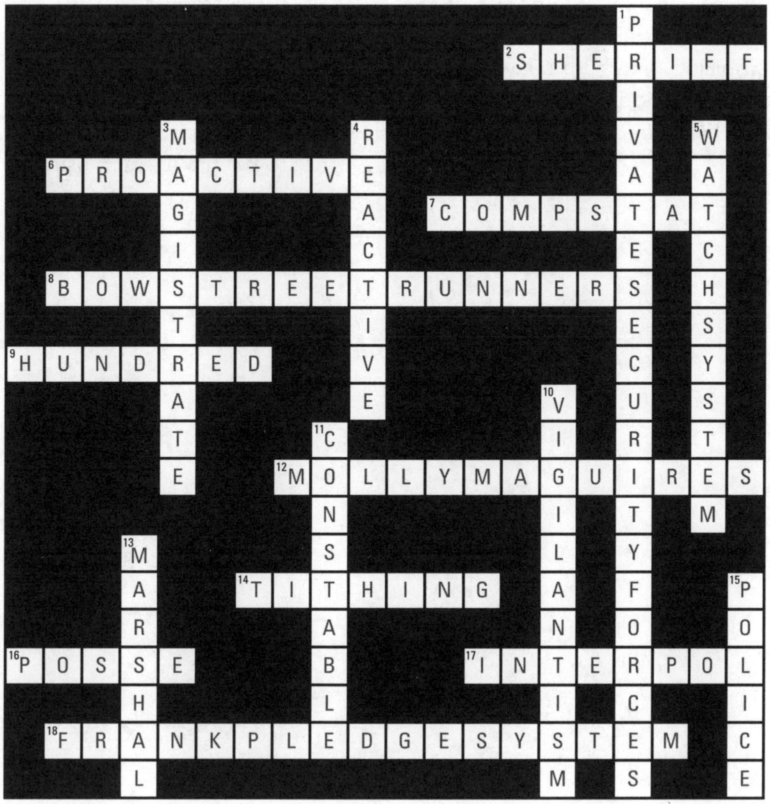

ACROSS

2 The chief law enforcement officer in a county, usually chosen by popular election.

6 In the problem-solving approach, ______ police should be more involved, taking the initiative in preventing crime.

7 "A goal-oriented strategic management process that uses computer technology, operational strategy and managerial accountability to structure the manner in which a police department provides crime-control services."

8 The mid-18th-century London system that gave the police powers of investigation and arrest to constables who were given some training and paid a portion of the fines in successfully prosecuted cases. (3 words, no spaces)

9 In English law, a combination of 10 tithings as part of the frankpledge system.

12 A powerful secret police organization in the 1870s in Pennsylvania. (2 words, no spaces)

14 In English history, a system of 10 families who had responsibility for the behavior of members over the age of 14.

16 The rural police system in which the sheriff may call into action any number of citizens over a certain age if they are needed to assist in law enforcement.

17 A world police organization that was established for the purpose of cooperation among nations involved in common policing problems.

18 In old English law, a system whereby the members of a tithing had corporate responsibility for the behavior of all members over 14 years old. (2 words, no spaces)

DOWN

1 Persons employed by private agencies instead of governmental ones to provide security from criminal activity. (3 words, no spaces)

3 A judge from the lower courts of the state or federal court system. Usually presides over arraignments, preliminary hearings, bail hearings, and minor offenses.

4 In the problem-solving approach, ______ police wait for others to call in complaints.

5 A system charged with the duties of overseeing, patrolling, or guarding an area or a person. (2 words, no spaces)

10 Literally, "watchman"; action by a person who is alert and on guard, cautious, suspicious, ready to take action to maintain and preserve peace; actions of citizens who take the law into their own hands in an effort to catch and punish criminals.

11 An officer of a municipal corporation who has duties similar to those of a sheriff, such as preserving the public peace, executing papers from the court, and maintaining the custody of juries.

13 A sworn law enforcement officer who performs the civil duties of the courts, such as the delivery of papers to begin civil proceedings.

15 A government official authorized to enforce the law and to maintain order, using physical, including deadly, force if necessary.

ANSWERS TO WORD SEARCH

Bow Street Runners
Department of Homeland Security
hundred
Law Enforcement Education Program
Molly Maguires
private security forces
sheriff
Transportation Security Administration
watch system
COMPSTAT
Federal Bureau of Investigation
INTERPOL
magistrate
police
proactive
shires
USA Patriot Act
constable
frankpledge system
Law Enforcement Assistance Administration
marshal
posse
reactive
tithing
vigilantism

POLICING IN A MODERN SOCIETY

LEARNING OBJECTIVES

After reading this chapter, you should be able to do the following:

- **Describe the importance of police recruitment and selection**
- **Discuss the role of higher education in policing**
- **Analyze the importance of police training**
- **Explain the meaning and importance of discretion in policing**
- **List and discuss the three major areas of police functions**
- **Present an overview of the major U.S. constitutional provisions that govern policing**
- **Discuss the implications of the USA Patriot Act**
- **Discuss recent U.S. Supreme Court decisions regarding traffic stops and searches**
- **Explain the difference between an investigatory stop and an arrest**
- **Assess the meaning and importance of racial profiling**
- **Discuss the meaning of probable cause, and explain the purpose of requiring a warrant for most searches**
- **Explain what police can and cannot do in searching a home, a vehicle, and a person**
- **Understand the importance of the prohibition against unreasonable searches and seizures, even in public school settings**
- **Compare the police role of interrogation with that of investigation**
- **Explain and evaluate the *Miranda* rule, its exceptions, and updates**

Criminal Justice Essentials: Study Guide, Ninth Edition. Shannon Barton-Bellessa.

CHAPTER OUTLINE

KEY TERMS

anticipatory search warrant
arrest
contraband
curtilage
frisk
harmless error
informant
Miranda warning
plain view doctrine
pretextual stop
probable cause
racial profiling
reversible error
search and seizure
search warrant
summary judgment
warrant

CHAPTER SUMMARY

Chapter 4 is the second of three on policing. The chapter began with a discussion on preparing for a job in law enforcement, which includes exploring the issues with **recruitment, selection, education,** and **training** of police. As noted in the chapter, one of the most difficult aspects of **recruiting and retaining** good officers is that the desired qualities and attributes of candidates are oftentimes difficult if not impossible to measure. Good officers must be intelligent and able to think independently, multi-task, understand and appreciate different cultures and subcultures, and be persons of the highest moral and ethical standards. One mechanism for encouraging these characteristics is through **education**. Although law enforcement agencies recognize the importance of having an educated workforce, only one-third report requiring some form of education as a requirement for employment. Once officers are hired, the screening process continues. Dating as far back as 1967, the Task Force on Police of the President's Commission emphasized the importance of **training** to prepare recruits to use discretion within the limits of the law, to be familiar with the role of the police, and to know the limits of the criminal justice system. The Commission further recommended the minimum number of **training** hours recruits should receive (e.g., 400 hours of classroom work spread over four to six months combined with field training). Increasing the amount and quality of training not only enhances community safety but also reduces the level of civil liability for the department.

The second section of the chapter reviews the role of **discretion** in law enforcement. Noting the critical nature of using discretion, the chapter reviews the magnitude of the decisions made on a daily basis by officers to question, detain, arrest, or ignore various behaviors of citizens. The process of **selective enforcement** is integral to not only the functioning of the agency but police–community relations as well. More specifically, this chapter focuses on what police do in a modern society, and how their role functions within the context of the discretion that police have in performing their jobs. The chapter devotes a section to the explanation and analysis of why discretion is necessary and how it might be abused. The decision-making process of officers is collapsed into four broad categories: **organization variables, neighborhood variables, situational variables**, and **officer characteristics**. Discretion cannot be eliminated; thus, controlling it is a necessity. The key to successful use of discretion is that the officer must be mindful to use legal rather than **extralegal factors** in making the decision to stop, arrest, or take other actions.

The next and primary focus of the chapter is on the functions that police must perform in an increasingly complex society. Those functions are numerous, but they are categorized as **law enforcement, order maintenance**, and **community service**. Although there is agreement that these are the three most important functions of law enforcement, communities may differ in what they choose to emphasize. Both order maintenance and community service are discussed before law enforcement.

Police are tasked with the responsibility to maintain order in a society. The presence of order is the absence of disorder. As noted by James Q. Wilson, the key to successful **order maintenance** activities is for officers is to manage conflict situations and to bring about a consensual resolution. Order maintenance may be the most crucial function of policing, as the absence of order may lead to law violations, even serious criminal acts, such as the violent crimes of aggravated assault and murder. Examples of order maintenance activities include dealing with noise complaints, public drunkenness, local ordinance violations, etc. Although some of these calls may result in law enforcement tasks, this is typically not an officer's primary function. Agencies receive far more calls for order maintenance than for law enforcement. In addition, research suggests that the greatest influence on increasing the public's overall satisfaction with police is to focus on order maintenance tasks as a mechanism for improving police–community relations. Police may also serve the community by assisting offenders with their reentry into society. As will be noted in later chapters, approximately 97 percent of all those incarcerated reenter society. This order maintenance function is important for successful reintegration. Likewise, the **community service function** of policing may prevent or reduce actions that might lead to law violations. Furthermore, many of the activities police are called upon to perform occur after hours, when other organizations have closed for the day. Despite the importance of the community service function, many officers do not like completing these tasks. One way to address the needs of the community through public service is to hire officers who are less educated, less trained, and with lower salaries but who are good at community involvement. Through these tasks, young people who are interested in law enforcement, but who may otherwise not qualify, can be provided with opportunities to perform an important policing function.

The section on **law enforcement** includes discussion of the following: the constitutional limitations on policing; the process of traffic control and enforcement of traffic laws; the investigatory stop; racial profiling; stop and frisk procedures; arrest, search, and seizure, including warrants and probable cause, home searches, vehicle searches, and body searches; interrogation; and investigation. This chapter summarizes a number of U.S. Supreme Court cases that establish the boundaries of police procedure and citizens' constitutional right to protection while observing the defendants' due process rights. U.S. criminal justice systems place great emphasis on the right of individuals to be free from unreasonable governmental intrusion. This does not mean, however, that police cannot arrest, search and seize, interrogate, and investigate, but only that these functions must be performed within the limits of state and federal statutes, constitutions, and court decisions. Those limits are being challenged in many cases.

There are three key Amendments to the U.S. Constitution's Bill of Rights that protect U.S. citizens from unlawful police practices: first, the **Fourth Amendment's** prohibition against unreasonable search and seizure; second, the **Fifth Amendment**'s provision that a person may not be forced to incriminate him- or herself; and, third, the **Sixth Amendment** right to counsel. These are the key constitutional bases of what police may and may not do in law enforcement. The investigatory stop, brief detention, arrest, and searching and seizing are important police activities regulated by constitutional requirements, court interpretations of those requirements, and departmental policies.

A look at a few key cases on the law of stop, arrest, search, and seizure should make it obvious that it is impossible to state what *the law* is in these areas. The facts of a particular case must be analyzed carefully in light of previous court decisions, statutes, and constitutional provisions. Reasonable minds may differ as to the conclusion in any given case. It is important to analyze case law carefully, looking at the rule of a case as well as the reasons for that rule.

In some situations, police are permitted to stop, arrest, search, and seize without a warrant, although the U.S. Supreme Court prefers warrants. In the case of *Terry v. Ohio*, the U.S. Supreme Court established the ***Terry* stop and frisk** rule that guides officers in considering the **totality of circumstances** to inform their decision to continue their search without a warrant. Again, it is impossible for police to know in every case whether they face exceptions to the warrant requirement. Other key concerns facing law enforcement officers are whether they have probable cause to search; whether evidence would fall under the plain view doctrine (*Mapp v. Ohio* and *Chimel v. California*); and to what extent the **exclusionary rule** applies. Similarly, law enforcement officers must decide when and what type of **search warrant** may be necessary to seek evidence. Frequently, law enforcement is ambiguous, leaving considerable discretion to the individual officer, who may be second-guessed by the courts. Despite the need to analyze individual cases in terms of their unique facts, some general principles of constitutional law govern the law enforcement function of policing. These are discussed in the chapter, with attention paid to some of the major U.S. Supreme Court cases governing each aspect of law enforcement, from the initial stop to the searching and seizing of homes, automobiles, and persons.

Interrogation is another important law enforcement function. Law enforcement officers must be able to interrogate suspects but also keep in mind the Fifth Amendment protection against bearing witness against oneself. The U.S. Supreme Court has decided many cases in this area. The ***Miranda*** warning must be given in cases in which a person might be deprived of his or her liberty, but it is not always clear when interrogation has begun and the warning must be given (**custodial interrogations**). Suspects may waive the right to counsel, but that waiver must be knowingly and intelligently made, and law enforcement officers may not initiate interrogations once that waiver has been made. Failure to comply with *Miranda* requirements may result in the exclusion of evidence from the trial.

Investigation is the final police function discussed in this chapter. In recent years, the field of law enforcement has seen advanced techniques involving science as a mechanism for detection and prosecution of criminal cases (DNA testing). As the goals of traditional law enforcement and the scientific community become less blurred, there are possibilities for increased conviction rates. Although some still question the use of DNA and it will continue to be challenged, the utilization of forensic techniques further illustrates the need for improved methodologies for solving crime.

KEY TERMS

anticipatory search warrant A warrant that is issued for a search at a particular place at a particular time *in the future*. It is based on evidence of a *triggering* event that gives probable cause to believe that the evidence, contraband, or fugitive will be at that place at that time.

arrest The act of taking an individual into custody in order to make a criminal charge against that person.

contraband Any item (such as weapons, alcohol, or other drugs), possession of which is illegal or violates prison rules.

curtilage The enclosed ground and buildings immediately around a dwelling.

frisk An action by a law enforcement officer, airport security officer, or a correctional officer in a penal setting, consisting of patting down or running one's hands quickly over a person's body to determine whether the individual has a weapon or other contraband. This is in contrast to a body search, which is a more careful and thorough examination of the person.

harmless error A minor or trivial error not deemed sufficient to harm the rights of the party who asserts the errors. Cases are not reversed on the basis of harmless errors.

informant A person who gives information to law enforcement officials about a crime or planned criminal activity.

***Miranda* warning** The rule, stemming from *Miranda* v. *Arizona*, that stipulates that anyone in custody for an offense that might result in a jail or prison term must be warned of certain rights before any questioning by law enforcement officials occurs. These rights include the right to remain silent, to be told that anything said can and will be held against the suspect, the right to counsel (which will be appointed if the suspect cannot afford to retain private counsel), and the right to cease talking at any time. If the warning is not given or is given and violated, any information obtained from the suspect may be inadmissible as evidence at trial. The rights may be waived if done so willingly and knowingly by one who has the legal capacity to waive them.

plain view doctrine The legal doctrine that permits a law enforcement officer who is legally searching a place for particular items to seize those that are in plain view but not listed on the search warrant.

pretextual stop A stop allegedly for a minor traffic offense but actually conducted as a pretense to look for a more serious offense, such as the possession of illegal drugs.

probable cause In search warrant cases, a set of facts and circumstances that leads to the reasonable belief that the items sought are located in a particular place. In arrest cases, the facts and circumstances lead to the reasonable belief that the suspect has committed a crime.

racial profiling The reaction by law enforcement officers to potential suspects based solely on their race or ethnicity.

reversible error An error in a legal proceeding, such as a trial, that is considered sufficient to require the reversal of a conviction or a sentence.

search and seizure The examination of a person or a person's property and the taking of items that may be evidence of criminal activity; generally requires a search warrant. Unreasonable searches and seizures are prohibited by the U.S. Constitution.

search warrant *See* **warrant.**

summary judgment A decision by a court based on legal issues rather than questions of fact that must be decided by the jury (or judge) after hearing evidence.

warrant A court issued document authorizing an officer to arrest a suspect or to search a person, personal property, or a place for specified reasons. A warrant should be issued only on a finding of probable cause.

STUDY QUESTIONS

These questions are found at the end of your chapter. Your instructor may wish to revisit these or assign them for points. These questions are a good way to integrate the material and to generate your own perspectives during class.

1 If you were in charge of recruiting persons into policing, what characteristics would you emphasize? What emphasis would you place on higher education and why? What type of training would you require and why? How would you assess the ethical and moral standards of recruits? What standards would you require for policing, and what efforts would you suggest for maintaining those standards within police forces?

2. What types of training would prepare police for such terrorist acts as those of 9/11 or the bombing of the federal building in Oklahoma City?
3. Discuss the importance of discretion in policing.
4. What is meant by *order maintenance* in policing?
5. What should be the role of police with regard to service functions within the communities they serve?
6. Explain briefly the constitutional provisions that govern policing.
7. What functions do police have in traffic control and the enforcement of traffic laws and ordinances? Discuss the recent U.S. Supreme Court cases in this area.
8. Under what circumstances may police stop, question, and arrest a suspect? When may police frisk?
9. Explain racial profiling and its implications.
10. Why are warrants usually required for arrest and search?
11. Under what circumstances may police search without a warrant? Arrest without a warrant?
12. What is the meaning of *probable cause*, and how may it be established?
13. When may police search a home? How much of the home may be searched? Explain the plain view doctrine, and define *curtilage*.
14. After knocking and announcing, how long must police wait before entering a home forcibly to execute a search warrant?
15. Do you believe police should be permitted to use drug-sniffing dogs at the scene of a normal traffic stop?
16. Explain the *plain feel* and the *plain view* doctrines.
17. Under what circumstances may a vehicle be searched?
18. Under what circumstances may body searches be conducted? Should special provisions exist for searching young persons?
19. What is the *Miranda* warning? Why is it important? Discuss the limitations, if any, placed on this right recently by the U.S. Supreme Court interpretations.
20. What is DNA testing and how is it used?

LEARNING ACTIVITIES

4.1 To better understand the characteristics and qualifications of various law enforcement agencies, this activity requires you either to use the Internet, newspapers, or library resources, or contact the following agency representative directly to find the answers.

Local/City Police Officer
County/Sheriff's Department Officer

State Police Officer
Private Security/Loss Prevention Officer
One Federal Policing Agency, e.g, Federal Bureau of Investigation, Drug Enforcement Agency, TSA, etc.
Once you have identified an agency for each of those listed above, answer the following questions:

a List the minimum qualifications
b Provide the starting pay
c Outline the organizational structure, e.g, Sgt, Lt., Chief, Director, Commander, etc.
d Summarize the areas of pre-employment qualifications (e.g., physical agility = x number of sit ups, etc.)
e Summarize the training hours and areas for each position, where available (e.g., law, criminal procedure, driving, police tactics, etc.)

a ____________________

____

____

____

____

____

____

b ____________________

____

____

____

____

____

____

c ____________________

____

____

____

____

____

____

d ____

e ____

4.2 In the debate regarding the necessity for law enforcement officers to seek higher education, many have argued against this proposition. Several states (e.g.., Michigan) have implemented programs within their curriculum that meet the requirements of the state law enforcement training boards to make students eligible for "certification" upon graduation. Find a website from a university criminal justice program at either the two- or the four-year degree level that offers a degree program whereby a student would be eligible to be certified upon graduation and one program where they would not. Compare these two programs, including general education/foundational studies requirements. What are the similarities and differences? What are the pros and cons of obtaining a degree from each of these universities? Imagine you are a Chief of Police and you have one opening. All other things being equal, which graduate are you most likely to hire, and why?

4.3 Issues of racial profiling continue to be of the utmost concern in communities across the United States. Review a reputable newspaper to find an article that discusses the issue of racial profiling. How was this incident handled by the media, the community, and law enforcement officials? What efforts might be made to reduce racial profiling?

4.4 Given the following scenario, what issues might confront a homicide investigator: A female between the ages of 18 and 25 was found dead in a male dormitory room. The victim was lying face down on the bed. Reports suggested that she may have been visiting a male student for the weekend. She and the male student were seen attending a fraternity party the night before. The room was a mess with sheets lying on the floor and books strewn across the room, potentially suggesting a struggle. There was some evidence of blood on the desk and a broken vodka bottle. However, there were no apparent signs of blood on the woman.

STUDENT STUDY GUIDE PRACTICE QUESTIONS

True or False

4.1 Good policing requires intelligence and the ability to think independently, to perform different roles and functions, to comprehend and accept other cultures and subcultures, and to understand the importance of freedom and the dangers of abusing authority.

4.2 The success of efforts to recruit persons with high moral and ethical stands into policing and to encourage them to maintain those standards is impossible to measure once recruits are hired.

4.3 A college education is mandated for all law enforcement agencies.

4.4 A 2007 publication by the RAND Corporation concluded that most police stops in New York City the previous year did constitute widespread evidence of racial profiling.

4.5 Some searches and seizures are permissible without a warrant, without probable cause, and without consent.

4.6 Persons arrested without a warrant are entitled to prompt judicial determination of whether probable cause existed. The U.S. Supreme Court has interpreted prompt to mean 72 hours under most circumstances.

4.7 In the 2009 case of *Arizona v. Gant*, the U.S. Supreme Court retracted its position regarding a warrantless vehicle search incident to an arrest stating that the 1981 case too broadly defined search incident to arrest.

4.8 In the case of *Illinois v. Caballes* (2005), the U.S. Supreme Court ruled that a well-trained narcotics-detection dog used to sniff only the outside of the vehicle during a legitimate traffic stop is not permitted by the Fourth Amendment.

4.9 Thc 1949 casc of *Rochin v. California* was the first case whereby the U.S. Supreme Court ruled on the issue of illegal body searches, defining the term shocking the conscience.

4.10 *Miranda* warnings apply only to custodial interrogations.

Multiple Choice

4.11 A debate over requiring education for law enforcement officers has raised a lot of criticisms. Which of the following is not a criticism toward requiring college education for police officers?

a Raising educational requirements might discriminate against minority applicants.
b The applicant pool may be too small.
c Unions are opposed to higher educational requirements.
d All are criticisms of requiring higher education for law enforcement officers.

4.12 The issue of "driving while black" is of serious concern to minorities in the United States and the public in general. In the case of *United States v. Montero-Camargo* (2000), the Ninth Circuit Court of Appeals heard the question of whether it was permissible for law enforcement officers to detain and question suspects solely based upon their race. In this case the Court of Appeals held that:

a It is permissible to use ethnicity as a fact in deciding whether to stop an individual suspected of a crime.
b It is not permissible to use ethnicity as a fact in deciding whether to stop an individual suspected of a crime.
c The Court of Appeals refused to hear the case therefore the original conviction stood.
d None of the above.

4.13 In the case of *Kolender et al. v. Lawson* (1983), the U.S. Supreme Court considered whether law enforcement officers had too much discretion in stops, even those involving nontraffic situations. In this case, the U.S. Supreme Court ruled that:

a Police may use a vague statute for purposes of stopping, questioning, and otherwise harassing individuals.
b Police may use a clearly defined statute only for purposes of stopping, questioning, and otherwise harassing individuals, but they may stop and question individuals.

c Police may not use a vague statute for purposes of stopping, questioning, and otherwise harassing individuals but they may stop and question individuals.
d Police may not use a vague statute for purposes of stopping, questioning, and otherwise harassing individuals but they may stop individuals.

4.14 In the case of *Illinois v. Lidster* (2001), the U.S. Supreme Court considered whether it was lawful for officers to stop motorists about whom they have no reason to suspect committed illegal acts. In this case, the U.S. Supreme Court ruled that:
a It is not constitutional for the police to establish "information-seeking checkpoints" in their efforts to combat crime, even if they are considering the totality of circumstances.
b It is constitutional for the police to establish "information-seeking checkpoints" in their efforts to combat crime as long as they are considering the totality of circumstances and not harassing motorists.
c It is not constitutional for the police to establish "information-seeking checkpoints" in their efforts to combat crime.
d It is constitutional for the police to establish "information-seeking checkpoints" in their efforts to combat crime.

4.15 In *Terry v. Ohio* (1968), the U.S. Supreme Court considered to what extent law enforcement officers had the discretion to stop and frisk an individual. In this case the U.S. Supreme Court ruled that:
a The "totality of circumstances" gives legal permission to officers to stop and frisk an individual based upon experience and safety of the community.
b The "totality of circumstances" does not give legal permission to officers to stop and frisk an individual based upon experience and safety of the community.
c The "totality of circumstances" gives legal permission to officers to stop and frisk an individual based upon extralegal factors only.
d The "totality of circumstances" does not give legal permission to officers to stop and frisk an individual based upon experience and safety of the community but rather this should be based upon "gut instinct."

4.16 In the 2009 decision of *Arizona v. Johnson*, the U.S. Supreme Court upheld the pat down search based on *Terry v. Ohio* stating that two conditions must occur before such searches do not constitute an unreasonable search and seizure.
a First, the officer must believe the person has committed a crime before stopping them and, second, the officer may use extralegal factors in considering whether or not to search the suspect.
b First, the initial stop must be lawful and, second, to conduct a frisk, the officer must have reason to believe that the suspect is armed and dangerous.
c First, the initial stop must be lawful and, second, the officer may use extralegal factors in considering whether or not to search the suspect.
d First, the officer must believe the person has committed a crime before stopping them and, second, to conduct a frisk, the officer must have reason to believe that the suspect is armed and dangerous.

4.17 Which Amendment to the U.S. Constitution prohibits unreasonable search and seizure?
a First Amendment
b Fourth Amendment
c Eighth Amendment
d Fourteenth Amendment

4.18 In *Mapp v. Ohio* (1961), the U.S. Supreme Court questioned the right to enter a home and search based upon information they had received that a person wanted for questioning in a bombing was hiding out in a two-family dwelling. In this case the U.S. Supreme Court:

- **a** Extended the use of the exclusionary rule to all 50 states, ensuring that individuals were guaranteed the Fourth Amendment protections against flagrant abuse and that individuals did have the right to privacy free from unreasonable state intrusion.
- **b** Ruled that the exclusionary rule applied only to federal violations of law ensuring that individuals were guaranteed the Fourth Amendment protections against flagrant abuse and that individuals did have the right to privacy free from unreasonable state intrusion.
- **c** Extended the use of the exclusionary rule to all 50 states, ensuring that individuals were guaranteed the Fourth Amendment protections against flagrant abuse but stated that individuals did not always have the right to privacy free from unreasonable state intrusion.
- **d** Ruled that the exclusionary rule applied only to federal violations of law, ensuring that individuals were guaranteed the Fourth Amendment protections against flagrant abuse but stated that individuals did not always have the right to privacy free from unreasonable state intrusion.

4.19 In *Escobedo v. Illinois* (1964), the U.S. Supreme Court considered whether an individual has a right to be advised by his (or her) lawyer of his privilege against self-incrimination. In this case, the U.S. Supreme Court ruled that:

- **a** An individual does not have the right to be advised by his lawyer of his privilege against self-incrimination.
- **b** An individual does have the right to be advised by his lawyer of his privilege against self-incrimination but only in federal cases.
- **c** An individual does not have the right to be advised by his lawyer of his privilege against self-incrimination unless certain conditions such as indigent status have been determined.
- **d** An individual does have the right to be advised by his lawyer of his privilege against self-incrimination.

4.20 In 1966, the U.S. Supreme Court considered when an individual suspect has a right to have the Fifth Amendment rights read to them and to voluntarily and knowingly not speak to authorities without the presence of an attorney. In this case, at what point in the process did the U.S. Supreme Court rule in *Miranda v. Arizona* that a suspect has the right to have their Fifth Amendment rights read to them and to voluntarily and knowingly not speak to authorities without the presence of an attorney.

- **a** A suspect has this right upon the initial confrontation.
- **b** A suspect has this right subsequent to arrest.
- **c** A suspect has this right prior to custodial interrogation.
- **d** A suspect has this right subsequent to being charged.

Fill-in-the-Blank

4.21 ______ factors are those elements outside of the law that may influence an officer's decision to stop and/or arrest a suspect.

4.22 Traffic stops in which persons are stopped for violations by police who have stereotyped them as more serious law violators because of their race or ethnicity are referred to by some as _____.

4.23 It is permissible for the police to conduct pat down searches, or _____ the suspect in some cases.

4.24 In the _____, the U.S. Supreme Court upheld that an officer may conduct a pat down search before concluding that the suspect is not armed if the officer feels an item "whose contour or mass makes its identity immediately apparent."

4.25 _____ refers to the facts of the situation that must be such that, upon hearing those facts, a reasonable person would conclude that in all probability a crime had been committed.

4.26 In 2006, the U.S. Supreme Court upheld the constitutionality of a(n) _____, referring to a warrant that is issued for a search at a particular place at a particular time in the future.

4.27 The U.S. Supreme Court in 1971 and later revisited in 1987 ruled that, according to the _____, police may seize evidence without a warrant while they are within the home to execute a lawful arrest and that probable cause exists to search.

4.28 _____ refers to the crime whereby a person smuggles contraband by carrying the contraband, usually illegal drugs, therein.

4.29 _____ is considered one of the most effective and widely used investigative techniques.

4.30 The process of using DNA to identify individuals that is close to 100 percent accurate is known as _____.

CROSSWORD

ACROSS

1 A minor or trivial error not deemed sufficient to harm the rights of the parties who assert the error. (2 words, no spaces)

4 A court-issued writ authorizing an officer to arrest a suspect or to search a person, personal property, or a place. (2 words, no spaces)

8 The enclosed ground and buildings immediately around a dwelling.

9 An action by a law enforcement officer or a correctional officer consisting of patting down or running one's hands quickly over a person's body to determine whether the suspect or inmate has a weapon or other contraband.

11 A person who gives information to law enforcement officials about a crime or planned criminal activity.

12 The legal doctrine that permits a law enforcement officer who is legally searching a place for particular items to seize those that are in plain view but not listed on a search warrant. (3 words, no spaces)

14 The rule stipulating that anyone in custody for an offense that might result in a jail or prison term must be warned of certain rights before any questioning by law enforcement officials occurs. (2 words, no spaces)

15 A court-issued writ authorizing an officer to arrest a suspect or to search a person, personal property, or a place.

16 The act of taking an individual into custody in order to make a criminal charge against that person.

17 In search warrant cases a set of facts and circumstances that leads to the reasonable belief that the items sought are located in a particular place. (2 words, no spaces)

DOWN

2 The reaction by law enforcement officers to potential suspects based solely on their race or ethnicity. (2 words, no spaces)

3 A warrant that is issued for a search at a particular place at a particular time in the future. (3 words, no spaces)

5 The examination of a person or a person's property and the taking of items that may be evidence of criminal activity; it generally requires a search warrant. (3 words, no spaces)

6 A decision by a court based on legal issues rather than questions of fact that must be decided by the jury (or judge) after hearing evidence. (2 words, no spaces)

7 An error in a legal proceeding, such as a trial, that is considered sufficient to require the reversal of a conviction or a sentence. (2 words, no spaces)

10 A stop allegedly for a minor traffic offense but actually conducted as a pretense to look for a more serious offense, such as the possession of illegal drugs. (2 words, no spaces)

13 Any item (such as weapons, alcohol or other drugs) possession of which is illegal or violates prison rules.

WORD SEARCH

n b c i n r t e i a a s a h n a a t t y a t w r g
a r s r a n l a a o s r d e o r c n r w r t j e g
p r o b a b l e c a u s e s n n r e h o s c f m d
a n i r t v i o l a b l e l l s u m e d s e e r d
e t r p r e t e x t u a l s t o p g u w u t s w a
h a r m l e s s e r r o r g e n c d r s s a c v r
w r n t e r e i n c o i c b i r j u r a w o a d e
y t e a d r r l h r t t c s o i i j r l n n f o r
r i s n o o r w b a g a i d i r k y z t o r a r r
p w t m i r a i r i m a e u t a o r r s i r w g t
r b d t e r u z i e s d n a h c r a e s g l z a u
i l v l r o t n e h t r e u a i b m k g p u a t c
r s a a g c r c d i e e e o n a r m o n n r b g a
a a n f b r s s o l i r i v n l a u e n u t b r e
m t c c u r e u y d h e o d e p e s r f n e o e r
u t c m g n i n r a w a d n a r i m e a b n s s a
d r n e c o r a e r e e f g l o n n n a i t u b r
p p a e e t m t i b a h i e r f f s u o a t e s d
i r h t t r u a p i e l l v a i o f s r n t g r f
l a l n a h i t e e i t n a n l r i w a j i e a l
s l n y a o g c c n s d r y r i m e u t s s s n n
o s f b s a n u w n u w v r s n a r n n e u b w d
o r e n x r i i o r e a a i o g n l r n a l a g k
t n a r r a w h c r a e s y r o t a p i c i t n a
p e g z b i t a y r t a u a n t r i i f p a s n r

anticipatory search warrant
curtilage
informant
pretextual stop
reversible error
summary judgment
arrest
frisk
Miranda warning
probable cause
search and seizure
warrant
contraband
harmless error
plain view doctrine
racial profiling
search warrant

ANSWERS TO CROSSWORD

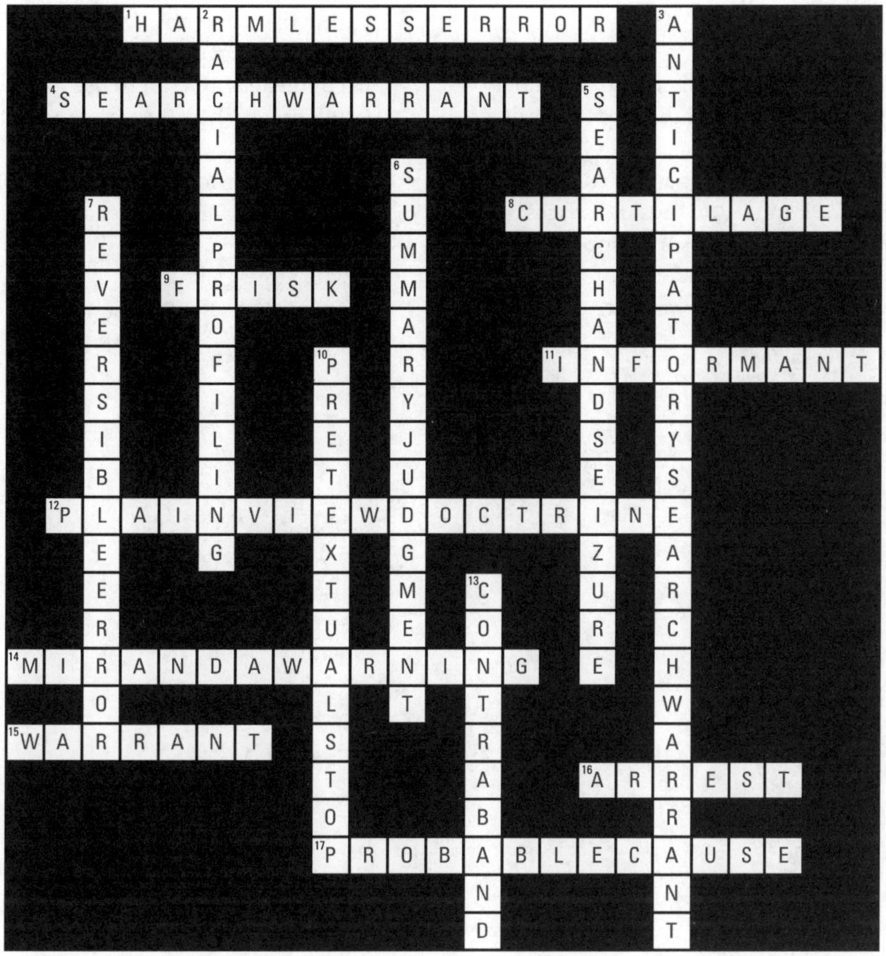

ACROSS

1 A minor or trivial error not deemed sufficient to harm the rights of the parties who assert the error. (2 words, no spaces)

4 A court-issued writ authorizing an officer to arrest a suspect or to search a person, personal property, or a place. (2 words, no spaces)

8 The enclosed ground and buildings immediately around a dwelling.

9 An action by a law enforcement officer or a correctional officer consisting of patting down or running one's hands quickly over a person's body to determine whether the suspect or inmate has a weapon or other contraband.

11 A person who gives information to law enforcement officials about a crime or planned criminal activity.

12 The legal doctrine that permits a law enforcement officer who is legally searching a place for particular items to seize those that are in plain view but not listed on a search warrant. (3 words, no spaces)

14 The rule stipulating that anyone in custody for an offense that might result in a jail or prison term must be warned of certain rights before any questioning by law enforcement officials occurs. (2 words, no spaces)

15 A court-issued writ authorizing an officer to arrest a suspect or to search a person, personal property, or a place.

16 The act of taking an individual into custody in order to make a criminal charge against that person.

17 In search warrant cases a set of facts and circumstances that leads to the reasonable belief that the items sought are located in a particular place. (2 words, no spaces)

DOWN

2 The reaction by law enforcement officers to potential suspects based solely on their race or ethnicity. (2 words, no spaces)

3 A warrant that is issued for a search at a particular place at a particular time in the future. (3 words, no spaces)

5 The examination of a person or a person's property and the taking of items that may be evidence of criminal activity; it generally requires a search warrant. (3 words, no spaces)

6 A decision by a court based on legal issues rather than questions of fact that must be decided by the jury (or judge) after hearing evidence. (2 words, no spaces)

7 An error in a legal proceeding, such as a trial, that is considered sufficient to require the reversal of a conviction or a sentence. (2 words, no spaces)

10 A stop allegedly for a minor traffic offense but actually conducted as a pretense to look for a more serious offense, such as the possession of illegal drugs. (2 words, no spaces)

13 Any item (such as weapons, alcohol or other drugs) possession of which is illegal or violates prison rules.

ANSWERS TO WORD SEARCH

n	b	c	i	n	r	t	e	i	a	a	s	a	h	n	a	a	t	t	y	a	t	w	r	g
a	r	s	r	a	n	l	a	a	o	s	r	d	e	o	r	c	n	r	w	r	t	j	e	g
p	r	o	b	a	b	l	e	c	a	u	s	e	s	n	n	r	e	h	o	s	c	f	m	d
a	n	i	r	t	v	i	o	l	a	b	l	e	l	l	s	u	m	e	d	s	e	e	r	d
e	t	r	p	r	e	t	e	x	t	u	a	l	s	t	o	p	g	u	w	u	t	s	w	a
h	a	r	m	l	e	s	s	e	r	r	o	r	g	e	n	c	d	r	s	s	a	c	v	r
w	r	n	t	e	r	e	i	n	c	o	i	c	b	i	r	j	u	r	a	w	o	a	d	e
y	t	e	a	d	r	r	l	h	r	t	t	c	s	o	i	i	j	r	l	n	n	f	o	r
r	i	s	n	o	o	r	w	b	a	g	a	i	d	i	r	k	y	z	t	o	r	a	r	r
p	w	t	m	i	r	a	i	r	i	m	a	e	u	t	a	o	r	r	s	i	r	w	g	t
r	b	d	t	e	r	u	z	i	e	s	d	n	a	h	c	r	a	e	s	g	l	z	a	u
i	l	v	l	r	o	t	n	e	h	t	r	e	u	a	i	b	m	k	g	p	u	a	t	c
r	s	a	a	g	c	r	c	d	i	e	e	e	o	n	a	r	m	o	n	n	r	b	g	a
a	a	n	f	b	r	s	s	o	l	i	r	i	v	n	l	a	u	e	n	u	t	b	r	e
m	t	c	c	u	r	e	u	y	d	h	e	o	d	e	p	e	s	r	f	n	e	o	e	r
u	t	c	m	g	n	i	n	r	a	w	a	d	n	a	r	i	m	e	a	b	n	s	s	a
d	r	n	e	c	o	r	a	e	r	e	e	f	g	l	o	n	n	n	a	i	t	u	b	r
p	p	a	e	e	t	m	t	i	b	a	h	i	e	r	f	f	s	u	o	a	t	e	s	d
i	r	h	t	t	r	u	a	p	i	e	l	l	v	a	i	o	f	s	r	n	t	g	r	f
l	a	l	n	a	h	i	t	e	e	i	t	n	a	n	l	r	i	w	a	j	i	e	a	l
s	l	n	y	a	o	g	c	c	n	s	d	r	y	r	i	m	e	u	t	s	s	s	n	n
o	s	f	b	s	a	n	u	w	n	u	w	v	r	s	n	a	r	n	n	e	u	b	w	d
o	r	e	n	x	r	i	i	o	r	e	a	a	i	o	g	n	l	r	n	a	l	a	g	k
t	n	a	r	r	a	w	h	c	r	a	e	s	y	r	o	t	a	p	i	c	i	t	n	a
p	e	g	z	b	i	t	a	y	r	t	a	u	a	n	t	r	i	i	f	p	a	s	n	r

anticipatory search warrant
curtilage
informant
pretextual stop
reversible error
summary judgment
arrest
frisk
Miranda warning
probable cause
search and seizure
warrant
contraband
harmless error
plain view doctrine
racial profiling
search warrant

P OBLEMS AND UES IN POLICING

LEARNING OBJECTIVES

After reading this chapter, you should be able to do the following:

- **Explain the meaning of dilemmas in policing**
- **Summarize the external political pressures of policing**
- **Explain time allocation pressures in policing**
- **Define *proactive* and *reactive* policing and discuss each in the context of domestic violence**
- **Assess the impact of various stressors in policing**
- **State what we can do to decrease domestic violence among police**
- **Explain and analyze the impact of police subcultures**
- **Discuss the nature and extent of police misconduct**
- **Explain the proper use of deadly force in the context of fleeing felons and vehicle pursuits**
- **Discuss the nature and implications of police brutality**
- **Discuss violence against police**
- **Explain how police activities may be controlled by police departments**
- **Explain and evaluate the exclusionary rule**
- **Suggest ways in which federal regulations might improve policing**
- **Discuss the control of policing by community relations and through civil actions**
- **Explain the legal actions that citizens may take if they are mistreated by negligently trained police officers**
- **Discuss the impact that affirmative action programs have had on policing and what might be expected in the future**

Criminal Justice Essentials: Study Guide, Ninth Edition. Shannon Barton-Bellessa.

CHAPTER OUTLINE

KEY TERMS

deadly force
domestic violence
exclusionary rule
fleeing felon rule
good faith exception
inevitable discovery rule
intimate partner violence (IPV)
statute of limitations
subculture

CHAPTER SUMMARY

Chapter 5 is the third of three on policing. This chapter focuses on problems and issues connected with policing in a complex society. The first section addresses the various dilemmas facing law enforcement officers. One dilemma facing law enforcement is the political pressure from within the department, along with pressure from the community and other outside forces. These pressures include competing for scarce resources; meeting community needs within legal boundaries; and ensuring the wide use of discretion does not result in abuse of power. Officers also confront internal pressure and role conflict when individual goals and means to achieve those goals are at odds with external constituents.

A second dilemma faced by the police is the allocation of time. As noted in the text, there is little agreement about how time spent on the three functions of policing (**law enforcement**, **order maintenance**, and **service**) should be allocated. This may create additional problems related to the role conflicts of policing. For example, most individuals attracted to the field of policing presume that their days will be spent enforcing the law. This belief is further perpetuated during training, where the majority of their time is spent on learning the various aspects of law enforcement and little attention is given to the functions of order maintenance and community service. This continues to be reinforced through the evaluation process, where superiors rate the effectiveness of the subordinates based upon their law enforcement responsibilities. Studies, however, reveal that officers spend less time in law enforcement than in other police functions. Likewise, the lines of responsibility and function are not always clear regarding law enforcement. For example, today most departments view domestic violence as a law enforcement issue, not a social problem, but not all police administrators, officers, or the public agree. Therefore, how officers respond creates conflict potentially both internally (for themselves) and externally (with the public).

As a third dilemma, the response to domestic violence or interpersonal violence is governed by laws that regulate **mandatory versus preferred arrests**. This may create various problems associated with addressing domestic violence calls for service or response. With the passage of the federal **Violence Against Women Act (VAWA)** in 1984 and findings from research studies such as the **Minneapolis Domestic Violence Experiment**, the move toward utilizing mandatory arrest practices has become more commonplace. Although domestic violence replication studies reveal inconsistent findings, domestic violence as a serious social concern has been incorporated into policing practices.

The fourth dilemma faced by officers is **stress**. On-the-job stress is a normal function of policing. Officers confront stressors on a daily basis, some as a result of community expectations and some as a result of the legal system itself. One impetus for these stressors may be the unrealistic expectations of citizens. Citizens expect officers to respond one way when they are in need of service and another when enforcing the laws. These expectations are difficult to meet when the police personality does not always provide opportunities for officers to switch in and out of these roles. Other stressors originate from the job itself, such as the inability to use full enforcement to uphold all laws; the conflict between maintaining an authoritarian stance while still being supportive, friendly, and approachable; and the expectations that officers should be able to handle all emergencies despite limited resources.

For some, the stress may be too much to handle, resulting in suicide. Other issues are related to the fear of being exposed to contagious deadly diseases such as AIDS. This is true both for the officer who is already infected and for those who are not. Other more recent issues such as concerns with planning for and responding to homeland security mandates create additional stressors that once either did not exist or at least did not exist to this extent. This has placed additional stress on law enforcement officers and administrators, who must now make decisions about allocating both resources and time differently than prior to 9/11. Many agencies have created formal mechanisms such as stress reduction programs, counseling, 24-hour help lines, and private agency collaborations as a way to assist officers with handling the stress of the job. Another more informal way officers cope with stressors on the job is through the development of a **police subculture**. The extent and importance of this subculture can be seen in the creation of the **blue code of silence**, whereby unwritten rules and practices state officers should not testify against one another or even report misbehavior. Some have argued that these practices, termed **testilying**, are commonplace, and may actually violate the law (e.g., perjury).

The existence and handling of **police misconduct** is another problem that has been studied extensively. The most reported form of misconduct is **corruption.** Reports vary as to the pervasiveness and nature of misconduct, but it is clear that at least some police are involved in drug transactions and other illegal acts. James Q. Wilson in his study of policing styles and corruption found that agencies characterized by the **watchman style**, in which they were expected to maintain order and not regulate behavior, were more prone to corruption than the **service or legalistic styles** of policing. Formal commissions to study the pervasiveness of corruption in New York City have been adopted. These include the **Knapp Commission** in 1970 (report issued in 1972) and the **Mollen Commission** in 1994. Findings from these studies revealed that although corruption exists, vast improvements were made to combat the behavior between the 1972 and 1994 study findings.

More specifically, police use of **deadly force** has become a critical issue in some departments. The fourth section of this chapter deals with issues related to violence and the amount of force permitted by law. Although police are permitted to use some force, it is the *abuse* of that responsibility that generates concern for both the department and the public. The **fleeing felon rule** was created during a time when officers did not have the technology available to them to stop or apprehend a suspect. This rule was challenged in the case of ***Tennessee v. Garner*** (1985). In this case, the U.S. Supreme Court ruled that in order for law enforcement officers to use deadly force to stop a fleeing felon, the actions must be reasonable to meet the following criteria: to prevent escape; to prevent the threat of death or serious injury to the suspect of others; and/or there is belief the suspect is involved in a case that has inflicted harm on another. With the evolution of court decisions requiring changes in the use of deadly force, some police departments have begun to place greater emphasis on proper training in the use of deadly force and the establishment of more detailed departmental policies on the use of vehicular pursuits. Despite these changes, some police use excessive force, leading to allegations of police brutality.

Law enforcement officers are at a higher risk for workplace violence than any other type of occupation. Not all police encounter violence on the job, but verbal hostility is a common occurrence. The issue of violence and brutality by police came into national focus in the widely publicized beating of Rodney King, an African American, by white police officers. The long-ranging effects of the widely publicized use of violence by white officers against a minority were best illustrated by the Los Angeles riots following the state acquittals of the officers tried in the King case. Recent allegations of police violence against citizens of all races, ethnicities, and ages have refocused attention on this serious policing problem, further illuminating the need for continuing to improve training and to respond to reports of violence by law enforcement agencies.

A variety of mechanisms exist to control improper policing. These include departmental regulations, court decisions, civil actions against police, and the improvement of community–police relations through the use of citizen review boards and other community efforts. One of the most controversial strategies passed by the U.S. Supreme Court in an attempt to minimize police corruption was the creation of the **exclusionary rule.** The exclusionary rule states that evidence obtained by police in violation of a suspect's constitutional rights may be excluded from that individual's trial. The exclusionary rule serves both a symbolic function and a real function as a mechanism to reduce the number of illegal searches and seizures. The U.S. Supreme Court has created some exceptions to the exclusionary rule, such as **good faith** and **inevitable discovery**, and retracted the rule in other ways. Under the good faith clause, illegally obtained evidence can still be submitted in court if it can be shown that the officer had reason to believe he or she was operating within the framework of the law. The concept of inevitable discovery states that illegally obtained evidence will be admitted at trial if it can be shown that eventually the evidence would have been discovered by legal methods. Civil actions against police may serve as a deterrent to improper police behavior, and an increasing number of these suits are being filed under the federal code.

Additional problems and issues in policing surround affirmative action programs aimed at employing more women and racial and ethnic minorities. Civil actions are brought under the **Civil Rights Act of 1964**, commonly called ***1983 actions***. These groups argue that the police cannot understand their problems and gain the support of their members unless the groups are represented adequately among police officers and administrators. Others argue that recruitment efforts have lowered standards or that court decisions upholding affirmative action programs for increasing the number of women and racial minorities in a police force are unfair and create internal problems for police. The U.S. Supreme Court's upholding of some affirmative action policies in 2003 gave a green light to universities and businesses – including law enforcement agencies – to attempt to achieve greater diversity in admissions and hiring. Civil suits may be brought against the police for negligence particularly in hiring and training. Despite problems in policing, however, many officers are satisfied with their profession.

KEY TERMS

deadly force Force likely to cause serious bodily injury or death.

domestic violence The causing of serious physical harm or the threatening of such harm to a member of one's family or household, including spouses, ex-spouses, parents, children, persons otherwise related by blood, persons living in the household, or persons who formerly lived there. May include relationships of persons who do not live together but who have had or currently have intimate relationships, such as courtship.

exclusionary rule Requirement that evidence secured as the result of illegal actions by law enforcement officers must be excluded from a legal proceeding, such as a trial.

fleeing felon rule The common law rule that permitted police to shoot at any fleeing felon. The rule has been modified to require circumstances involving (1) the threat of serious injury to or death of an officer or others, (2) the prevention of an escape if the suspect threatens the officer with a gun, or (3) the officer's having probable cause to believe that the suspect has committed or has threatened to commit serious bodily harm.

good faith exception The provision that illegally obtained evidence will not be excluded from a subsequent trial if it can be shown that law enforcement officers secured the evidence in good faith, meaning that they had a reasonable belief that they were acting in accordance with the law.

inevitable discovery rule Evidence secured illegally by police will not be excluded from the suspect's trial, provided it can be shown that the evidence would have been discovered anyway under legal means.

intimate partner violence (IPV) Violence toward a current or former spouse, or other persons with whom one has had an intimate relationship; also referred to as *courtship violence.*

statute of limitations The time limit in which to bring a charge for a crime. The statute of limitations may differ from jurisdiction to jurisdiction but usually does not apply to murder charges, which may be brought at any time.

subculture A group of significant size whose behavior differs significantly from the behavior of the dominant groups in society.

STUDY QUESTIONS

These questions are found at the end of your chapter. Your instructor may wish to revisit these or assign them for points. These questions are a good way to integrate the material and to generate your own perspectives during class.

1. What external political situations might affect policing?
2. How should police spend most of their time? Why?
3. What is meant by *proactive* and *reactive* policing, and what changes are being made in the former?
4. What is the relationship between domestic violence and policing?
5. What are the major stressors in policing?
6. What is meant by a *subculture*? How does that concept apply to policing?
7. Discuss the extent and result of police corruption, with particular reference to the influence of drugs.
8. What is the *fleeing felon rule*? Contrast its historical meaning with the U.S. Supreme Court's ruling currently in effect.
9. Analyze the reasons for and concern with police vehicle pursuits.
10. Discuss police brutality in the context of a recent example.
11. What is the relationship, if any, between violence against the police and violence by the police?
12. Distinguish between police department regulations and civil lawsuits as methods of controlling policing.
13. How have changes in federal regulations affected law enforcement?
14. State the purpose of the *exclusionary rule* and analyze whether that purpose is being met. What exceptions has the U.S. Supreme Court recognized?

15 Discuss civil liability that may result from inadequate police training.

16 What has been the result of efforts to recruit women and racial minorities into policing? Do you think this is important? If so, why? If not, why not? What effect, if any, will recent U.S. Supreme Court decisions have on affirmative action recruiting in policing?

LEARNING ACTIVITIES

5.1 In examining the functions of law enforcement and time spent on the job, research suggests that the majority or a significant amount of time on the job is spent responding to calls for service or calls for information. How might administrative personnel recruit officers in a truthful manner that increases their overall level of satisfaction with the job?

5.2 As noted in the chapter, law enforcement officers continually confront situations and persons contributing to high levels of stress, such as the potential for violence, long hours, rotating shifts, exposure to HIV/AIDS, potential for terrorist attacks, work–family conflict, etc. Assume that you are in a leadership position within a law enforcement agency. You have been appointed by your Chief of Police to create a program to reduce the stress experienced by officers in your department. How would you create this program? Describe the program. What things do you need to take into consideration when developing this program? How would you ensure that your officers take advantage of these opportunities?

5.3 Domestic violence as an offense continues to draw attention from law enforcement officers. In reviewing policies related to the handling of domestic violence calls, you will find that there is no one set of standards across the country or even within states. For this activity, you are responsible for contacting the following agencies: one local, one county, and one state law enforcement agency. When contacting them, ask them the following questions:

a How many calls for service for domestic violence does your agency receive on an annual basis?

b What is the arrest policy for domestic violence calls for service in your agency, e.g., mandatory, preferred?

c Once you have compiled the information from a and b above, compare the results. How are the agency policies similar? How are they different? These responses can reflect not only the policies but the number of calls for service as well.

a ______________________________

b ______________________________

c ______________________________

5.4 The issue of police misconduct is one that permeates all law enforcement communities. To better understand the impact of law enforcement corruption, select and peruse a reputable newspaper within the past two years for an example of a law enforcement officer violating the law. Briefly describe the crime. What was the outcome for the offense? Describe the potential impact of violations of law by police officers on police–community relations. How might you as a Police Chief respond to this incident?

____

____

____

____

____

____

____

STUDENT STUDY GUIDE PRACTICE QUESTIONS

True or False

5.1 In a classic 1966 study conducted by James Q. Wilson, he found that the majority of calls to law enforcement officers were for order maintenance-related functions.

5.2 The wide discretion police have in law enforcement typically is not influenced by political pressures.

5.3 Most police work is proactive not reactive.

5.4 In communities with mandatory arrest policies, women are more likely to be arrested and detained in domestic violence cases than men.

5.5 Law enforcement officials are concerned that the diversion of FBI agents to counterterrorism task forces deemphasizes the efforts on drug-related offenses and bank robberies, therefore increasing pressure on local departments to provide law enforcement in their areas.

5.6 The term *testilying* was coined by the Mollen Commission to characterize the pervasive falsifications of testimony, etc., by the New York City Police Department.

5.7 Law enforcement officers are not at a higher risk of workplace violence than other types of employee.

5.8 In an effort to curb police misconduct, law enforcement agencies should both actively and fairly enforce departmental policies.

5.9 Since the U.S. Supreme Court adopted the good faith exception to the exclusionary rule, some state courts have held that it does not apply under their state constitutions, and thus all illegally seized evidence must be excluded at trial, regardless of the motivation of the officer who seized the evidence.

5.10 In 1989, the U.S. Supreme Court ruled that inadequate police training may result in civil liability of the municipality under which the police department operates.

Multiple Choice

5.11 Results from the Minneapolis Domestic Violence Experiment changed the way law enforcement officers respond to domestic violence incidents. How did this experiment alter responses to domestic violence calls?

a When officers counseled both parties at the scene then left, subsequent calls for domestic violence were reduced.

b When officers mandated the perpetrator to leave, subsequent calls for domestic violence were reduced.

c When officers mandated both parties to leave the residence, subsequent calls for domestic violence were reduced.

d When officers made an arrest, subsequent calls for domestic violence were reduced.

5.12 Which of the following characteristics has not been identified as part of the police subculture?

a Empathetic

b Cynical

c Assertive

d Impulsive risk takers

5.13 In James Q. Wilson's study on police corruption, he found that corruption is most likely found in agencies that emphasize which type of policing style:

a Watchman style

b Legalistic style

c Service style

d None of the above

5.14 In 1970, the Knapp Commission was formed in response to allegations of corruption within the New York City Police Department. What were the findings from this commission?

a No evidence of corruption

b Little evidence that officers participated in lower levels of corruption

c Evidence that corruption was pervasive but was centered on lower level crimes such as falsification and theft from drug dealers on routine traffic stops

d Widespread evidence that officers participated in organized crime, payoffs or traffic citations, and acceptance of money for overlooking violations of licensing ordinance.

5.15 The *Tennessee v. Garner* case (1985) established the fleeing felon rule. What is the fleeing felon rule?

a This rule articulates when it is lawful for an officer to use deadly force to apprehend a suspect.

b This rule articulates that it is lawful for an officer to use deadly force to apprehend a suspect regardless of the circumstances.

c This rule articulates when it is lawful for an officer to use deadly force to apprehend a suspect when they believe a suspect is going to flee.

d This rule articulates when it is lawful for an officer to use deadly force to apprehend a suspect when they believe the suspect is younger and faster than them.

5.16 Preliminary data from 2010 reveal that ______ law enforcement officers were killed in the line of duty.

- a 22
- b 37
- c 56
- d 53

5.17 Which rule of law states that if police seize evidence illegally or secure confessions improperly, the evidence may be excluded from trial.

- a Inevitable discovery
- b Exclusionary rule
- c Good faith exception
- d *Habeas corpus*

5.18 Which rule of law allows for illegally obtained evidence to be presented at trial if it can be shown that police had a reasonable belief that they were acting in accordance with the law?

- a Inevitable discovery
- b Exclusionary rule
- c Good faith exception
- d *Habeas corpus*

5.19 Which rule of law allows illegally seized evidence to be admitted at trial if it can be shown that, eventually, the evidence would have been discovered by legal methods?

- a Inevitable discovery
- b Exclusionary rule
- c Good faith exception
- d *Habeas corpus*

5.20 In the latest available published data by the BJS, women represented ______ percent of all local officers, while racial and ethnic minorities accounted for ______ percent.

- a 16.4% (women); 30.4% (racial and ethnic minorities)
- b 21.2% (women); 33.2% (racial and ethnic minorities)
- c 10.2% (women); 21.2% (racial and ethnic minorities)
- d 11.8% (women); 25.3% (racial and ethnic minorities)

Fill-in-the-Blank

5.21 In recent years, more attention has been paid to ______, which involves spouses abusing each other, parents abusing children, and children abusing each other or their parents.

5.22 According to ______ policies, law enforcement officers must arrest the alleged perpetrator of domestic violence if there is sufficient evidence that violence has occurred.

5.23 In an effort to address the high demands of the law enforcement occupation, many agencies have created ______ programs to provide peer support, mental counseling, 24-hour help lines, and interagency and public–private collaborations.

5.24 The ______ has values and expectations that distinguish it from the dominant culture and that solidify its members.

5.25 The ______ refers to the police subculture that states that police will not testify against each other or even report any improper behavior.

5.26 Police use of ______ has been defined as "such force as under normal circumstances poses a high risk of death or serious injury to its human target, regardless of whether or not death, serious injury, or any harm actually result."

5.27 According to the ______ rule, police use of deadly force is considered lawful and reasonable in the following situations: to prevent escape; threat of injury to the officer or others; and probable cause to believe the individual has committed a crime involving the infliction or threatened infliction of serious physical harm.

5.28 According to the Police Executive Research Forum (PERF), approximately one-fourth of the larger law enforcement agencies have a(n) ______, which is designed to detect officers who might abuse their power.

5.29 In 1967, the Supreme Court articulated the ______ rule, which holds that, if a confession is coerced, it must be excluded at trial.

5.30 Civil actions are brought under the Civil Rights Act of 1964 and are commonly called ______ after the section of the U.S. Code in which the provision for such actions is codified.

CROSSWORD

ACROSS

3 The causing of serious physical harm or the threatening of such harm to a member of one's family or household, including spouses, ex-spouses, parents, children, persons otherwise related by blood, persons living in the household, or persons who lived there formerly. (2 words, no spaces)

5 A technical rule that requires a case to be filed within a certain period of time. (3 words, no spaces)

7 The provision that evidence secured as a result of illegal actions by law enforcement officers should be excluded from a trial. (2 words, no spaces)

8 The common law rule that permitted police to shoot at any fleeing felon. (3 words, no spaces)

DOWN

1 The provision that evidence secured illegally by police will not be excluded from the suspect's trial, provided it can be shown that the evidence would have been discovered anyway under legal means. (3 words, no spaces)

2 The provision that illegally obtained evidence will not be excluded from a subsequent trial if it can be shown that the police secured the evidence in good faith, meaning that they had a reasonable belief that they were acting in accordance with the law. (3 words, no spaces)

4 Force likely to cause serious bodily injury or death. (2 words, no spaces)

6 A group of significant size whose behavior differs significantly from the behavior of the dominant groups of society.

WORD SEARCH

a u s o y c r t y s t x r l e f c f i t a d f

e c n e l o i v r e n t r a p e t a m i t n i

x e o e a u e o e e o o n e l u e e e s p t l

c a i v v v e o v f t x e t i e e e c u v e t

l e t i e i i i o t r s t i u m r b t b e a y

u e a i l t i o c c s u e e i e i n b c a e e

s e t l e n r o s g r y e t b i o x n u a r m

i i i o u e l o i n t e o c x c a e o l r n o

o a m g i s l u d r g l o i r e l e c t a e m

n o i t p e c x e h t i a f d o o g r u o t s

a o l e e i f t l y i g u t i n f c c r t v o

r n f e u t s n b i t e r v o l c y n e r g t

y n o y r e o t a t o i c m e a i t l i b c s

r a e l s e g u t e y i m r d e a l i d m r a

u n t n i i y n i e t i f a e f v t m t a u i

l e u i e y l f v s u e o t u u d c t c m e a

e m t i t f l e e i n g f e l o n r u l e e d

l s a n i d s m n l d a i i p a o v l t f g s

i o t i i f o s i f e a a c u l e r n p o g u

d r s i e d l e a e b o o l a e e e v y g b i

r i d o u t s e u m t e d t r t l e c e l n r

e l o a a t t e h y l a e l c u d i s m c c t

r t a i n e d n e i i l e c o x c i e l e t t

deadly force
fleeing felon rule
intimate partner violence

domestic violence
good faith exception
statute of limitations

exclusionary rule
inevitable discovery
subculture

ANSWERS TO CROSSWORD

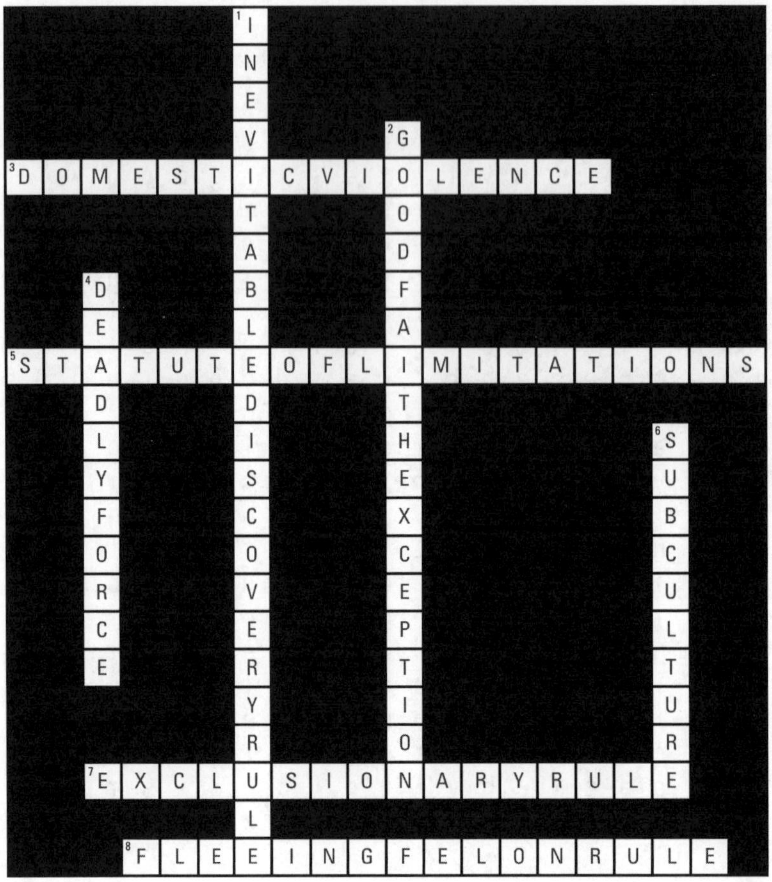

ACROSS

3 The causing of serious physical harm or the threatening of such harm to a member of one's family or household, including spouses, ex-spouses, parents, children, persons otherwise related by blood, persons living in the household, or persons who lived there formerly. (2 words, no spaces)

5 A technical rule that requires a case to be filed within a certain period of time. (3 words, no spaces)

7 The provision that evidence secured as a result of illegal actions by law enforcement officers should be excluded from a trial. (2 words, no spaces)

8 The common law rule that permitted police to shoot at any fleeing felon. (3 words, no spaces)

DOWN

1 The provision that evidence secured illegally by police will not be excluded from the suspect's trial, provided it can be shown that the evidence would have been discovered anyway under legal means. (3 words, no spaces)

2 The provision that illegally obtained evidence will not be excluded from a subsequent trial if it can be shown that the police secured the evidence in good faith, meaning that they had a reasonable belief that they were acting in accordance with the law. (3 words, no spaces)

4 Force likely to cause serious bodily injury or death. (2 words, no spaces)

6 A group of significant size whose behavior differs significantly from the behavior of the dominant groups of society.

ANSWERS TO WORD SEARCH

a u s o y c r t y s t x r l e f c f i t a d f
e c n e l o i v r e n t r a p e t a m i t n i
x e o e a u e o e e o o n e l u e e e s p t l
c a i v v v e o v f t x e t i e e e c u v e t
l e t i e i i i o t r s t i u m r b t b e a y
u e a i l t i o c c s u e e i e i n b c a e e
s e t l e n r o s g r y e t b i o x n u a r m
i i i o u e l o i n t e o c x c a e o l r n o
o a m g i s l u d r g l o i r e l e c t a e m
n o i t p e c x e h t i a f d o o g r u o t s
a o l e e i f t l y i g u t i n f c c r t v o
r n f e u t s n b i t e r v o l c y n e r g t
y n o y r e o t a t o i c m e a i t l i b c s
r a e l s e g u t e y i m r d e a l i d m r a
u n t n i i y n i e t i f a e f v t m t a u i
l e u i e y l f v s u e o t u u d c t c m e a
e m t i t f l e e i n g f e l o n r u l e e d
l s a n i d s m n l d a i i p a o v l t f g s
i o t i i f o s i f e a a c u l e r n p o g u
d r s i e d l e a e b o o l a e e e v y g b i
r i d o u t s e u m t e d t r t l e c e l n r
e l o a a t t e h y l a e l c u d i s m c c t
r t a i n e d n e i i l e c o x c i e l e t t

deadly force
fleeing felon rule
intimate partner violence
domestic violence
good faith exception
statute of limitations
exclusionary rule
inevitable discovery
subculture

OCESSING A
IMINAL CASE:
INAL COURT
EMS

MINAL COURT S STEMS

LEARNING OBJECTIVES

After reading this chapter, you should be able to do the following:

- **Discuss the judicial branch of government, define basic legal terminology regarding courts, and distinguish between trial and appellate courts**
- **Diagram the levels of state and federal court systems, and explain what happens at each level**
- **Discuss the history and purpose of the U.S. Supreme Court, and explain and evaluate its functions and operations**
- **Describe the role of judges in criminal trials**
- **Explain and evaluate the sentencing role of trial judges**
- **Contrast the role of an appellate judge with that of a trial judge**
- **List and explain two methods for selecting judges**
- **Explain briefly the training, retention, and control of judges**
- **Describe court congestion and suggest remedies**

CHAPTER OUTLINE

KEY TERMS

acquittal
appeal
appellant
appellee
concurring opinion
continuance
de novo
dicta
expert witness
judge
judicial review
moot
recusal
stare decisis
writ of *certiorari*

CHAPTER SUMMARY

This chapter is the first in three to discuss the role of the courts in processing cases through the criminal justice system. This chapter sets the framework for understanding the legal concepts necessary for a case to be processed through the system. The chapter begins with an examination of the judicial branch of government. Definitions of legal terms are presented, beginning with jurisdiction. **Jurisdiction** refers to a court's power to hear and decide a case and is given by the constitution or statute that created the court. Without jurisdiction a court has no legal framework from which to hear and decide a case. There are four different types of jurisdiction: original, concurrent, exclusive, and appellate. **Original jurisdiction** refers to the jurisdiction of the court that may hear a case first. **Concurrent jurisdiction** refers to the authority of more than one court to hear a case; while **exclusive jurisdiction** refers to the authority of only one court to hear the case. **Appellate jurisdiction** refers to the jurisdiction of the court that may hear the case on appeal.

Next, the chapter discusses the differences between trial and appellate courts. **Trial courts** try the facts of the case, and **appellate courts** are concerned only with law. Trial courts are the major fact finders. The judge oversees the operation of the court while the prosecution and defense make their case before a jury. After the judge or jury make their decision at the trial level, the defendant, if found guilty, may appeal that decision. Appeal cases are heard by judges or justices, not juries. The purpose of the appellate court is to ensure that no errors were committed during the trial. The appellate court has the option to **affirm** the lower decision; reverse the case **with prejudice**; or **reverse and remand** the decision back to the trial court.

Next the chapter, reviews the concept of duality in the United States court system with the **federal and state courts**. The federal and state courts constitute separate systems and may only hear those cases over which they have jurisdiction. In rare cases both state and federal law are violated. In these instances, the defendant may be tried in a state or federal court or both. The state court systems vary in their organization and jurisdiction. As the author notes, however, the organization of these systems may be divided into four broad categories: courts of limited jurisdiction, general trial courts, intermediate appellate courts, and highest state appellate courts. **Courts of limited jurisdiction** typically hear civil or minor criminal cases. **General trial courts** have a wider jurisdiction and cover a broader geographic area and may be divided by case type, e.g., traffic, domestic, probate, civil, etc. **Intermediate appellate courts** provide for at least one appeal. These courts are usually called the **court of appeals**. The **highest state appellate court** is known as the **state supreme court**. This court has the final decision on cases involving legal issues pertaining to the constitution or statutes of the state in which the case is brought. If the case involves any federal issues, the defendant may appeal to the U.S. Supreme Court.

The federal system is divided into three broad categories: U.S. district courts; circuit court of appeals; and U.S. Supreme Court. The **U.S. district courts** are the lower level trial courts. These courts hear cases in which individuals have been accused of violating federal criminal laws. **Circuit court of appeals** hear cases from federal district courts. Decisions of the federal appellate courts are not binding on state courts unless they involve federally created procedural rights, nor are they binding on another federal appellate court. The **U.S. Supreme Court** is the only court created by the federal Constitution. The basic function of the U.S. Supreme Court is to interpret federal laws and the federal Constitution. Nine justices (one chief justice and eight associate justices) sit on the U.S. Supreme Court. The U.S. Supreme Court is the only court in the land that has the option to hear a case. A case gets before the U.S. Supreme Court if the Court grants a **writ of *certiorari***.

The role of the judge in the court process is then discussed. Judges are involved with the case long before the trial begins. They grant warrants. They hear and rule on motions by attorneys before, during, and after trial. At the appellate level, they determine whether cases should be reversed or affirmed. **Trial judges** function essentially as referees for the process. They ensure that the legal process is upheld and evaluate the admissibility of expert witness testimony. They determine whether there is enough evidence for a case to stand trial. They instruct the jury regarding the law in the case it must decide. The judge then decides whether to accept a jury verdict. Finally, if a finding of guilty is accepted, the judge administers the sentence. **Appellate judges** and justices are often faced with interpreting the laws and constitutions of their jurisdictions in ways that will have an effect on more than the parties before the court.

One of the most important issues regarding judges is how they are selected, trained, and retained. Because of the authority given to the judge, they should be able to meet very high standards. Judges should be impartial and fair; they should be objective and open-minded; they should be well educated in substantive and procedural law and the rules of evidence; they should have high moral and ethical standards; and they should be in good physical, mental, and emotional health. States vary in how judges come to the bench. Most states use the election process to select judges. States differ in their mandate for party affiliation, but election by popular vote still occurs. Another method for selecting judges, known as the **merit plan** (**Missouri plan**), varies extensively from state to state, but most plans include a nonpartisan commission, which solicits, investigates, and screens candidates when a judicial opening occurs. Normally three to five names are sent forward to the executive branch. A new judge is appointed from this list to serve a probationary period (usually one year). At the end of this year, the judge's name goes to the voters, who simply choose whether or not the judge should remain in office. Most jurisdictions do not have formal training for judges but do offer and in some instances require continuing education while on the bench. Salaries for judges vary by system and jurisdiction, with federal judges receiving the best compensation. The lower paid the judge, the more likely there will be turnover. Judges, like most individuals in the criminal justice system, experience a high rate of stress. Stress in this position originates from multiple sources, but the most frequently cited include the judicial code of conduct and the potential for violence in the courtroom. Diversity on the judicial bench is important to ensure fairness of the system. Issues related to age, gender, disability, race, and ethnicity are noted in the chapter. One issue confronting the system as well is not only how to recruit and retain good judges but also how to get rid of bad ones. It is difficult to unseat judges. There are, however, processes in existence to do so.

The chapter concludes with a discussion on the crisis in the courts. One crisis discussed is the impact of state budget shortfalls on the ability to process cases in a timely manner. The result of this shortfall is an increase in delays in the court process and in the number of cases that are backlogged in the system. Delays have many sources, such as court congestion, the issuing of continuances (postponement notices), decreases in resources and court personnel, etc. As noted by the author, courts must be analyzed and altered in the total social context in which they operate.

KEY TERMS

acquittal Legal decision regarding the failure of the prosecution to prove the guilt of a defendant in a criminal trial.

appeal The stage in a judicial proceeding in which a higher court is asked to review a decision by a lower court.

appellant: The losing party in a lower court, who seeks a review of the decision by a higher appellate court.

appellee The winning party in a lower court, who argues on appeal against reversing the lower court's decision.

concurring opinion A judge's written opinion agreeing with the result in a case but presenting other reasons for the decision or emphasizing some of the reasons stated by the majority opinion.

continuance The adjournment of a trial or another legal proceeding until a later date.

de novo Literally, anew; afresh. A *trial de novo* is a case that is tried again, as if no decision had been previously rendered. In some jurisdictions the first appeal from a lower court may be a trial *de novo*. The term may also be used to refer to other proceedings, such as a *hearing de novo*.

dicta Statements by a judge or justice that go beyond the facts of a case and are thus not part of the actual ruling of the court. These statements are not legally binding precedents for future court decisions, although they may be indicative of how that judge would vote in a particular case.

expert witness A person with extensive training or education in a particular field, such as medicine, who testifies at depositions or at trials concerning a critical issue of that case, such as what caused the death of the deceased.

judge An elected or appointed officer who presides over a court of law; the final and neutral arbiter of law who is responsible for all activities within that court system.

judicial review The authority of an appellate court to review the decisions of lower courts and the executive and legislative branches of government within its jurisdiction in order to determine whether any of those acts are in violation of that jurisdiction's case, statutory, or constitutional law.

moot The term used to describe a controversy that has ended or evolved to the stage at which a court decision is no longer relevant or necessary as it would not have an impact on the legal rights of the parties before the court.

recusal The removal of oneself from a proceeding, such as by a judge who has a conflict of interest in a case.

stare decisis Literally, "let the decision stand." The doctrine that courts will abide by or adhere to the rulings of previous court decisions when deciding cases having substantially the same facts.

writ of *certiorari* *Certiorari* literally means "to be informed of." A *writ* is an order from a court giving authority for an act to be done or ordering that it be done; a writ of *certiorari* is used by courts that have discretion to determine which cases they will hear. Today this writ is most commonly associated with the U.S. Supreme Court.

STUDY QUESTIONS

These questions are found at the end of your chapter. Your instructor may wish to revisit these or assign them for points. These questions are a good way to integrate the material and to generate your own perspectives during class.

1 Distinguish the judicial branch from other branches of government.

2 What is meant by *jurisdiction*? How does it apply to the dual court system?

3 What is the difference between trial and appellate courts?

4 What is the relationship between state and federal courts?

5 What are the levels of courts in each of the two main court systems, state and federal?

6 What is the purpose of the U.S. Supreme Court, and how does a case get before the Court? What happens to a case that is appealed to but not accepted by the Court?

7 What are the main roles of judges in trial courts and appellate courts?

8 How are judges and justices selected? What are the advantages and disadvantages of each method?

9 Should an effort be made to recruit more female and minority judges? Why or why not? What methods do you suggest if you think more should be recruited?

10 What actions do you think should be sufficient to disqualify a person for a state judgeship, a federal judgeship, or appointment to the U.S. Supreme Court?

11 To what extent, if any, should public opinion be permitted to influence judicial appointments or judicial retention?

12 How would you suggest that the current caseload crisis in trial and appellate courts be resolved?

LEARNING ACTIVITIES

6.1 In order to gain a better appreciation of the court process, it is important to spend a day or at least some time in the courtroom. For this activity, choose a local court. Attend at least **one hour** of court. Answer the following questions:

a Identify the court including location and type, e.g., superior, circuit, appellate, day, time, and length of attendance. You must also identify whether it is federal or state. Identify the name of the judge.

b Describe what occurred, e.g.., arraignment, pre-trials, etc.

c Identify and discuss at least three cases.

d Identify who was present in court, e.g, prosecutor, defense attorney, plaintiff, defendant, etc. When possible list their names.

e What problems did you encounter in completing this activity?

a

b

c

d

e

6.2 According to the text, judges should be well educated in substantive and procedural law and the rules of evidence; be able to think and write clearly; have high moral and ethical standards; be in good physical, mental, and emotional health; be good managers; and assume power sensibly, without abuse, and exercise leadership in social reform where necessary and desirable. Unfortunately, cases exist where these standards/requirements have been violated. Searching a reputable media source, locate such a case where a judge has been accused of violating one of the above standards. Complete the following activities:

a Summarize the case.
b What was the outcome in the case?
c Why is it important to ensure that the standards identified by the author are met?
d Are there any other standards not listed that you believe should be included in the requirements to sit on the bench? If yes, list those and explain why. If no, why not?

a

b

c

d

6.3 One important area discussed in this chapter is how judges come to the bench. Keeping in mind there are a variety of different mechanisms, answer the following for your state:

- a How do judges come to the bench in your state?
- b If elected, are they allowed to be party affiliated?
- c If not elected, what is the process?
- d Do judges have to be attorneys in your state to sit on the bench? Explain your response.

a

b

c ____

d ____

6.4 Given the economic crises of the time, how have budget shortfalls or concerns in your state affected the state and local administration of court services?

STUDENT STUDY GUIDE PRACTICE QUESTIONS

True or False

6.1 Trial courts are only concerned with law, while the appellate courts try the facts of the case.

6.2 The decision of one federal court of appeals is not binding on other federal appellate courts.

6.3 The U.S. Supreme Court is one of three specific courts established by the federal Constitution, which designates a few cases in which the Supreme Court has original jurisdiction.

6.4 At trial, judges serve as the referees.

6.5 The prosecutor in a case decides whether expert witness testimony may be admitted into court.

6.6 Federal judges along with U.S. Supreme Court justices are elected.

6.7 Most U.S. court jurisdictions do not have required formal training for judges.

6.8 According to a study published in 2009 entitled "A Disturbing Trend in Law School Admission," minority representation in law schools has diminished since 1993.

6.9 Research on diversity in criminal court cases found that men vote more conservatively in criminal procedure cases than women.

6.10 It is not easy to unseat judges, even after they have been convicted of a crime.

Multiple Choice

6.11 Which jurisdiction gives the authority of the court that may hear a case first – that is, the court that may try the facts?
- a Exclusive
- b Original
- c Appellate
- d Concurrent

6.12 Which jurisdiction gives the authority of more than one court to hear a case?
- a Exclusive
- b Original
- c Appellate
- d Concurrent

6.13 Which jurisdiction gives the authority of only one court to hear a case?
- a Exclusive
- b Original
- c Appellate
- d Concurrent

6.14 Which jurisdiction gives the authority of the court to hear the case on appeal?
- a Exclusive
- b Original
- c Appellate
- d Concurrent

6.15 How many justices sit on the U.S. Supreme Court?
- a 5
- b 7
- c 9
- d 15

6.16 In today's society, most states use ______ to select judges for the bench.
- a the merit system
- b the Missouri Plan
- c election
- d appointment

6.17 Which of the following statements about federal judicial compensation is not true?

a Inadequate compensation directly threatens the vitality of life tenure, and if tenure in office is made uncertain, the strength and independence judges need to uphold the rule of law – even when it is unpopular to do so – will be seriously eroded.

b If judicial appointment ceases to be the capstone of a distinguished career and instead becomes a stepping stone to a lucrative position in private practice, the Framers' goal of a truly independent judiciary will be placed in serious jeopardy.

c Judicial salaries may never compete with those in private practice, and some highly qualified attorneys will not be attracted to judicial positions as a result, but it is reasonable to expect that the prestige of being a federal judge, along with a job for life, is appealing.

d All are true.

6.18 At the federal level, which act provides some avenues for disciplining judges:

a The Judicial Councils Reform and Judicial Conduct and Disability Act of 1980
b The Judicial Conduct and Disability Act of 1981
c The Judicial Reform and Conduct Act of 1982
d None of the above

6.19 By November 2008, 31 states faced budget shortfalls in the justice system because of shifting a number of federal cases to the state courts. What are some of the problems associated with budget shortfalls?

a Backlogged cases
b Overcrowded jails
c Court congestion
d All are problems associated with budget shortfalls

6.20 Which of the following has not been offered as a solution to solving court congestion?

a Reduce the number of offenses covered by criminal law
b Better management of court proceedings
c Use lay judges
d Shift court cases back to federal jurisdiction

Fill-in-the-Blank

6.21 ______ refers to a court's power to hear and decide a case.

6.22 A(n) ______ is granted once the U.S. Supreme Court agrees to hear a case on appeal.

6.23 Judges who, for some reason, may find themselves unable to be impartial and fair in a court case should remove themselves from the case in a process known as ______

6.24 Once the verdict of ______ has been entered, the defendant may not be retried on the same charge.

6.25 The role of the trial judge at ______ is one of the most important of all judicial functions.

6.26 The first merit selection plan for judges was implemented in ______ in 1940 and is known as the ______.

6.27 ______ plans for judicial selection typically include a nonpartisan commission, which solicits, investigates, and screens candidates when judicial openings occur. A list of three to five names is sent to the executive branch, where appointment is made. The new judge serves a probationary period and then his or her name is placed on a general election ballot for approval.

6.28 In addition to concerns associated with disparities in salary compensation for judges, another problem is ______ which may result from feelings of isolation; the judicial code of conduct; and fear of violence.

6.29 By 2009, most states had entered budget crisis mode, with the state of ______ topping the list.

6.30 ______ are frequently used in the criminal court process as a means to guarantee a fair hearing.

CROSSWORD

ACROSS

4 The winning party in a lower court, who argues on appeal against reversing the lower court's decision.
6 Controversy that has ended or evolved to the stage at which a court decision on that case is no longer relevant or necessary.
9 The loser in a court case, who seeks a review of the decision by a higher appellate court.
11 The authority of a court to check the power of the executive and legislative branches of government. (2 words, 1 space)
14 "Let the decision stand." (2 words, 1 space)
15 Literally "anew" or "afresh." (2 words, 1 space)
16 Legal verification of the innocence of a person in a criminal trial.

DOWN

1 A judge's written opinion agreeing with the result in a case but disagreeing with the reasoning of the majority opinion. (2 words, 1 space)
2 The written portions of a judge's opinion that are not part of the actual ruling of the court and are not legally binding precedents for future court decisions.
3 An elected or appointed officer of the court who presides over a court of law.
5 A person with extensive training or education in a particular field who testifies at depositions or at trials concerning a critical issue of that case. (2 words, 1 space)
7 The adjournment of a trial or another legal proceeding until a later date.
8 The stage in a judicial proceeding in which a higher court is asked to review a decision of a lower court.
10 The removal of oneself from a proceeding.
12 "To be informed of."
13 An order from a court giving authority for an act to be done or ordering that it be done.

WORD SEARCH

```
l q a l w i n n n t u u u o u c r
t a d t r u s l s a u w p u t e a
n o i n i p o g n i r r u c n o c
a c o n t v c c e r j n i o o v o
l o g m o t c o t i s u t i r f r
l s l n f l i n e e t n d o e a n
e u e a c p d t n a a a v g w u t
p d s s e n t i w t r e p x e g e
p w a p r p n n c e e l l e p p a
a e p u t g p u a t d n i p n e r
i j u d i c i a l r e v i e w a n
n p c j o a c n l c c a t t j i t
r i c r r a a c q u i t t a l i n
c r c j a t r e c u s a l c s e n
e c o c r p e a a s i a w i i l l
c e r d i r o c o o s u a e l d c
o e i p a t p i l d a n x n r d e
```

acquittal
appellee
de novo
judge
recusal

appeal
concurring opinion
dicta
judicial review
stare decisis

appellant
continuance
expert witness
moot
writ of certiorari

ANSWERS TO CROSSWORD

ACROSS

4 The winning party in a lower court, who argues on appeal against reversing the lower court's decision.
6 Controversy that has ended or evolved to the stage at which a court decision on that case is no longer relevant or necessary.
9 The loser in a court case, who seeks a review of the decision by a higher appellate court.
11 The authority of a court to check the power of the executive and legislative branches of government. (2 words, 1 space)
14 "Let the decision stand." (2 words, 1 space)
15 Literally "anew" or "afresh." (2 words, 1 space)
16 Legal verification of the innocence of a person in a criminal trial.

DOWN

1 A judge's written opinion agreeing with the result in a case but disagreeing with the reasoning of the majority opinion. (2 words, 1 space)
2 The written portions of a judge's opinion that are not part of the actual ruling of the court and are not legally binding precedents for future court decisions.
3 An elected or appointed officer of the court who presides over a court of law.
5 A person with extensive training or education in a particular field who testifies at depositions or at trials concerning a critical issue of that case. (2 words, 1 space)
7 The adjournment of a trial or another legal proceeding until a later date.
8 The stage in a judicial proceeding in which a higher court is asked to review a decision of a lower court.
10 The removal of oneself from a proceeding.
12 "To be informed of."
13 An order from a court giving authority for an act to be done or ordering that it be done.

ANSWERS TO WORD SEARCH

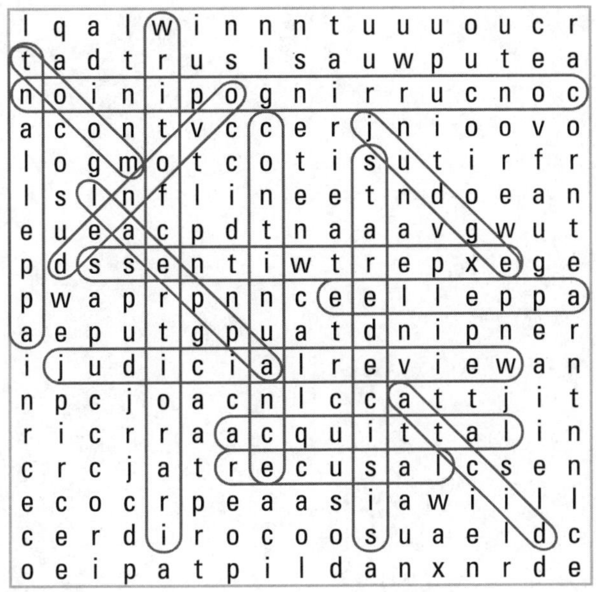

acquittal
appeal
appellant
appellee
concurring opinion
continuance
de novo
dicta
expert witness
judge
judicial review
moot
recusal
stare decisis
writ of certiorari

PROSECUTION, DEFENSE, AND PRETRIAL PROCEDURES

LEARNING OBJECTIVES

After reading this chapter, you should be able to do the following:

- **Discuss briefly the historical background of the legal profession**
- **Explain the organization and structure of prosecutorial systems**
- **Recognize the importance and problems of prosecutorial discretion regarding whether to prosecute**
- **Evaluate ways to control prosecutorial discretion and especially prosecutorial misconduct**
- **Explain the role of the defense attorney**
- **Explain and analyze the right to be represented by defense counsel**
- **Discuss the reasons for private defense counsel in contrast to public defense counsel**
- **Distinguish among public defender programs, assigned counsel programs, and contract programs for providing defense counsel**
- **Explain the meaning of effective assistance of counsel and the right to refuse counsel**
- **List and explain the major steps in the criminal justice pretrial process**
- **Explain the importance of bail to defendants**
- **List and explain the ways in which a defendant may be released pending trial**
- **Explain the process of entering a plea in a criminal case**
- **Discuss the arguments for and against plea bargaining**

CHAPTER OUTLINE

KEY TERMS

arraignment
assigned counsel
bail
bond
booking
community prosecution
contract system
defendant
defense attorney
deposition
discovery
grand jury
habeas corpus
indictment
information
initial appearance
interrogatories
lineup
motion
nolo contendere
plea bargaining
preliminary hearing
presentment
pretrial detention
preventive detention
pro se
prosecuting attorney
prosecution
public defender
right to counsel
showup
subpoena
true bill
venue
waiver

CHAPTER SUMMARY

Chapter 7 is the second of three reviewing the court process. This chapter discusses the attorneys who prosecute and defend in criminal cases, and then provides an overview of the pretrial procedures in which they engage.

The chapter begins with a historical overview of the need for lawyers and the legal profession. During the 17th century, the American colonies operated the legal system without lawyers. It was not until legal matters became more complex that colonists began to recognize the need for representation during proceedings by individuals trained in the legal system and the law. The legal profession flourished before the American Revolution. However, between 1830 and 1870, it fell out of favor. It was not until after 1870, when there was a movement toward professionalization, that lawyers became more educated and the practice of licensing began, along with higher law school admission standards and the beginning of a strong bar association. Public criticism toward lawyers may originate from the public's lack of understanding of the **adversary system**. Underlying the adversary philosophy is the belief that the best way to obtain the facts of a criminal case is for each side to have an advocate, or attorney, to present evidence and cross-examine the witnesses on the opposing side. Attacks toward attorneys come not only from the public but from within the profession itself as well. Despite these attacks and the potential for distrust, the need for attorneys remains.

Next, the chapter discusses the role of the prosecutor in the system. **Prosecution** of a criminal case is the process by which formal charges are brought against a person accused of committing a crime on behalf of the state. Most local and state prosecutors are elected officials, although the elected prosecutor may appoint attorneys to serve as deputy (or assistant) prosecutors within the office. Prosecution systems may be categorized as local, state, or federal. First, **local prosecution systems** exist at the rural, suburban, and urban levels. Each of these caseloads is different and the mechanisms for resolving conflicts differ based upon case type and resource availability. Second, the **state level systems** differ from state to state but most are headed by an attorney general who is an elected official and serves as the chief prosecutor for the state. The final level of prosecution is the **federal level**, which was provided for by the **Judiciary Act of 1789**. Federal prosecutors, or **U.S. attorneys**, are appointed by the president and approved by the Senate. U.S. attorneys report to the **U.S. attorney general**. Another variation of prosecution is **community prosecution**. Community prosecution is similar to community-oriented policing, focusing on quality of life issues, such as prostitution, disorderly conduct, drug solicitation, vandalism, and graffiti. In these instances, the prosecutor seeks input from the community along with public and private agencies and law enforcement.

The chapter next discusses the role of the prosecutor. The duty of the prosecuting attorney is to seek justice, not merely convict. The prosecutor is responsible for charging the accused with a crime; working with the defense to plea bargain a case; if the case goes to trial, developing and presenting the evidence against the accused; and participating at the sentencing phase of the process. The prosecutor has a great deal of discretion in deciding whether to bring charges against an individual. Despite the public's perception of the duty to prosecute, prosecutors have the authority to decide not to prosecute, especially if there is not enough evidence to suggest that a conviction would be obtained. A variety of other factors influence a prosecutor's decision to prosecute. These may include **extralegal factors**, such as race, ethnicity, gender or sexual orientation, and political influence. Once a prosecutor decides to prosecute, they must decide what charges to bring. The law specifies where and how formal charges are brought. This may include the filing of an **informa-**

tion or the filing of an **indictment** by a grand jury. Charging decisions may be based on intuition, personal beliefs about the usefulness of punishment, the relation of the crime to the possible penalty, and even personal bias or prejudice. There are at least three goals of charging the accused: first, crime reduction; second, efficient use of resources in the prosecutor's office; and, third, rehabilitation of the defendant. In recognition of the vast discretion a prosecutor maintains in the system, processes have been implemented to control its misuse. This includes the implementation of a **judicial review** process to ensure that the prosecutor has not participated in any misconduct. One form of prosecutorial misconduct for which judicial review may be a remedy is the act of **overcharging**. Prosecutors may overcharge defendants, as well as being blamed for the lack of convictions. Considerable attention has been given to the role of extralegal factors as well as the conscious decision for selective enforcement of certain laws.

Next, the chapter discusses the role of the defense attorney in the process. The **defense attorney** is charged with the responsibility of protecting defendants' constitutional rights at all stages of the legal proceedings, which begin long before trial. If an individual has not secured a private attorney, the judge will appoint counsel at the **first court appearance**. The defense attorney is responsible for interviewing their client; collecting and understanding the evidence of the case; developing a strategy for defense; ensuring that the case stays on schedule; and preparing an appeal should the defendant lose their case. The process of providing defense in a criminal case is crucial to the adversary system. The most important aspect of the defense of a criminal case is that the accused has a **right to counsel** provided in the **Sixth Amendment** to the U.S. Constitution. Should a defendant not be able to afford their own attorney, they have a right to have one appointed for them. The critical U.S. Supreme Court cases addressing this issue of indigency include *Gideon v. Wainwright* (1963), which upheld the right to representation in felony cases; and *Argersinger v. Hamlin* (1972), which upheld the right to representation in misdemeanor cases where incarceration even for a short time may be a possibility. The accused also has the right to refuse counsel via a **waiver**, but they must demonstrate that the decision to refuse was made voluntarily and knowingly. This protection for defendants is provided in an effort to eliminate the disadvantage of appearing ***pro se*** (i.e. as one's own attorney) in the system. Defendants also have the right to hire their own private attorney. As noted in the chapter, the right to counsel implies a right to effective counsel, which the U.S. Supreme Court defined in *Strickland* v. *Washington* (1984) as involving a two-pronged test. The defendant must show that counsel was deficient and that the deficiency resulted in prejudice to the defendant, who as a result did not get a fair trial. This standard is very difficult to prove, but the courts must consider the totality of the circumstances in making their decisions concerning whether a defendant had effective assistance of counsel. The chapter updates the issue of effective assistance of counsel by looking at cases decided since *Strickland*. To accommodate the needs of indigent defendants, three systems for providing representation exist. These indigent defense systems include **public defender systems**, **assigned counsel systems**, and **contract attorney systems**.

The last section of the chapter overviews the **pretrial process**, including the decision to grant bail and plea bargaining. The decision to grant **bail** to defendants awaiting trial continues to be controversial. The procedure to release defendants on bail varies by state and jurisdictions. The **Eighth Amendment** to the U.S. Constitution prohibits excessive bail. This Amendment does not guarantee the right to bail but rather provides protections against bail that is deemed unreasonable. Until recently, the only purpose of bail was to secure the return of the individual to court for their appearance. The U.S. Supreme Court upheld in the case of the *United States v. Salerno* (1987), however, that **preventive detention** is permissible as a mechanism to ensure the safety of the community and the individual.

As seen in the chapter, **plea bargaining** is a very controversial process within the system. Questions are raised concerning the need for justice from a community and victim stance and the need to continue to keep cases flowing through the system. Although the prosecution and defense may negotiate a plea bargain that they both believe meets the needs for justice, the judge may refuse to accept the plea deal. The process of plea bargaining provides a necessary function in the criminal court system to help reduce the amount of backlog with cases and as a tool for reducing overcrowding in the jails and prisons.

KEY TERMS

arraignment A hearing before a judge, during which the defendant is identified, hears the formal reading of the charges, is read his or her legal rights, and may enter a plea to the charges.

assigned counsel An attorney appointed by and paid for by the court to represent a defendant who does not have funds to retain a private attorney.

bail Money or property posted to guarantee that a defendant will appear for a legal proceeding, such as a trial, sentencing, or imprisonment. If the defendant does not appear, the court may require that the money or property be forfeited.

bond A written document indicating that the defendant or his or her sureties assure the presence of that defendant at a criminal proceeding and that, if the defendant is not present, the court may require that the security posted for the bond be forfeited.

booking The official recording of the name, photograph, and fingerprints of a suspect, along with the offense charged and the name of the officer who made the arrest.

community-oriented prosecution Similar to community-oriented policing (COPS), utilizes a more integrated, solution-based approach to crime, going beyond traditional criminal justice systems to look at such issues as quality of life.

contract system System for providing defense attorneys in which a governmental agency contracts with a local bar association, a private law firm, or a private attorney to provide legal services for indigent defendants.

defendant A person charged with a crime and against whom a criminal proceeding has begun or is pending.

defense attorney The counsel for the defendant in a criminal proceeding, whose main function is to protect the legal rights of the accused.

deposition Oral testimony taken from the opposing party or a witness for the opposing party. Depositions are taken out of court but under oath. They are recorded verbatim, usually by a court reporter. Attorneys for both sides are present. Depositions may be used when the deposed is not able to appear in court. They may also be used to impeach the testimony of a witness in court.

discovery: The process of revealing to opposing counsel the documents and other evidence that are intended for use in the forthcoming trial, along with a list of witnesses counsel proposes to call to testify.

grand jury A group of citizens, convened by legal authority, who evaluate evidence to ascertain whether a crime has been committed and whether there is sufficient evidence against the accused to justify prosecution. If so, the grand jury may return an *indictment*. In some jurisdictions grand juries are empowered to conduct investigations into alleged criminal activities.

habeas corpus Technically, a written court order requiring that the accused be taken to court to determine the legality of custody and confinement; also refers to actions filed by inmates regarding the alleged illegality of their confinement, or the conditions of that confinement. *See also* **writ**.

indictment The written accusation of a grand jury, formally stating that probable cause exists to believe that the suspect committed a specified felony.

information A formal written document used to charge a person with a specific offense. Prosecutors issue informations, in contrast to an *indictment* issued by a grand jury.

initial appearance The first appearance of the accused before a magistrate; if the accused is detained in jail immediately after arrest, he or she must be taken quickly to a magistrate for the initial appearance. At that point the magistrate decides whether there is probable cause to detain the suspect and, if so, tells the suspect of the charges and of his or her constitutional rights, including the right to an attorney.

interrogatories A set of questions given to a party thought to have pertinent information that may be used at a trial or other legal proceeding. The party completing the interrogatories must sign an oath that the statements are correct.

lineup A procedure in which a group of people are placed together in a line to allow the complainant or an eyewitness to the crime to identify the alleged offender.

motion A written document (or a verbal request) submitted to the court, asking for an order or a ruling.

nolo contendere Literally, "I will not contest it." In a criminal case, this plea has the legal effect of a guilty plea, but it cannot be used against the defendant in a civil action based on the same act. The plea might be used in a case involving a felony charge of driving while intoxicated. A guilty plea could be used as evidence of liability in a civil action of wrongful death filed by the family of a victim who died in the accident, whereas a *nolo* plea requires that the plaintiff in the civil action prove liability.

plea bargaining The process of negotiation between the defense and the prosecution before or during the trial of a defendant. The process may involve reducing or dropping some charges or a recommendation for leniency in exchange for a plea of guilty on another charge(s). Plea bargaining may also result in no changes in the charges or sentence recommendation. Any bargain must be approved by the judge.

preliminary hearing An appearance before a lower court judge to determine whether there is sufficient evidence to submit the case to the grand jury or to the trial court. Preliminary hearings may include the bail decision.

presentment A document issued by a grand jury that states that probable cause exists to believe that the suspect committed the crime. Presentments are issued without the participation of the prosecutor. *See also* **indictment.**

pretrial detention The detention of a person in jail (or some other approved facility) between arrest and trial, either because the judge has refused bail or the defendant cannot meet the requirements of bail. Generally the purpose of detention is to assure the presence of the accused at trial. Defendants may also be detained because they are thought to present a danger to themselves, to others, or to both if they are released pending trial or other judicial proceedings. Such detention is referred to as *preventive detention*.

preventive detention *See* **pretrial detention.**

pro se Literally, "on behalf of self"; acting as one's own attorney.

prosecuting attorney A government official responsible for representing the state (or federal government) against an offender in criminal proceedings.

prosecution The process that occurs when the state (or federal government) begins the formal process in a criminal case. The action is taken by a prosecuting attorney.

public defender An attorney retained and paid by the government to represent indigent defendants in criminal proceedings.

right to counsel The right to be represented by an attorney at crucial stages in the criminal justice system. Indigent defendants have the right to counsel provided by the state (or, in the case of a federal offense, the federal government).

showup An identification procedure during a police investigation; it involves showing the alleged victim only one person rather than several, as in a *lineup*; it is permitted only in extraordinary circumstances.

subpoena A command, issued by a court, ordering a person to appear in court (or at another designated place) at a specified time and place for the purpose of giving testimony on a specified issue. Persons may be ordered to bring documents pertinent to the case; that order is called a subpoena *duces tecum*.

true bill The prosecutor's indictment returned with the approval of the grand jury. After hearing the prosecutor's evidence, the grand jury determines that the indictment is accurate: that is, it is a *true bill*.

venue The location of a trial; a *change of venue* is the removal of a trial from the location where it would normally be held to another location, either to avoid public pressure or to obtain an impartial jury.

waiver In criminal law, the giving up of one's legal rights, such as the right to counsel or to a jury trial. Waivers must be made knowingly and intelligently: that is, the defendant must understand what is being relinquished. Some rights may not be waived.

STUDY QUESTIONS

These questions are found at the end of your chapter. Your instructor may wish to revisit these or assign them for points. These questions are a good way to integrate the material and to generate your own perspectives during class.

1 How have lawyers been viewed by the public historically?

2 Why did a system of public prosecution develop, and what is the difference between public and private prosecution? Which system do you think is better?

3 Compare local, state, and federal prosecution systems.

4 What is meant by *community prosecution*?

5 What is the main function of a prosecutor? Why is the prosecutor allowed so much discretion in fulfilling that role? What are the problems with allowing such discretion?

6 How can prosecutorial discretion be kept within reasonable limits? Evaluate one example of prosecutorial misconduct discussed in the chapter.

7 What is meant by the *right to counsel*? Describe briefly what that right means today, compared with its historical meaning in the United States.

8 What is the importance of the *Gideon* case?

9 What is the scope of the right to appointed counsel? Should it be expanded? Should it apply to the detention of those suspected of terrorist acts? If not, why not? If so, under what circumstances?

10 Do you think a defendant should have the right to refuse counsel? Explain your answer.

11 What does the U.S. Supreme Court mean by *effective assistance of counsel*? If you had the opportunity to define that term for the Court, what would you include?

12 Enumerate and explain the three major systems by which appointed counsel is provided. Explain current legal developments regarding public defender systems.

13 How would you suggest improving the availability and quality of legal defense counsel?

14 Would you prefer to be a defense attorney or a prosecuting attorney? Why?

15 Define each of the major steps in the criminal justice process before trial.

16 What restrictions are placed on the securing of physical evidence from a suspect?

17 Describe the main purposes of the *initial appearance*, *preliminary hearing*, and *arraignment*.

18 What is a *grand jury indictment*? How does that process differ from a prosecutor's information?

19 Distinguish between *depositions* and *interrogatories*.

20 What should be considered in deciding whether to release a defendant prior to trial?

21 What is the *bail bond system*, and why is it controversial today?

22 Which of the alternatives to a bail bond system do you think is most feasible? Why?

23 What should be the goals and purposes of detention prior to trial? Should foreign nationals be treated differently from others? Should it make a difference where they are detained? How did the U.S. Supreme Court rule on this issue?

24 Describe the process of pleading guilty before trial. Does it make any difference whether the plea is a negotiated one?

25 Do you think plea bargaining should be abolished? Why? If it is, what might be the result?

26 Evaluate some of the recent high-profile cases involving plea bargaining.

LEARNING ACTIVITIES

7.1 In 1975, a Louis Harris public opinion poll found that "the public had more confidence in garbage collectors than in lawyers, or doctors or teachers." Since that time, has the public opinion of lawyers changed? Provide evidence to support your arguments. Why do you believe there has historically been so much distrust with attorneys?

7.2 Imagine you are a newly elected county prosecutor. One of the platforms you ran on was to eliminate the "good ol' boy system" (also known as the courtroom workgroup), which has a tendency to be too lenient during the plea bargaining process. Address the following questions:

a Define the courtroom workgroup.
b Who belongs to this group?
c How might you go about eliminating the courtroom workgroup?
d What are some of the benefits and consequences of eliminating the courtroom workgroup?

a

b

c

d

7.3 Although not guaranteed by the U.S. Constitution, the lower courts have agreed not only that individuals should be guaranteed the right to representation when the possibility for confinement exists, but also that the representation should be effective. Within this context, answer the following questions:

a Which method(s) for appointing indigent defendants counsel is(are) used in your local community (public defender, assigned counsel, or contract attorneys)?

b Given what you know about the defense counsel system, do you believe indigent defendants are typically provided effective counsel? Explain your response.

c How might – or should – this system for appointing attorneys be improved?

a

b

c

7.4 An ongoing debate in the field of criminal justice exists regarding the use of plea bargaining. Using library resources, locate an article discussing the effectiveness of plea bargaining in criminal case processing. Answer the following questions:

a Based upon this article and what you have read in the text, should the criminal court system continue to use plea bargaining as an option to the criminal trial process?

b What would happen to the current system if the use of plea bargaining were eliminated?

c How might the current plea bargaining process be modified to be more fair and efficient?

d What role do the victims of crime play in the plea bargaining process?

a

b ____

____

____

____

____

____

____

c ____

____

____

____

____

____

____

d ____

____

____

____

____

____

____

STUDENT STUDY GUIDE PRACTICE QUESTIONS

True or False

7.1 The 17th century was the first time the colonies began using lawyers in the legal system.

7.2 Between 1830 and 1870, Michigan and Illinois permitted any male voter of good moral character to practice law.

7.3 Most local and state prosecutors are elected officials.

7.4 According to the American Bar Association, the duty of the prosecuting attorney is to "seek justice, not merely to convict."

7.5 The prosecutor in most jurisdictions has extensive discretion in deciding whether to bring formal charges against the accused.

7.6 The primary job of a defense attorney is to protect the defendant's legal rights and thereby preserve the adversary system.

7.7 Approximately 50 percent of jail inmates and 60 percent of prison inmates are represented by court-appointed attorneys.

7.8 During the process of booking, the court will hold a hearing for the purpose of having the court determine whether there is probable cause to charge the suspect with the crime.

7.9 In theory, the grand jury serves as a check on judicial review.

7.10 The U.S. Constitution does not guarantee a legal right to a plea bargain.

Multiple Choice

7.11 The passage of the Judiciary Act of 1789 provided for:
- a Indigent defense
- b The right to council
- c Prosecution at the state level
- d Prosecution at the federal level

7.12 Which of the following does not characterize an advantage of maintaining a rural prosecuting system?
- a Caseloads are lighter.
- b Case processing may be more informal.
- c Most cases go to trial.
- d Most cases are handled individually.

7.13 According to your text, which of the following might be a remedy for the prosecutorial abuse of overcharging?
- a Case law review
- b Civil law review
- c Judicial review
- d Law enforcement review

7.14 Which of the following is not considered a general goal of charging individuals with a crime?
- a Crime displacement
- b Crime reduction
- c Efficient use of resources
- d Rehabilitation of the defendant

7.15 Which Amendment to the U.S. Constitution states that "in all criminal prosecutions, the accused shall enjoy the right . . . to have the Assistance of Counsel for his defense"?
- a Second
- b Fourth
- c Fifth
- d Sixth

7.16 Which of the following is the first responsibility of the defense attorney?
- a Keep track of the scheduled procedures for the remainder of the time the case is in the criminal justice system.
- b Interview the client and obtain as many facts as possible.
- c Advise the defendant concerning the strategy that could be used in the case.
- d Talk to the clients' families and inform them of what to expect during the initial stages of the criminal justice process.

7.17 In 1962, the U.S. Supreme Court ruled in ______ that "in our adversary system of criminal justice, any person haled into court, who is too poor to hire a lawyer, cannot be assured a fair trial unless counsel is provided for him." This ruling applied the right to counsel in state felony cases.
- a *Betts v. Brady*
- b *Gideon v. Wainwright*
- c *Argersinger v. Hamlin*
- d *Scott v. Illinois*

7.18 In this 1972 case, the U.S. Supreme Court extended the right to counsel for indigent defendants to misdemeanor offenses for which a conviction might result in the "actual deprivation of a person's liberty," e.g., imprisonment.
- a *Betts v. Brady*
- b *Gideon v. Wainwright*
- c *Argersinger v. Hamlin*
- d *Scott v. Illinois*

7.19 The ______ Amendment to the U.S. Constitution prohibits requiring excessive bail.
- a Fourth
- b Fifth
- c Sixth
- d Eighth

7.20 In the 1987 case of ______, the U.S. Supreme Court upheld the Bail Reform Act's provision of preventive detention pretrial.
- a *United States v. Salerno*
- b *Gideon v. Wainwright*
- c *Argersinger v. Hamlin*
- d *Schall v. Martin*

Fill-in-the-Blank

7.21 The ______ of a criminal case is the process by which formal charges are brought against a person accused of committing a crime.

7.22 ______ involves a long-term, proactive partnership among the prosecutor's office, law enforcement, the community, and public and private organizations, whereby the authority of the prosecutor's office is used to solve problems, improve public safety, and enhance the quality of life of community members.

7.23 The prosecutor prepares a(n) ______, a document that names a specific person and the specific charge(s) against that individual.

7.24 Appealing a prosecutor's decision is difficult and rarely successful – unless the prosecutor has ______ or ______.

7.25 _____ occurs when prosecutors abuse their discretion and file charges that are not reasonable in light of the evidence available at the time those charges are filed.

7.26 The right to counsel involves a right to refuse counsel, but a(n) _____ of the right to counsel must be made voluntarily and knowingly.

7.27 An indictment returned by a grand jury is known as a(n) _____.

7.28 It is common for the defense to file a motion requiring the prosecutor to produce evidence, a process called _____

7.29 If a case has received considerable media attention, the defense may succeed with the argument that the defendant could not get a fair trial in that jurisdiction, and, therefore, a change of _____ should be granted.

7.30 _____ are informal meetings with the prosecution and the defense discussing the status of the case and enumerating the issues on which they agree so that no court time is wasted on arguing issues that are not in dispute.

CROSSWORD

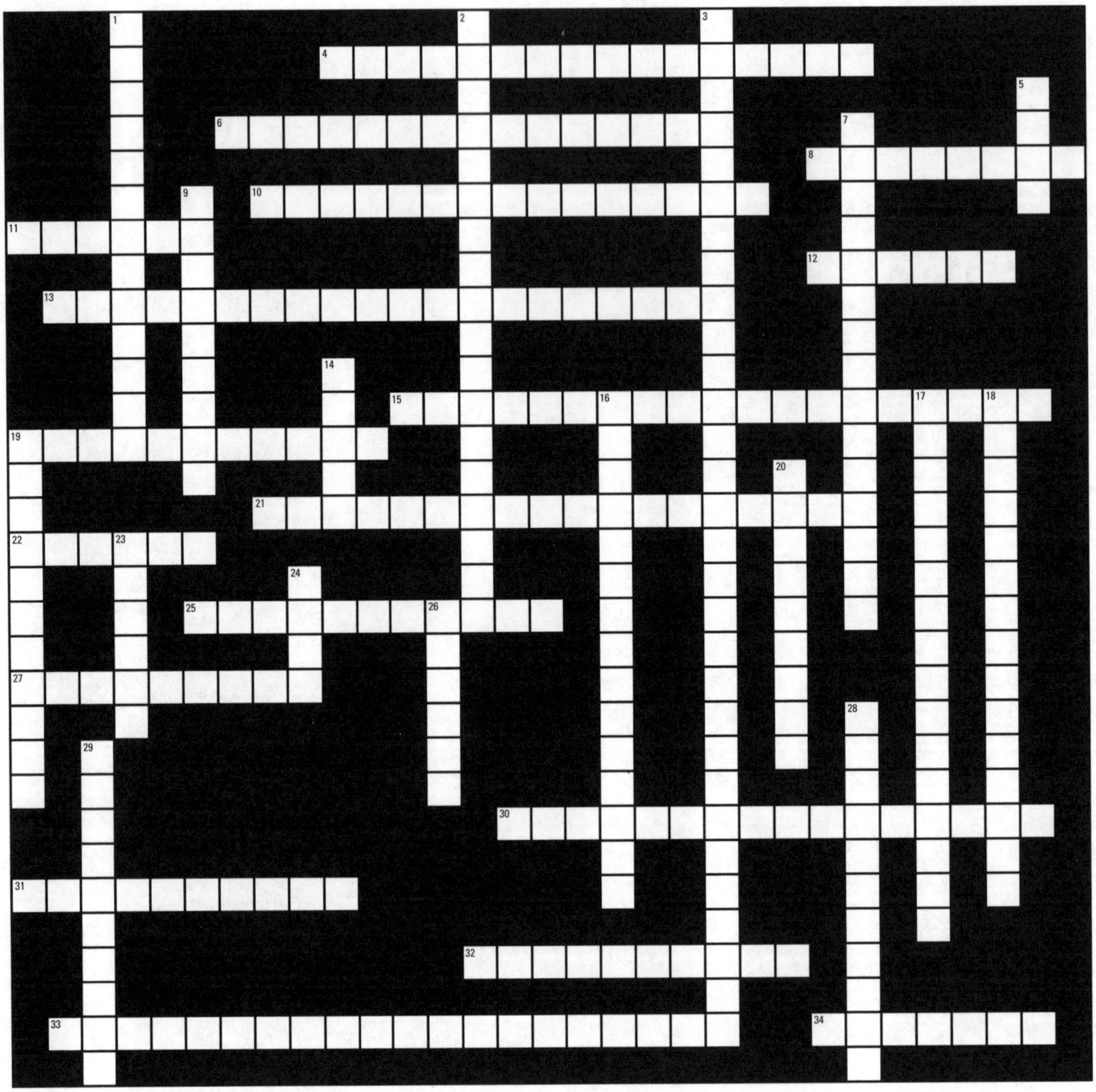

ACROSS

4 The counsel for the defendant in a criminal proceeding, whose main function is to protect the legal rights of the accused. (2 words, 1 space)

6 A way of organizing the provision of defense counsel for indigent defendants. (2 words, 1 space)

8 A command issued by a court, ordering a person to appear in court.

10 The process of negotiation between the defense and the prosecution before or during the trial of a defendant. (2 words, 1 space)

11 Literally, "on behalf of self"; acting as one's own attorney. (2 words, 1 space)

12 A procedure in which a group of people are placed together in a line to allow the complainant or an eyewitness to point out the alleged offender.

13 A government official responsible for representing the state or federal government against an offender in criminal proceedings. (2 words, 1 space)

15 An appearance before a lower-court judge to determine whether there is sufficient evidence to submit the case to the grand jury or to the trial court. (2 words, 1 space)

19 A document issued by a grand jury that states that probable cause exists to believe that the suspect committed the crime.

21 The detention of a defendant in jail between arrest and trial, either because the judge has refused bail or because the defendant cannot meet the requirements of bail. (2 words, 1 space)

22 An identification procedure during a police investigation.

25 A hearing before a judge, during which the defendant is identified, hears the formal reading of the charges, is read his or her legal rights, and enters a plea to the charges.

27 The prosecutor's indictment returned with the approval of the grand jury. (2 words, 1 space)

30 An attorney appointed by and paid for by the court to represent a defendant who does not have funds to retain a private attorney. (2 words, 1 space)

31 The written accusation of a grand jury, formally stating that probable cause exists to believe that the suspect committed a specified felony.

32 Oral testimony taken from the opposing party or a witness for the opposing party.

33 Detention of defendants who are detained because they are thought to present a danger to themselves, to others, or to both if released pending trial. (2 words, 1 space)

34 Official recording of the name, photograph, and fingerprints of a suspect, along with the offense charged and the name of the officer who made the arrest.

DOWN

1 A written court order requiring that the accused be taken to court to determine the legality of custody and confinement. (2 words, 1 space)

2 The first appearance of the accused before a magistrate. (2 words, 1 space)

3 A strategy of prosecution that goes beyond traditional criminal justice systems to look at such issues as quality of life. (3 words, 1 hyphen, 1 space).

5 A written document indicating that the defendant or his or her sureties assure the presence of that defendant at a criminal proceeding.

7 An attorney retained and paid by the government to represent indigent defendants in criminal proceedings. (2 words, 1 space)

9 The person charged with a crime and against whom a criminal proceeding has begun or is pending.

14 The location of a trial.

16 A set of questions given to a party thought to have pertinent information that may be used at a trial or other legal proceedings.

17 The right to be represented by an attorney at crucial stages in the criminal justice system. (3 words, 2 spaces)

18 Literally, "I will not contest it." (2 words, 1 space)

19 The process that occurs when the state (or federal government) begins the formal process in a criminal case.

20 A legal motion requesting the disclosure of information held by the opposing counsel and intended for use in the forthcoming trial.

23 The giving up of one's rights, such as the right to counsel or to a jury trial.

24 Money or property posted by the defendant (or a surety) to guarantee that he or she will appear for trial, sentencing, or imprisonment.

26 A document submitted to the court, asking for an order or a rule.

28 A formal written document used to charge a person with a specific offense.

29 A group of citizens, convened by legal authority, who evaluate evidence to ascertain whether a crime has been committed and whether there is sufficient evidence against the accused to justify prosecution. (2 words, 1 space)

WORD SEARCH

```
w t n l n t n e r b i e i u i n e g o t a e a n s l o i
n p w r o a o e i i p g t t t o n o p e e n r a o s a n
a c v a o s i o y r e v o c s i d e c n y m r n b a a n
u i n d i c t m e n t d u l r a n a i e e l t y p i t n
m n o e o v n s p l e a b a r g a i n i n g i p d p n s
n o i t u c e s o r p d e t n e i r o y t i n u m m o c
c l t t n n t r o l g h o i f e o i i s o a i b n b i d
r o u i t e e p i a y t n i n t t t u n y e t l l r t n
b c c m o d d v b r e r r r t o n r r y e c i i b o i i
o o e c i n e m a n e m i a a r e r l e g m a c u i s r
i n s g s m v n a s s i g n e d c o u n s e l d l e o n
t t o r n n i i c p b n h p n w e f e r s r a e n n p c
n e r t o m t n b u i t t c g t e r s o n y p f n o e y
e n p p i i n o i t n e t e d l a i r t e r p e o i d p
i d o l t e e d u p i r o a a i a p s t n c e n p a n i
i e e i a i v c t c s r c y r u j d n a r g a d u a n n
o r s n m e e i y a i o o d n c w n e e d p r e m r n b
p e d h r s r s i t p g u t m e t s y s t c a r t n o c
p u e e o n p o e e e a n a r r a i g n m e n t i s i p
a i e r f w s a t t t t s i y u h a b e a s c o r p u s
e m p n n e u o d a p o e g k b e a n f f i e o i r t l
r u r v i s n p e e t r l a e o i b i e l e i a s g i o
o n o p i l i d o m o i f u o l o i i d o i c n i t r i
a l y t e n n b a j d e n n n n r b t l i p b e n i o u
a r i a t s i d f n o s e m d v a v e o l e b e a i o p
e d s n e n c r e f t c m r e n t l p g e e n u a s e e
t n a s t n i d a e f a t a o n i y r r n n y i s e d s
r u n m s o e t o i e h a e e i a t v r s p r o p e g m
```

arraignment
assigned counsel
bail
bond
booking
community-oriented prosecution
contract system
defendant
defense attorney
deposition
discovery
grand jury
habeas corpus
indictment
information
initial appearance
interrogatories
lineup
motion
nolo contendere
plea bargaining
preliminary hearing
presentment
pretrial detention
preventive detention
pro se
prosecuting attorney
prosecution
public defender
right to counsel
showup
subpoena
true bill
venue
waiver

ANSWERS TO CROSSWORD

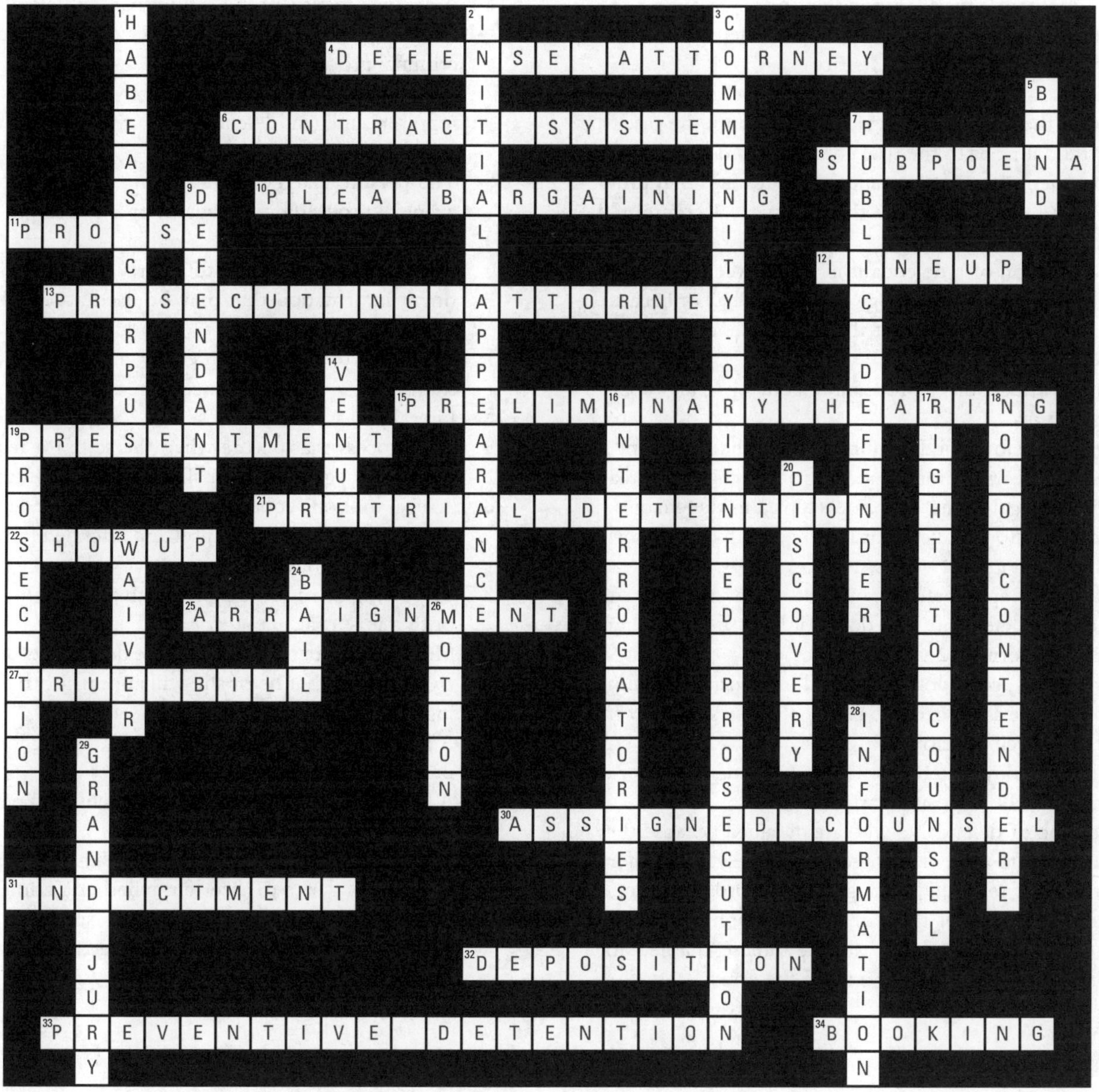

ACROSS

4 The counsel for the defendant in a criminal proceeding, whose main function is to protect the legal rights of the accused. (2 words, 1 space)

6 A way of organizing the provision of defense counsel for indigent defendants. (2 words, 1 space)

8 A command issued by a court, ordering a person to appear in court.

10 The process of negotiation between the defense and the prosecution before or during the trial of a defendant. (2 words, 1 space)

11 Literally, "on behalf of self"; acting as one's own attorney. (2 words, 1 space)

12 A procedure in which a group of people are placed together in a line to allow the complainant or an eyewitness to point out the alleged offender.

13 A government official responsible for representing the state or federal government against an offender in criminal proceedings. (2 words, 1 space)

15 An appearance before a lower-court judge to determine whether there is sufficient evidence to submit the case to the grand jury or to the trial court. (2 words, 1 space)

19 A document issued by a grand jury that states that probable cause exists to believe that the suspect committed the crime.

21 The detention of a defendant in jail between arrest and trial, either because the judge has refused bail or because the defendant cannot meet the requirements of bail. (2 words, 1 space)

22 An identification procedure during a police investigation.

25 A hearing before a judge, during which the defendant is identified, hears the formal reading of the charges, is read his or her legal rights, and enters a plea to the charges.

27 The prosecutor's indictment returned with the approval of the grand jury. (2 words, 1 space)

30 An attorney appointed by and paid for by the court to represent a defendant who does not have funds to retain a private attorney. (2 words, 1 space)

31 The written accusation of a grand jury, formally stating that probable cause exists to believe that the suspect committed a specified felony.

32 Oral testimony taken from the opposing party or a witness for the opposing party.

33 Detention of defendants who are detained because they are thought to present a danger to themselves, to others, or to both if released pending trial. (2 words, 1 space)

34 Official recording of the name, photograph, and fingerprints of a suspect, along with the offense charged and the name of the officer who made the arrest.

DOWN

1 A written court order requiring that the accused be taken to court to determine the legality of custody and confinement. (2 words, 1 space)

2 The first appearance of the accused before a magistrate. (2 words, 1 space)

3 A strategy of prosecution that goes beyond traditional criminal justice systems to look at such issues as quality of life. (3 words, 1 hyphen, 1 space).

5 A written document indicating that the defendant or his or her sureties assure the presence of that defendant at a criminal proceeding.

7 An attorney retained and paid by the government to represent indigent defendants in criminal proceedings. (2 words, 1 space)

9 The person charged with a crime and against whom a criminal proceeding has begun or is pending.

14 The location of a trial.

16 A set of questions given to a party thought to have pertinent information that may be used at a trial or other legal proceedings.

17 The right to be represented by an attorney at crucial stages in the criminal justice system. (3 words, 2 spaces)

18 Literally, "I will not contest it." (2 words, 1 space)

19 The process that occurs when the state (or federal government) begins the formal process in a criminal case.

20 A legal motion requesting the disclosure of information held by the opposing counsel and intended for use in the forthcoming trial.

23 The giving up of one's rights, such as the right to counsel or to a jury trial.

24 Money or property posted by the defendant (or a surety) to guarantee that he or she will appear for trial, sentencing, or imprisonment.

26 A document submitted to the court, asking for an order or a rule.

28 A formal written document used to charge a person with a specific offense.

29 A group of citizens, convened by legal authority, who evaluate evidence to ascertain whether a crime has been committed and whether there is sufficient evidence against the accused to justify prosecution. (2 words, 1 space)

ANSWERS TO WORD SEARCH

```
w t n l n t n e r b i e i u i n e g o t a e a n s l o i
n p w r o a o e i i p g t t t o n o p e e n r a o s a n
a c v a o s i o y r e v o c s i d e c n y m r n b a a n
u i n d i c t m e n t d u l r a n a i e e l t y p i t n
m n o e o v n s p l e a b a r g a i n i n g i p d p n s
n o i t u c e s o r p d e t n e i r o y t i n u m m o c
c l t t n n t r o l g h o i f e o i i s o a i b n b i d
r o u i t e e p i a y t n i n t t t u n y e t l l r t n
b c c m o d d v b r e r r r t o n r r y e c i i b o i i
o o e c i n e m a n e m i a a r e r l e g m a c u i s r
i n s g s m v n a s s i g n e d c o u n s e l d l e o n
t t o r n n i i c p b n h p n w e f e r s r a e n n p c
n e r t o m t n b u i t t c g t e r s o n y p f n o e y
e n p p i i n o i t n e t e d l a i r t e r p e o i d p
i d o l t e e d u p i r o a a i a p s t n c e n p a n i
i e e i a i v c t c s r c y r u j d n a r g a d u a n n
o r s n m e e i y a i o o d n c w n e e d p r e m r n b
p e d h r s r s i t p g u t m e t s y s t c a r t n o c
p u e e o n p o e e e a n a r r a i g n m e n t i s i p
a i e r f w s a t t t t s i y u h a b e a s c o r p u s
e m p n n e u o d a p o e g k b e a n f f i e o i r t l
r u r v i s n p e e t r l a e o i b i e l e i a s g i o
o n o p i l i d o m o i f u o l o i i d o i c n i t r i
a l y t e n n b a j d e n n n n r b t l i p b e n i o u
a r i a t s i d f n o s e m d v a v e o l e b e a i o p
e d s n e n c r e f t c m r e n t l p g e e n u a s e e
t n a s t n i d a e f a t a o n i y r r n n y i s e d s
r u n m s o e t o i e h a e e i a t v r s p r o p e g m
```

arraignment
bond
contract system
deposition
habeas corpus
initial appearance
motion
preliminary hearing
preventive detention
prosecution
showup
venue
assigned counsel
booking
defendant
discovery
indictment
interrogatories
nolo contendere
presentment
pro se
public defender
subpoena
waiver
bail
community-oriented prosecution
defense attorney
grand jury
information
lineup
plea bargaining
pretrial detention
prosecuting attorney
right to counsel
true bill

AL, SENTENCING
A D APPEAL

LEARNING OBJECTIVES

After reading this chapter, you should be able to do the following:

- **State an overview of defendants' constitutional rights**
- **Explain a defendant's right to a speedy, public trial by an impartial jury**
- **Discuss the variables of gender, race (and ethnicity), age, and disability in jury selection**
- **List and explain the stages in the trial and appeal of a criminal case in the United States**
- **Explain how evidence is presented in a criminal trial, and discuss the various types of evidence and objections to evidence**
- **Distinguish the prosecution's case from that of the defense**
- **Discuss the role of the jury in deciding a criminal case**
- **Explain and analyze the concept and process of sentencing and sentencing strategies**
- **Discuss the sentencing hearing and decision**
- **List and define the major types of sentences**
- **Describe the use of sentencing guidelines by states and the federal government**
- **Explain the difference between indeterminate and determinate sentencing and evaluate each**
- **Explore the meaning, causes, and consequences of sentence disparity**
- **Discuss the meaning and impact of three strikes and truth-in-sentencing legislation**
- **Consider the impact of a treatment approach to sentencing**
- **Describe appeals and writs**

Criminal Justice Essentials: Study Guide, Ninth Edition. Shannon Barton-Bellessa.

CHAPTER OUTLINE

KEY TERMS

aggravating circumstances
beyond a reasonable doubt
capital punishment
circumstantial evidence
community work service
concurrent sentence
consecutive sentence
contempt of court
corporal punishment
cross-examination
demonstrative evidence
determinate sentence
directed verdict
direct evidence
direct examination
fine
good time credits
hearsay evidence
incarceration
indeterminate sentence
jury
mandatory sentence
mistrial
mitigating circumstances
pardon
peremptory challenge
petit jury
prejudicial errors
presentence investigation (PSI)
presumption of innocence
presumptive sentence
sentence
sentence disparity
summons
three strikes and you're out
trial
truth in sentencing
voir dire
writ

CHAPTER SUMMARY

This chapter is the last of three focusing on the court system. More specifically, this chapter concentrates on the criminal processes during the stages of trial, sentencing, and appeal.

As was found in the chapters on policing, so here, too, constitutional issues guide practice, in this case the trial process. It was noted previously that the Sixth Amendment to the U.S. Constitution guarantees the right to representation during the court process. Embodied within this guarantee is the right to a speedy trial. In 1974, Congress passed the **Speedy Trial Act**. This act establishes a timeframe for suspects in federal cases only, stating that an indictment or an information charging the suspect must be filed within 30 days of the arrest or of the time when the suspect is served with a summons on the charge. That timeframe may be extended for 30 days in a felony charge if the grand jury was not in session during that time. Although this act does not address timeframes within states, they do typically provide for some variation of the Speedy Trial Act within their constitution. The Sixth Amendment also guarantees the right to a **public trial.** This does not mean, however, that the defendant should be tried by the media. A true balancing act occurs between the right to an impartial public trial and the First Amendment guarantee of freedom of speech. Should an impartial jury not be found, the defense and/or prosecution can request a **change of venue** or to **sequester the jury**. Similarly, defendants have the right to be notified of the charges against them; have the right to have the charges read to them at trial; have the right to compel witnesses to testify on their behalf; and the right to confront and to cross-examine witnesses who testify against them.

In the next section of the chapter, each stage of the criminal trial is explained and discussed, beginning with the opening of the court session, in which charges against the defendant are read, through jury selection, the presentation of evidence, the final arguments, and the verdict. Those defendants pleading not guilty and proceeding on to trial have the right to have their case heard in front of a jury of their peers. This has been deemed to be an unbiased jury that resembles the composition of the population as closely as possible. To select the jury, prosecutors and defense attorneys question the potential members through a process known as ***voir dire***. Jury members may be excluded from the pool for one of two reasons: for **cause** (i.e., a bias is assumed) or through a **peremptory challenge** (i.e., no reason need be given) . The number of challenges provided to both the prosecution and defense is established by statute. Once a jury has been seated, the trial process begins with opening statements by both the prosecution and the defense. The next stage of the process is the presentation of evidence by the prosecution and then the defense. An important evidentiary rule is that of **discovery**, which refers to the process during which one side obtains the information that will be presented in court by the other side. There are several forms of evidence that may be presented at trial. These include **demonstrative evidence**, **testimonial evidence** (i.e., victim-witness, eyewitness, expert witness), **hearsay evidence**, **direct evidence**, and **circumstantial evidence**. Following the presentation of the case by both the prosecution and the defense, closing statements are given. Once this process concludes, the case is submitted to the jury for consideration. In criminal cases, the jury is tasked with deciding whether the prosecution's case met the **burden of proof** standard of **proof beyond a reasonable doubt**. In civil cases, the prosecution is charged with presenting its case in a manner whereby there is a **preponderance of evidence** to suggest that the defendant committed the offense. Upon a finding of guilty, the court imposes a **sentence**. In all of these stages, the defense, the prosecution, and the judge are primary figures in assuring that proper procedures are followed. Following proper procedures, however, does not end the matter. It is important to consider and reconsider the issues involved in U.S. criminal justice systems.

Next, the chapter discusses the sentencing process, ranging from the sentencing hearing to the formal stage of imposing the sentence on the convicted defendant. This process may involve numerous issues and problems. The major sentencing strategies, which include **indeterminate**, **presumptive**, **mandatory**, and **determinate sentences**, are examined in this section. The sentencing hearing is reviewed, along with some of the procedures and issues involved in the decision-making process of sentencing, including the use of the **presentence investigation** (**PSI**) report. The role of the victim in the process is also reviewed. The use of the **Victim Impact Statement** (**VIS**) has been challenged in the courts. However, the U.S. Supreme Court has ruled that it is constitutional for a VIS to be read during capital sentencing hearings.

The type of sentence a defendant receives varies by jurisdiction, state, and crime type. In general, the sentencing options range from the least restrictive, a fine, to the most restrictive, capital punishment. In most jurisdictions, judges have the option of using one or a combination of possibilities, such as fines, restitution, community work service, probation, incarceration, etc. Because there is so much discretion given to judges even within the legal framework to sentence offenders, there is great concern about sentencing disparity between and within states. The concern with alleged sentence disparity led to a return to determinate sentences, many of which are longer than previously allowed. **Sentencing guidelines** have been created in an effort to reduce the amount of judicial discretion and the disparities that occur. The current concept of **three strikes and you're out,** which creates mandatory penalties for certain offenders and offenses, and **truth in sentencing** laws, which are designed to ensure that offenders serve a specified amount of time behind bars (interpreted as 85 percent of the original sentence at the federal level), embody this return to longer and more determinate sentences. More recently, however, some jurisdictions have turned to treatment rather than punishment in an attempt to balance budgets and reduce crime.

The next section of the chapter addresses the use of **appeals** and **writs**. As noted in the previous chapter, individuals convicted of crimes have the right to appeal errors in law. In addition to an appeal, those convicted of a crime may also file a writ, which is a court order giving permission to do whatever was requested or orders someone to do something specific. A writ commonly filed by offenders is the **writ of *habeas corpus***. The writ of *habeas corpus* is often filed questioning the confinement of the individual.

The chapter concludes with a discussion of **wrongful convictions** – a subject that epitomizes the failure of the criminal justice system. As noted in the chapter, 138 persons on death row have been exonerated. Not all wrongful convictions are found on death row, however. In many instances those wrongly convicted have served many years behind prison walls seeking to prove their innocence. The collateral damage caused by wrongfully convicting and detaining an individual continues to be of the utmost concern to the criminal justice system.

KEY TERMS

aggravating circumstances Circumstances that are above and beyond those required for the crime but that make the crime more serious; may be used in reference to many crimes, but the concept is critical in capital punishment cases, where it is required.

beyond a reasonable doubt The standard for evidence required for a conviction in an adult criminal court or processing in a juvenile court; a lack of uncertainty; the facts presented to the judge or jury are sufficient to lead a reasonable person to conclude without question that the accused committed the act(s) charged.

capital punishment Punishment by death for those convicted of capital crimes.

circumstantial evidence Evidence that may be inferred from a fact or a series of facts. *See also* **direct evidence**.

community work service Punishment assigning the offender to community service or work projects; may be combined with restitution or probation.

concurrent sentence A sentence for more than one offense served at the same time. For example, if an offender receives a three-year prison term for robbery and a five-year prison term for assault, these sentences to be served concurrently, the total prison sentence is five years.

consecutive sentence A term of imprisonment for more than one offense that must be served one following the other. Thus, if an offender receives a three-year term for robbery and a five-year term for assault, the defendant has an eight-year term.

contempt of court An act (usually committed in violation of a court order or rule) considered as embarrassing, humiliating, or as undermining the power of the court; may be civil or criminal.

corporal punishment Physical punishment, such as beatings or whippings; such punishments are no longer permitted in U.S. correctional facilities.

cross-examination The questioning of a court witness by adversary counsel after one attorney concludes the *direct examination*.

demonstrative evidence Real evidence; the kind of evidence that is apparent to the senses, in contrast to evidence presented by the testimony of other people.

determinate sentence A sentence for a specific crime and determined by the legislature; the parole board, correctional officials, or a judge cannot make changes in the sentence length. In some jurisdictions the trial judge may have the power to suspend the sentence or to impose probation rather than the legislatively specified prison term.

directed verdict Upon a finding of insufficient evidence to convict a defendant, the judge may direct the jury to return a verdict of not guilty. The judge may not direct a verdict of guilty.

direct evidence Evidence offered by an eyewitness who testifies to what he or she saw, heard, tasted, smelled, or touched.

direct examination The verbal examination in a court proceeding of a witness, which is conducted by the attorney who called that witness to testify. *See also* **cross-examination**.

fine The payment of a sum of money to a court by a convicted defendant in addition to or instead of other punishment(s).

good time credits Credits for hours or days awarded for satisfactory behavior in prison and resulting in a reduction of prison time that must be served.

hearsay evidence Evidence of which witnesses do not have personal knowledge but merely repeat what they have heard others say. Hearsay evidence must be excluded from a trial unless it meets one of the legally recognized exceptions to the hearsay rule.

incarceration Imprisonment in a jail, a prison, or another type of penal institution.

indeterminate sentence A sentence to confinement without a definite term. Parole boards or professionals determine when the offender should be released.

jury In a criminal case, a group of people who have sworn to listen to the evidence during a trial and to decide whether the defendant is guilty or not guilty. In some jurisdictions, after a conviction, a jury may also recommend or even determine the sentence.

mandatory sentence A sentence having a length imposed by the legislature, with no discretion given to the trial judge. If the defendant is convicted, the specified sentence must be imposed.

mistrial A trial that is invalid and thus cannot stand. Judges may call a mistrial for such reasons as an error on the part of the prosecution or the defense, the illness or death of any of the parties participating in the legal proceedings, jury tampering, or the jury's inability to reach a verdict.

mitigating circumstances Circumstances that do not justify or excuse a crime but that, because of justice and fairness, make the crime less reprehensible; they may be used to reduce a charge to a lesser offense, such as to reduce murder to manslaughter. Mitigating circumstances must be considered before the death penalty can be imposed. *See also* **aggravating circumstances**.

pardon An act by a state governor or the U.S. president (in federal cases) that exempts a convicted offender from punishment or, in the case of those already serving terms, further punishment, and removes the legal consequences of the conviction. Pardons may also be granted after a person is released from prison. Pardons may be absolute or conditional; individual or granted to a group, or class, of offenders; and may be full or partial, in which case the pardon remits only part of the punishment or removes some of the legal disabilities resulting from the conviction.

peremptory challenge A challenge that may be used by the prosecution or the defense to excuse a potential juror from the jury panel without stating a reason. Each attorney gets a specified number of peremptory challenges. Peremptory challenges are distinguished from *challenges for cause*, which are unlimited and based on a reason for disqualification, such as a conflict of interest with the case.

petit jury *Petit* literally means "small, minor, or inconsiderate"; a trial jury, in contrast to a grand jury. *See also* **jury.**

prejudicial errors Errors made during legal proceedings that substantially affect the rights of parties and thus may result in the reversal of a case.

presentence investigation (PSI) An investigation of the background and characteristics of the defendant; it may include information that would not be admissible at the trial; it is presented to the court to be used in determining sentence.

presumption of innocence A cornerstone of the adversary system; provides that a defendant is innocent unless and until the prosecution proves guilt beyond a reasonable doubt.

presumptive sentence The normal sentence is specified by statute for each offense; judges are permitted to deviate from that sentence but usually may do so only under specified circumstances or must give reasons for the deviation.

restitution Punishment that requires an offender to repay the victim with services or money. This punishment may be imposed instead of or in addition to other punishment or fines and may be a requirement of parole.

sentence The punishment imposed by the court on a convicted offender.

sentence disparity Inequalities and differences in sentencing as, for example, when people found guilty of the same crime receive sentences varying in length and type, without reasonable justification for those differences.

summons A formal document issued by the court to notify a person that his or her presence is required in court for a particular reason at a specified time and date.

three strikes and you're out Name of legislation enacted in recent years and designed to impose long sentences on persons who commit three or more serious crimes.

trial In criminal law, court proceeding during which a judge, a jury, or both listen to the evidence as presented by the defense and the prosecution and determine whether the defendant is guilty beyond a reasonable doubt, or should be acquitted. *See also* **mistrial**.

truth in sentencing The concept requiring that actual time served by offenders is closer to the time allocated for the sentence. Many jurisdictions are establishing 85 percent as their goal, meaning that offenders may not be released for any reason until they have served 85 percent of their sentences.

voir dire To speak the truth; the process of questioning prospective jurors to determine their qualifications and desirability for serving on a jury.

writ An order from a court. *See also* **writ of *certiorari*** and ***habeas corpus***.

STUDY QUESTIONS

These questions are found at the end of your chapter. Your instructor may wish to revisit these or assign them for points. These questions are a good way to integrate the material and to generate your own perspectives during class.

1 Explain the importance of constitutional rights in a criminal trial.

2 What is the purpose of the Speedy Trial Act of 1974? What kinds of delays does it permit?

3 Why is the right to a public trial important to defendants? What are the legal problems and issues with public trials as far as the media are concerned?

4 Why is the jury system considered important in the United States? Should it be abolished? Why or why not? Do you think a fair and impartial jury can be selected in high-publicity trials?

5 What are the requirements for jury size and the selection of names for the jury pool? What is meant by an *impartial jury* and a *jury of peers*?

6 What is the role of the judge in controlling the conduct of defendants at trial?

7 Should people who are chosen for the jury pool be permitted to be excused from jury duty at their own request, or should all persons called be required to serve? Which, if any, requests should be honored? Which reasons should not be considered?

8 What is the significance of *Batson v. Kentucky*? Does the case apply to gender?

9 How do opening statements differ from closing statements? Are both required for the prosecution and the defense?

10 Define *demonstrative evidence*. How does it differ from witness testimony as evidence?

11 What is the *hearsay rule*?

12 What is the difference between direct and circumstantial evidence?

13 What is meant by *direct examination*, *cross examination*, and *redirect* examination?

14 Contrast the prosecution's case with that of the defense.

15 Describe the role of the judge in presenting the case to the jury.

16 Describe and evaluate the role of the jury in a criminal trial.

17 Discuss the importance of sentencing, and explain sentencing strategies.

18 Is a sentencing hearing necessary? Is it required? What occurs in a sentencing hearing? What is the value of a presentence investigation? Should the presentence investigation be available to the prosecution and the defense, as well as the judge? Why or why not?

19 What are the legal issues concerning the role of victims in the sentencing process? What is your opinion regarding the role victims should be permitted to play?

20 Should capital punishment be abolished? Why or why not?

21 What is meant by *sentence disparity*? Discuss the issues of gender and racial discrimination in sentencing.

22 What problems have arisen with federal sentencing guidelines?

23 What is the difference between *determinate* and *indeterminate sentences*?

24 What do you think will be the effect of three strikes and you're out legislation? Evaluate the U.S. Supreme Court's recent decision on this concept. What is the effect of truth in sentencing?

25 What is a *wobbler*, and what is its significance? Should we treat rather than punish? Discuss.

26 Explain the meaning of *appeals* and *writs*.

27 What is a wrongful conviction and what measures should be taken when it occurs?

LEARNING ACTIVITIES

8.1 Using the links provided on the supplemental webpage, locate your state's Speedy Trial Act. How does your state's statute compare to the federal Speedy Trial Act? What, if any, mechanisms are put in place to exceed the maximum time allowed?

8.2 Currently states vary in the roles that victims play in the criminal justice process. Using your state's current victim advocacy programs, answer the following questions:

- **a** To what extent are victims allowed to participate in the criminal justice court process?
- **b** Describe the victim compensation programs offered in your state.
- **c** Are there any mechanisms for recourse for victims when offenders fail to compensate them?

a

b

c

8.3 As noted in Chapter 1, there are a variety of different purposes of the criminal justice system, i.e., rehabilitation, retribution, just deserts, incapacitation, deterrence, etc. Many states and the federal government have focused their attention on the deterrence and retribution strategies for sentencing. These strategies result in increasing the use of punishment and decreasing opportunities for rehabilitation. Describe the potential long-term impact of having punishment as the reason for incarceration as opposed to rehabilitation. What are some of the potential costs and benefits (i.e., economic, emotional, collateral) to this approach?

8.4 The issue of sentencing and sentencing guidelines continues to be at the forefront of the majority of state court and correctional systems. These concerns are exacerbated with growing economic deficits and budget shortfalls. In 2001, the U.S. Department of Justice published an article entitled "Sentencing Guidelines: Reflections on the Future." For this activity you should read the article found at the following link: http://www.ncjrs.gov/pdffiles1/nij/186480.pdf. After reading the article, answer the following questions:

a Look to your state. Are sentencing guidelines currently used? If so describe them.

b According to the statutes in your state, what is the guiding purpose of sentencing?

c Using the article, do you think the propositions put forward still remain in today's criminal justice system?

a

b

c

STUDENT STUDY GUIDE PRACTICE QUESTIONS

True or False

8.1 The 1974 Speedy Trial Act applies to both federal and state court cases.

8.2 The Sixth Amendment guarantees the right to a public trial.

8.3 The U.S. Constitution specifies how many jurors must be present for the defendant's right to a jury trial to be legal.

8.4 The presentence investigation (PSI) is completed prior to the trial in an effort to expedite the sentencing phase if the defendant is found guilty.

8.5 In civil cases, the standard of proof is the preponderance of evidence.

8.6 The U.S. Supreme Court ruled in *Payne v. Tennessee* (1991) that Victim Impact Statements could be used at capital sentencing hearings.

8.7 Probation is used nearly five times as often as incarceration.

8.8 All truth in sentencing laws require that inmates serve 85 percent of their sentences before they are released from prison.

8.9 Writs of *habeas corpus*, which means "you have the body," are oftentimes used by inmates who are questioning the legality of their confinement.

8.10 The ultimate wrongful conviction is the execution of an innocent person. According to the author, 257 persons on death row have been exonerated.

Multiple Choice

8.11 The right to a speedy trial is embodied in the _____ Amendment to the U.S. Constitution.

- a First
- b Second
- c Sixth
- d Fifth

8.12 Which of the following observations is incorrect?

- a Some delays are permissible under the Speedy Trial Act.
- b The Speedy Trial Act applies to prosecutions in federal and state courts.
- c The right to a speedy trial is embodied in the Sixth Amendment to the U.S. Constitution.
- d The Speedy Trial Act permits delays caused by continuances requested by the defense when they are granted to serve the ends of justice.

8.13 Identify the term that refers to a challenge that does not require the attorney to state a reason.

- a Judicial challenge
- b Disposition
- c Peremptory challenge
- d a and b

8.14 Which of the following is a correct observation?

- a The U.S. Supreme Court has held that defendants have a right to a jury of peers of their own age.
- b Juries must be representative of the community.
- c Juries must mirror the community and reflect the various distinctive groups in the population.
- d The U.S. Supreme Court held that the use of peremptory challenges by the prosecution to exclude men from the jury was constitutional.

8.15 _____ evidence is real to the senses, in contrast to evidence presented by the testimony of other people.

- a Hearsay
- b Demonstrative
- c Testimonial
- d Collected

8.16 Which of the following is a preferred type of testimonial evidence?
- a Eyewitness
- b Victim-witness
- c Expert witness
- d Hearsay

8.17 Which of the following is not admissible?
- a Dying declaration
- b Demonstrative evidence
- c Hearsay evidence
- d Victim-witness testimonial evidence

8.18 Evidence inferred from a fact or series of facts is called ______.
- a perceived evidence
- b circumstantial evidence
- c demonstrative evidence
- d hearsay evidence

8.19 After the defense cross-examines a prosecution witness, the prosecutor may follow with additional questions, in a process called ______ examination.
- a redirect
- b direct
- c cross
- d indirect

8.20 In ______ sentencing the normal sentence is specified for each offense, but judges are permitted to deviate from that norm.
- a indeterminate
- b mandatory
- c determinate
- d presumptive

Fill-in-the-Blank

8.21 A(n) ______sentence must be imposed upon conviction and usually involves a prison term.

8.22 A(n) ______ sentence involves legislative specifications of sentence ranges that permit judges to exercise discretion in determining actual sentences.

8.23 ______ requires offenders to reimburse victims financially or with services.

8.24 Technically the jury that sits in a trial is called the ______

8.25 Questioning of the potential jurors follows a process called ______, which means "to tell the truth."

8.26 Jurors are excused from jury duty in two ways: ______ and ______.

8.27 A witness who testifies that he or she saw the defendant using the alleged weapon is providing ______ evidence, while evidence that is inferred from a fact or series of facts is called ______ evidence.

8.28 The ______ is an important principle in the court process that means the prosecution has the responsibility of proving every element required for conviction and that the defendant does not have to prove innocence.

8.29 Determinate sentences may include provisions for raising (______ circumstances) or lowering (______ circumstances) the sentence.

8.30 With a(n) ______ sentence, the defendant satisfies the terms of all sentences at the same time. With a(n) ______ sentence, the defendant will serve all counts one after another.

CROSSWORD

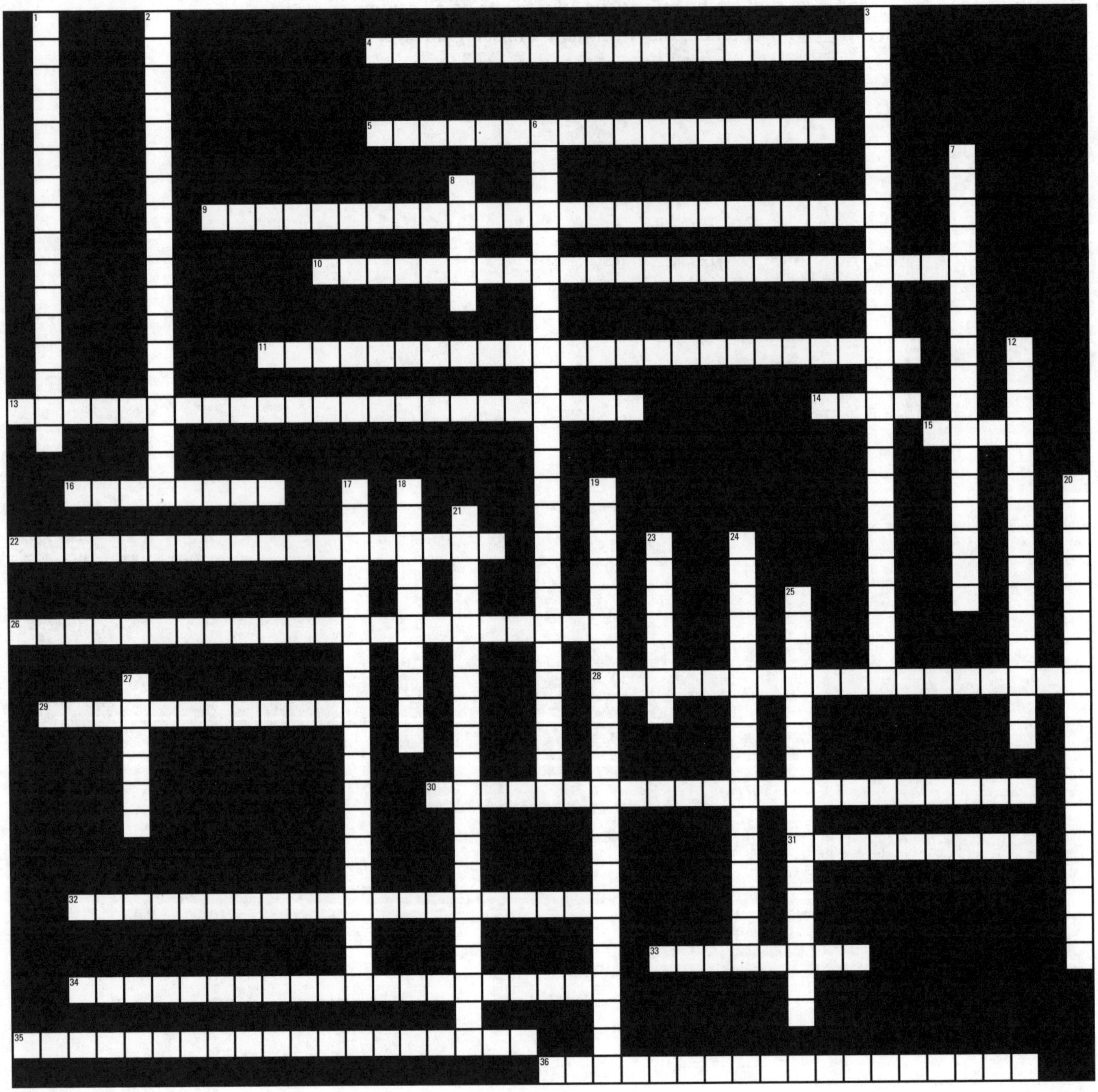

ACROSS

4 The concept requiring that actual time served by offenders is closer to the time allocated for the sentence. (3 words, 2 spaces)

5 An act (usually committed in violation of a court order or rule) considered as embarrassing, humiliating, or undermining the power of the court; may be civil or criminal. (3 words, 2 spaces)

9 The standard for evidence required for a conviction in an adult criminal court or a juvenile court. (4 words, 3 spaces)

10 Circumstances that do not justify or excuse a crime but that, because of justice and fairness, make the crime less reprehensible. (2 words, 1 space)
11 A cornerstone of the adversary system. (3 words, 2 spaces)
13 Evidence that may be inferred from a fact or a series of facts. (2 words, 1 space)
14 A group of people who have been sworn in at court to listen to a trial and to decide whether the defendant is guilty or not guilty.
15 The payment of a sum of money to a court by the convicted defendant in addition to or instead of other punishment(s).
16 A trial that cannot stand, that is invalid.
22 The examination of a witness, which is conducted by the attorney who called the witness to testify. (2 words, 1 space)
26 Punishment assigning the offender to community service or work projects. (3 words, 2 spaces)
28 A sentence having a length imposed by the legislature with no discretion given to the trial judge. (2 words, 1 space)
29 Imprisonment in a jail, a prison, or another type of penal institution.
30 Real evidence; the kind of evidence that is apparent to the senses, in contrast to evidence presented by the testimony of other people. (2 words, 1 space)
31 To speak the truth. (2 words, 1 space)
32 A sentence for a specific crime and determined by the legislature. (2 words, 1 space)
33 The punishment imposed by the court on a convicted offender.
34 The normal sentence is specified by statute for each offense. (2 words, 1 space)
35 Physical punishment, such as beatings or whippings. (2 words, 1 space)
36 Errors made during legal proceedings that affect the rights of parties substantially and thus may result in the reversal of a case. (2 words, 1 space)

DOWN

1 Credit resulting in a reduction of prison time. (3 words, 2 spaces)
2 Punishment by death for those convicted of capital crimes. (2 words, 1 space)
3 Circumstances that are above and beyond those required for the crime but make the crime more serious. (2 words, 1 space)
6 An investigation of the background and characteristics of the defendant. (2 words, 1 space)
7 The questioning of a court witness by adversary counsel after one attorney concludes the direct examination. (2 words, hyphen)
8 Court proceedings during which a judge, a jury, or both listen to the evidence as presented by the defense and the prosecution and determine whether the defendant is guilty beyond a reasonable doubt.
12 Evidence offered by an eyewitness who testifies to what he or she saw, heard, tasted, smelled, or touched. (2 words, 1 space)
17 A sentence for more than one offense served at the same time. (2 words, 1 space)
18 A trial jury, its name meaning literally, "small, minor, or inconsiderate." (2 words, 1 space)
19 A sentence to confinement without a definite term. (2 words, 1 space)
20 Inequalities and differences that result when people found guilty of the same crime receive sentences varying in length and type, without reasonable justification for those differences. (2 words, 1 space)
21 A term of imprisonment for more than one offense that must be served one following the other. (2 words, 1 space)
23 Formal document issued by the court to notify a person that his or her presence is required in court for a particular reason at a specified time and date.
24 Upon a finding of insufficient evidence to convict a defendant, the judge may direct the jury to return a verdict of not guilty. (2 words, 1 space)
25 Secondhand evidence of which the witness does not have personal knowledge but merely repeats something the witness says he or she heard another person say. (2 words, 1 space)
27 An act by a state governor or the president of the United States (in federal cases) that exempts a convicted offender from punishment or, in the case of those already serving terms, further punishment and removes the legal consequences of the conviction.

WORD SEARCH

```
v j p e t u o e r u o y d n a s e k i r t s e e r h t r e
n n y c c r n u r a q i n t a c p u y n c t o p n e d y e
o o t n i a f t g n i c n e t n e s n i h t u r t e i s u
a i i e r p r e s u m p t i v e s e n t e n c e r g e c e
o t r t r b e t c i d r e v d e t c e r i d r c c n p t u
o a a n a i e e i n d e t e r m i n a t e s e n t e n c e
o n p e r g d y e j e e u n s n o a a v s a t e c l r a c
c i s s d f i r o e a d e c e u i t e i c i n n a l p j i
r m i t i g a t i n g c i r c u m s t a n c e s i a r d v
o a d n r o i v s o d s d v i e r m v c e c n a r h e e r
s x e e e o e r i e v a d e e h d u o i o c o d i c j m e
s e c r c d e l t t v g r e a l t c p n n o o p i y u o s
e t n r t t u c n m m n t e h h a r n s s n n e n r d n k
x c e u e i e u n e o i i v a p r i n s d s n n n o i s r
a e t c v m h g v e o d e e i s f c t e e e s u v t c t o
m r n n i e x i s n d l c t c o o g n n a c a u e p i r w
i i e o d c y e d s d i a e n n p n o l a u r v i m a a y
n d s c e r y t r r e l v o t a e i a t e t t w m e l t t
a d c t n e t r n i p e i e t a t t s b s i s h c r e i i
t e n a c d s i u u t t m n y r r a n m l v p m c e r v n
i r p x e i n e n j p p n k e a i v n e i e m r u p r e u
o l a i r t s i m m t d f c c n s a t e s s d p e c o e m
n i o e n n s i u o n i r a a y e r l n s e m o t m r v m
m i i s k h r s f e e a t n o o e g a e y n r a u a s i o
a e r n m r e c a s c j i e d t y g o e e t e p n b c d c
e t m e e r o k n n n i u n p c c a l e h e s d c v t e a
e o n p p u i o i m m c o r p o r a l p u n i s h m e n t
o t i e r s m a n d a t o r y s e n t e n c e i p m d c r
d r c t i r w e n d e t e r m i n a t e s e n t e n c e t
```

aggravating circumstances
beyond a reasonable doubt
capital punishment
circumstantial evidence
community work service
concurrent sentence
consecutive sentence
contempt of court
corporal punishment
cross-examination
demonstrative evidence
determinate sentence
directed verdict
direct evidence
direct examination
fine
good time credit
hearsay evidence
incarcertion
indeterminate sentence
jury
mandatory sentence
mistrial
mitigating circumstances
pardon
peremptory challenge
petit jury
prejudicial errors
presentence investigation
presumption of innocence
presumptive sentence
sentence
sentence disparity
summons
three strikes and you're out
trial
truth in sentencing
voir dire
writ

ANSWERS TO CROSSWORD

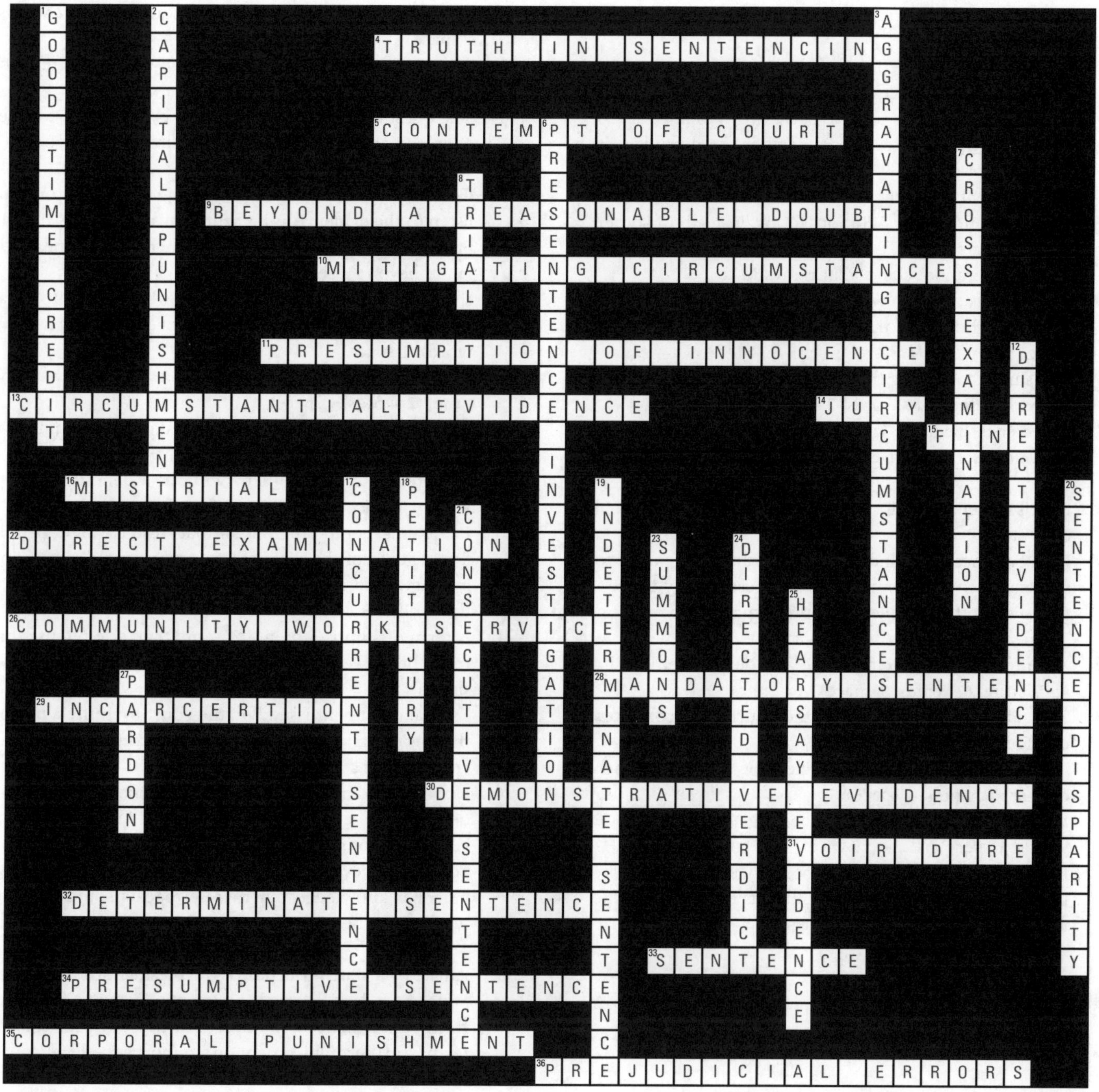

ACROSS

4 The concept requiring that actual time served by offenders is closer to the time allocated for the sentence. (3 words, 2 spaces)

5 An act (usually committed in violation of a court order or rule) considered as embarrassing, humiliating, or undermining the power of the court; may be civil or criminal. (3 words, 2 spaces)

9 The standard for evidence required for a conviction in an adult criminal court or a juvenile court. (4 words, 3 spaces)

10 Circumstances that do not justify or excuse a crime but that, because of justice and fairness, make the crime less reprehensible. (2 words, 1 space)

11 A cornerstone of the adversary system. (3 words, 2 spaces)

13 Evidence that may be inferred from a fact or a series of facts. (2 words, 1 space)

14 A group of people who have been sworn in at court to listen to a trial and to decide whether the defendant is guilty or not guilty.

15 The payment of a sum of money to a court by the convicted defendant in addition to or instead of other punishment(s).

16 A trial that cannot stand, that is invalid.

22 The examination of a witness, which is conducted by the attorney who called the witness to testify. (2 words, 1 space)

26 Punishment assigning the offender to community service or work projects. (3 words, 2 spaces)

28 A sentence having a length imposed by the legislature with no discretion given to the trial judge. (2 words, 1 space)

29 Imprisonment in a jail, a prison, or another type of penal institution.

30 Real evidence; the kind of evidence that is apparent to the senses, in contrast to evidence presented by the testimony of other people. (2 words, 1 space)

31 To speak the truth. (2 words, 1 space)

32 A sentence for a specific crime and determined by the legislature. (2 words, 1 space)

33 The punishment imposed by the court on a convicted offender.

34 The normal sentence is specified by statute for each offense. (2 words, 1 space)

35 Physical punishment, such as beatings or whippings. (2 words, 1 space)

36 Errors made during legal proceedings that affect the rights of parties substantially and thus may result in the reversal of a case. (2 words, 1 space)

DOWN

1 Credit resulting in a reduction of prison time. (3 words, 2 spaces)

2 Punishment by death for those convicted of capital crimes. (2 words, 1 space)

3 Circumstances that are above and beyond those required for the crime but make the crime more serious. (2 words, 1 space)

6 An investigation of the background and characteristics of the defendant. (2 words, 1 space)

7 The questioning of a court witness by adversary counsel after one attorney concludes the direct examination. (2 words, hyphen)

8 Court proceedings during which a judge, a jury, or both listen to the evidence as presented by the defense and the prosecution and determine whether the defendant is guilty beyond a reasonable doubt.

12 Evidence offered by an eyewitness who testifies to what he or she saw, heard, tasted, smelled, or touched. (2 words, 1 space)

17 A sentence for more than one offense served at the same time. (2 words, 1 space)

18 A trial jury, its name meaning literally, "small, minor, or inconsiderate." (2 words, 1 space)

19 A sentence to confinement without a definite term. (2 words, 1 space)

20 Inequalities and differences that result when people found guilty of the same crime receive sentences varying in length and type, without reasonable justification for those differences. (2 words, 1 space)

21 A term of imprisonment for more than one offense that must be served one following the other. (2 words, 1 space)

23 Formal document issued by the court to notify a person that his or her presence is required in court for a particular reason at a specified time and date.

24 Upon a finding of insufficient evidence to convict a defendant, the judge may direct the jury to return a verdict of not guilty. (2 words, 1 space)

25 Secondhand evidence of which the witness does not have personal knowledge but merely repeats something the witness says he or she heard another person say. (2 words, 1 space)

27 An act by a state governor or the president of the United States (in federal cases) that exempts a convicted offender from punishment or, in the case of those already serving terms, further punishment and removes the legal consequences of the conviction.

ANSWERS TO WORD SEARCH

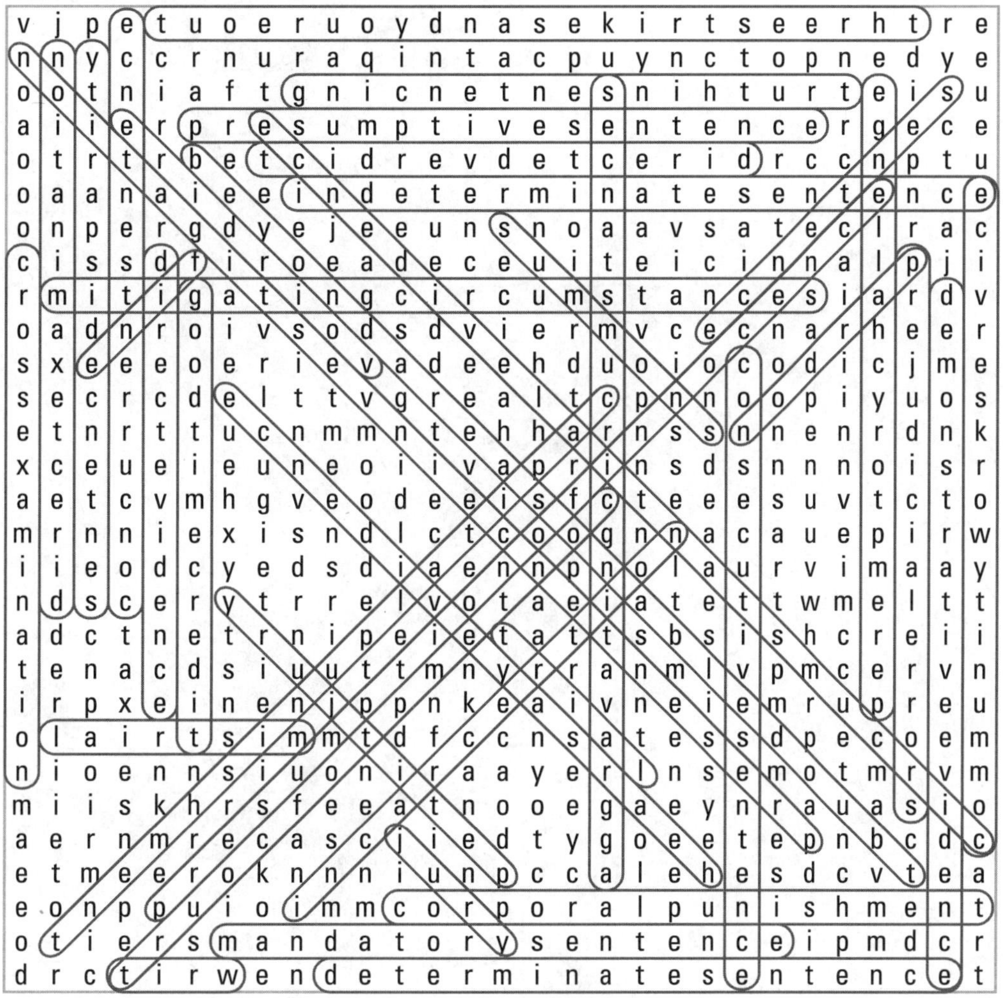

aggravating circumstances
beyond a reasonable doubt
capital punishment
circumstantial evidence
community work service
concurrent sentence
consecutive sentence
contempt of court
corporal punishment
cross-examination
demonstrative evidence
determinate sentence
directed verdict
direct evidence
direct examination
fine
good time credit
hearsay evidence
incarcertion
indeterminate sentence
jury
mandatory sentence
mistrial
mitigating circumstances
pardon
peremptory challenge
petit jury
prejudicial errors
presentence investigation
presumption of innocence
presumptive sentence
sentence
sentence disparity
summons
three strikes and you're out
trial
truth in sentencing
voir dire
writ

NFINEMENT AND RRECTIONS

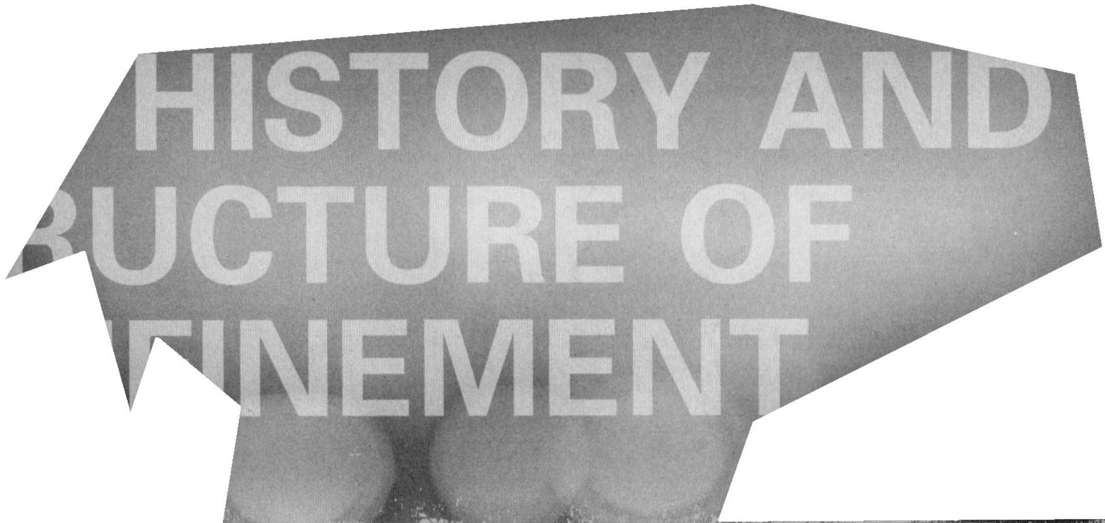

HISTORY AND UCTURE OF INEMENT

LEARNING OBJECTIVES

After reading this chapter, you should be able to do the following:

- **Explain the reasons for the emergence of institutions for confining offenders**
- **Explain the significance of the Walnut Street Jail**
- **Distinguish the Pennsylvania system from the Auburn system, and evaluate the contributions of each**
- **Recall the contributions of Europeans to the emergence and development of prisons**
- **Explain the relevance of the Elmira Reformatory**
- **Summarize the development of modern U.S. prison systems**
- **Distinguish among jails, prisons, and community corrections**
- **List and describe the purposes of prison security levels**
- **Analyze the differences between prisons for men and women**
- **Describe state and federal prison systems, and evaluate the differences between them**
- **Discuss the distinguishing features of jails, and analyze the role of the federal government in local jails**
- **Discuss the implications of the growth in jail and prison populations, with particular attention to the effects of overcrowding**
- **Analyze the role of privatization in correctional facilities**

Criminal Justice Essentials: Study Guide, Ninth Edition. Shannon Barton-Bellessa.

CHAPTER OUTLINE

KEY TERMS

classification
community-based correction facility
custody
humanitarianism
inmates
jail
offenders
open prison
penitentiary
prison
reformatory
silent system
transportation
wardens
workhouse

CHAPTER SUMMARY

Chapter 9 is the first of three addressing the issues related to incarceration. More specifically, a discussion of life in prison and community corrections is provided. The historical development of corrections in the United States is presented as a foundation for understanding incarceration today. Like the historical development of law enforcement and the court system, corrections has its roots in Europe. Those immigrating to the United States brought with them ideological viewpoints for addressing violators in the community that emphasized harsh punishment for minor offenses (by today's standards), unsanitary conditions, and deprivation of liberties. During the 17th and 18th centuries in Europe, those responsible for the creation of laws and enforcement of punishments believed that all individuals were **free will thinkers**. Therefore, if someone committed a crime, they should be punished for the harm caused to society as opposed to punishing the offender with rehabilitation in mind. Despite the harsh conditions and treatment of law violators, attention must be given to the reform efforts of **John Howard**, who is credited with the following: founding the penitentiary system; suggesting that inmates should be housed individually, in sanitary facilities, and provided clean clothing; arguing that women, men, and children prisoners should be segregated from each other; and advocating that jailers should be trained and well paid. Howard's ideas were influential in America, particularly with the **Quakers**, who led the movement toward incarceration where offenders were to seek penance by reading the Bible and reflecting upon their transgressions. The Quaker alternative was intended as a milder sanction to replace the death penalty and the inhumane methods of corporal punishment that prevailed in U.S. criminal justice systems.

The **Walnut Street Jail**, which opened its doors in 1790, is recognized as the first facility to open in the United States that classified and separated offenders by gender and whether there were pre- or post-sentence. This facility further focused on individualized treatment and prison labor so that prison could be self-supporting. This system relied on solitary confinement, with offenders working an 8- to 10-hour day and receiving religious instruction. Some have argued, however, that Connecticut's **Newgate Prison** is the first true colonial prison. Despite their efforts at reform, funding became a challenge for these institutions requiring solitary confinement. Because of the losses incurred, the entire prison system was at risk of being eliminated. In response to these problems, two separate systems emerged in the United States: **the Pennsylvania system**, with its emphasis on solitary confinement, and the **Auburn system**, with its emphasis on the silent system. The influence of the systems is still seen today both in the United States and in Europe. For example, many of our maximum-security prisons, built in the late 1800s and early 1900s, reflect an architectural design typical of the Auburn system and many prisons built on the architectural model of the Pennsylvania system remain in use in Europe.

Disagreement over which method of imprisonment should be used served as the impetus for future reformation. Again borrowing from the European movement, reformation of the overall system in the United States was influenced by the works of **Captain Alexander Maconochie**, a Scotsman, and **Sir Walter Crofton**, an Irishman. These two individuals developed and instituted a **system of marks**, **indeterminate sentences**, **work training, parole**, and **education.** American reformers visited the Irish prison system run on Crofton's principles and returned with great enthusiasm. A meeting of penologists in Cincinnati, Ohio, in 1870 to settle the dispute between the Pennsylvania and Auburn systems led to the development of the **National Prison Association**. The group drafted 37 principles calling for changes in the system such as indeterminate sentences, cultivation of inmates' self-respect, inmate **classification**, and advancement of the philosophy of reformation rather than punishment. The first institution to implement these reform efforts was the **Elmira Reformatory**, established in 1876. Although the architecture was similar to the Auburn system, the focus was on young offenders and reformation through education and work. These programs were intended to lead to greater prison discipline, indeterminate sentences, and parole. The use of prisoners to perform various work-related tasks led to an outpouring of dislike from private industry. The efforts of private industry leaders eventually led to the passage of the **Hawes–Cooper Act** in 1929 and the **Ashurst–Summers Act** in 1935, which restricts the sale of prison goods.

The next section of the chapter discusses the modern-day prison system and confinement. Each **prison** and **jail** has its own unique system; even so, there still exist similarities in organization and structure that can be compared. Although the terms "jail" and "prison" are often used synonymously, they do perform differing roles and functions in the correctional system. Jails are designed to be short-term holding facilities either for those awaiting a court appearance or for those who typically receive less than a year of confinement on their sentence. The prison system is designed for more serious offenders who have received sentences of more than one year. Just as with law enforcement and the courts, correctional systems are divided into the federal and state systems. The federal system is viewed as the most efficient and effective but continues to be the fastest growing. Today, men, women, and juveniles are housed in separate facilities. Where co-ed facilities exist, inmates are kept separate on the grounds. The federal system of separate confinement opened its doors in 1930 and was known as the **Bureau of Prisons** (BOP). The head of the BOP is known as a director and that person reports to the Department of Justice. For most systems, security levels are divided into three main categories: **maximum**, **medium**, and **minimum** custody. Attempts to confine the most serious offenders were instituted throughout the 20th century. Examples of **open systems** that use the natural environment as a mechanism for control have been used at great cost to the system. The most famous example of an open system is **Alcatraz Island** off the cost of San Francisco. Recent efforts to confine the most serious offenders have been realized in the creation of **super-maximum-security** facilities. These facilities are closed systems sometimes being built underground in an effort to confine those inmates who cannot function in the regular prison environment, or those who are deemed the greatest threat to security. Most systems continue to experience problems associated with overcrowding that have led to riots and inmate lawsuits. There are only two ways to address the issues of overcrowding: first, build more facilities; or, second, reduce the prison population. Both methods for reducing the population have met with uncertainty and criticisms.

The next section of the chapter discusses the role of the jail. As previously mentioned, jails are designed as short-term holding facilities for offenders typically sentenced to less than one year in prison or those who are awaiting their court appearance. The typical jail is locally financed and administered by the sheriff's department. The American Correctional Association has sponsored the **Commission on Accreditation for Corrections**, which developed jail standards and certified jails that meet those standards.

Over the past two decades, the prison population has increased exponentially, with over 1.6 million offenders incarcerated at year-end 2009. Despite the continued growth, however, the overall incarcerated populations appear to be slowing. By midyear 2010, jail populations had declined by 2.4 percent, representing only the second time a decline has occurred since 1982. One way correctional systems attempt to address the needs of the growing prison populations is through the use of private alternatives to incarceration, which is the subject of the final section in the chapter. The private sector contracts with corrections in three main areas: (1) prison work programs; (2) the financing of construction; and (3) the management of facilities. The **Corrections Corporation of America** (CCA) is the sixth largest correctional system in the United States. Despite serving as a potential viable alternative to state systems, the private sector has come under some scrutiny and will more than likely continue to do so.

KEY TERMS

classification In corrections, the assignment of new inmates to the housing, security status, and treatment programs that best fit their individual needs.

community-based correction facility Treatment and other correctional programs that emphasize assimilation of offenders into the community. Instead of imprisonment, the offender may be put on probation or placed on work release, education release, or in drug treatment programs, or assigned to halfway houses. Any of these arrangements may be combined with a furlough or parole release plan.

custody Legal control over a person or property; physical responsibility for a person or thing.

humanitarianism In penal philosophy, the doctrine advocating the removal of harsh, severe, and painful conditions in penal institutions.

inmates Convicted persons who are confined in jails, prisons, or other penal facilities.

jail A local, regional, or federal facility used to confine persons awaiting a legal proceeding, as well as those serving short sentences.

offenders Persons who have committed a criminal offense and either entered a guilty plea or have been adjudicated as guilty by a court of law.

open prison A prison that makes use of the natural environment for security purposes. For example, the prison might be located on an island surrounded by treacherous waters, as in the case of Alcatraz, located in San Francisco Bay and once used as a maximum-security federal prison.

penitentiary Historically, an institution intended to isolate convicted offenders from one another, giving them time to reflect on their bad acts and become penitent; later, synonymous with prison.

prison A federal or state penal facility for detaining adult offenders (although juvenile offenders are also incarcerated in adult facilities on occasion) sentenced to a year or longer after conviction of crimes.

reformatory An early correctional facility, which was less physically secure than prisons and in which the emphasis was on changing or reforming the offender. Today the term is normally used to refer to institutions for the confinement of juveniles who have been adjudicated in a juvenile court.

silent system In penitentiaries, the historical practice of not permitting inmates to speak with one another. In some institutions inmates communicated by use of sign language.

transportation Historically the practice of punishing criminals by exiling them to another country.

wardens Historically, the chief administrative officer in a correctional facility, most generally a prison.

workhouse An English institution used to confine and punish offenders who were forced to work at unpleasant tasks. The term is used in some places today to refer to institutions that emphasize reformation or rehabilitation through work.

STUDY QUESTIONS

These questions are found at the end of your chapter. Your instructor may wish to revisit these or assign them for points. These questions are a good way to integrate the material and to generate your own perspectives during class.

1. Explain why prisons emerged in Europe, and relate your discussion to the contributions of John Howard.
2. What characterized the emergence of prisons in the United States, and how did the Walnut Street Jail contribute to this development?
3. Compare and contrast the Pennsylvania and the Auburn systems.
4. What is a reformatory? Why were they developed? Explain the importance of European reformers to this development. How did European reform programs influence the emergence of the Elmira Reformatory?
5. How do jails differ from prisons and from community-based correction facilities?
6. What is the difference between prisons centered on a philosophy of custody and those that focus on rehabilitation?
7. Distinguish among the levels of prison security. What is meant by a *supermax* or a *maxi-maxi* prison? Evaluate.
8. Explore the general and unique features of prisons for women, and compare them with the features of those for men. Discuss the issues with regard to inmate children and suggest ways to solve those problems.
9. Distinguish between the state and federal prison systems, and analyze population growth in each.
10. How does the present-day purpose of jails compare with their historical purpose? What are the problems of administering jails? What role, if any, should the federal government play in the administration of local jails?
11. What are the effects of prison and jail overcrowding?
12. Discuss recent efforts in California and Florida to handle prison overcrowding.
13. What is the place of the private sector in jails and prisons, and in other security areas?

LEARNING ACTIVITIES

9.1 Search your state's Department of Correction(s) website and the state Criminal Code. Based upon what you find, what do you believe is the state's purpose of imprisonment? Based upon what you know about the correctional system and modern-day society, what do you believe should be the purpose of incarceration? What are the benefits of your chosen purpose over the others? What are some of the potential problems?

9.2 In 1777, John Howard published his classic work, *State of Prisons*. In this work he suggested that inmates should be housed individually, in sanitary facilities, and provided clean clothing, that women, men, and children should be segregated from each other, and that jailers should be trained and well paid. There is some evidence to suggest that states have begun to reinstitute some of the methods of solitary confinement, etc., for punishment. What are some of the problems associated with this response? Why was this approach abandoned for a congregate system? How do you think John Howard would respond to this approach? To what extent does your state use solitary confinement in its prison system?

9.3 As we enter the 21st century, there is evidence of continuing differences in how men and women are classified and treated or punished in the correctional system for successful reintegration. Search your library resources to find an empirical peer-reviewed article illustrating this fact. Summarize the article. Based on these findings, how do the authors suggest men and women should be treated differently by the criminal justice system, if at all? Given what you know, how might you respond to the governor on whether men and women should be treated differently in the prison system?

9.4 The issue of prison overcrowding and the increase in the prison population (despite a small decrease at the state level between 2008 and 2009) continues to be a growing concern at both the state and federal level. You have been appointed to a task force in your state by the governor to reduce the overall size of the prison/jail population. You have been charged with a variety of different tasks to complete. These include:

a Identify the number of persons incarcerated in prisons and jails in your state.

b What percentage of the state's overall budget goes toward confining offenders?

c Based upon what you know about the current economic situation in your state, what steps might you recommend should be taken to reduce the prison/jail population(s)?

d What are some of the potential benefits of this approach? What are some of the potential limitations?

e How might the governor address the populace in both explaining and convincing them of this approach to reducing the prison population?

a

b

c

d

e

STUDENT STUDY GUIDE PRACTICE QUESTIONS

True or False

9.1 The first formal prison institution in the United States codifying the principle of solitary confinement was opened in 1790 and known as the Elmira Reformatory.

9.2 During the 1800s there were two types of prison systems that developed: the Pennsylvania, or separate, system, based on solitary confinement; and the New York, or Auburn, system, known as the silent system.

9.3 The Auburn system of punishment was also known as the separate system.

9.4 The works of Captain John Augustus and Sir Walter Crofton were credited for the beginnings of a reformatory movement.

9.5 The National Prison Association drafted 37 principles calling for changes in the correctional system that included such things as indeterminate sentences and cultivation of inmates' self-respect.

9.6 There are no distinguishable differences between jails and prisons.

9.7 Prison security levels are typically divided into three main categories: maximum, medium, and minimum custody.

9.8 The famous former prison known as Alcatraz serves as a good example of an open prison.

9.9 In 1873, the first separate prison for women, the Illinois Women's Prison, was opened.

9.10 On 14 May, 1930, President Herbert Hoover signed the law that created the federal Bureau of Prisons (BOP).

Multiple Choice

9.11 Who was credited with the beginning of the penitentiary system?
- a James Wilson
- b August Vollmer
- c John Howard
- d Henry Fielding

9.12 Which of the following is often cited as the first U.S. prison?
- a Eastern Penitentiary
- b Western Penitentiary
- c Auburn Prison
- d The Walnut Street Jail

9.13 The Walnut Street Jail and other early prisons faced serious problems. Despite the thick walls and high security, inmates escaped. What solution was implemented by some wardens to combat this problem?
- a Higher walls
- b Early release programs
- c Work provided in cells
- d Uniforms for inmates

9.14 Which of the following is an incorrect observation regarding the Auburn system?
- a Discipline was strictly enforced.
- b Silent system was strictly enforced.
- c It featured congregate work during the day.
- d Work was provided for inmates in their cells.

9.15 What were the objectives of the Hawes–Cooper Act of 1929 and the Ashurst–Summers Act of 1935?
- a To restrict the sale of prison goods
- b To provide adequate funding for inmate employment
- c To improve prison conditions
- d To provide assistance for juvenile prisons

9.16 The Irish system was recognized for its emphasis on _____.
- a a reward system
- b individual influence of the prison administrators on the inmates
- c gradual release from restrictions
- d All of the above

9.17 In recent years, rehabilitation has been replaced by an emphasis on deterrence and _____.
- a reformation
- b isolation
- c retribution
- d restitution

9.18 Which of the following is an example of an open prison?
- a Walnut Street Jail
- b Alcatraz Island
- c San Quentin
- d Newgate Prison

9.19 All states have correctional systems; most are centralized and headed by a(n) _____, who reports to the governor.
- a superintendent
- b director
- c president
- d administrator

9.20 In corrections, which of the following is not a main area in which the private sector is involved?
- a Prison work programs
- b The financing of construction
- c The management of facilities
- d Administration of punishment

Fill-in-the-Blank

9.21 The unique contribution of America was the substitution of _____ for corporal punishment, an innovation of the Quakers of West Jersey and Pennsylvania in the 18th century.

9.22 The Auburn system was also known as the _____ system.

9.23 Supposedly prisons emerged as places in which inmates could be reformed. However, the early reform approach was abandoned eventually in favor of a(n) _____ philosophy.

9.24 _____ are used primarily for the incarceration of offenders sentenced for lengthy terms (usually over one year) and for more serious offenses, such as felonies.

9.25 Social scientists and federal judges have noted that jail and prison overcrowding has created a _____ impact on its inmates.

9.26 The first separate system prison was opened in Pittsburgh in 1826 and was known as the _____.

9.27 The Irish system of handling offenders was recognized for its emphasis on what four factors: (1) ______; (2)______; (3)______; and (4) ______.

9.28 In 1929 the ______ Act and in 1935 the ______ Act were passed in an effort to restrict the sale of prison goods.

9.29 In 1557, Western Europe experienced a significant increase in pauperism and public begging. To combat this problem, a workhouse called the ______ was established in London.

9.30 Name the three areas where the private sector is involved in corrections: (1)______; (2)______; and (3)______.

CROSSWORD

ACROSS

4 Historically an institution intended to isolate convicted offenders from one another, giving them time to reflect on their bad acts and become penitent; later, synonymous with prison.

5 An early corrections facility, which was less physically secure and which emphasized changing or reforming the offender; usually used to refer to an institution.

7 A prison that makes use of the natural environment for security. (2 words, 1 space)

9 The assignment of new inmates to the housing, security status, and treatment programs that best fit their individual needs.

10 A federal or state penal facility for detaining adult offenders sentenced to a year or longer after conviction of crimes.

11 Historically, the chief administrative officers in corrections facilities.

12 An English institution used to confine offenders who were forced to work at unpleasant tasks; offenders were punished physically as well.

14 In penal philosophy, the doctrine advocating the removal of harsh, severe, and painful conditions in penal institutions.

DOWN

1 A facility in which the punishment emphasizes assimilation into the community. (4 words, 1 hyphen, 2 spaces)

2 Persons who have committed a criminal offense.

3 Convicted persons whose freedom has been replaced by confinement in a prison, mental ward, or similar institution.

6 Historically the practice of punishing criminals by exiling them to another country, usually far away.

8 In penitentiaries, the historical practice of not allowing offenders to speak with one another. (2 words, 1 space)

9 Legal control over a person or property; physical responsibility for a person or thing.

13 A local, regional, or federal facility used to confine persons awaiting trial, as well as those serving short sentences.

WORD SEARCH

y l a i v y m n r c j p s t y

i i l c i s o n y l p o r s l

w a r d e n s t o a e a o y s

p j e y m o r s s s n d s d e

o f f e n d e r s s i i i o s

v a j r o t f i p i t r n t u

s i i i s h o o s f e s p s o

m s i n a i r a t i n a m u h

r e r n m t m i s c t h d c k

e i s r a a a d e a i p o m r

r a y t r m t p u t a s h i o

t s i m n a o e t i r e y p w

m o i n s p r n s o y t n o o

n u m e t s y s t n e l i s s

o p e n p r i s o n e y t c o

classification
inmates
open prison
reformatory
wardens
custody
jail
penitentiary
silent system
workhouse
humanitarianism
offenders
prison
transportation

ANSWERS TO CROSSWORD

ACROSS

4 Historically an institution intended to isolate convicted offenders from one another, giving them time to reflect on their bad acts and become penitent; later, synonymous with prison.

5 An early corrections facility, which was less physically secure and which emphasized changing or reforming the offender; usually used to refer to an institution.

7 A prison that makes use of the natural environment for security. (2 words, 1 space)

9 The assignment of new inmates to the housing, security status, and treatment programs that best fit their individual needs.

10 A federal or state penal facility for detaining adult offenders sentenced to a year or longer after conviction of crimes.

11 Historically, the chief administrative officers in corrections facilities.

12 An English institution used to confine offenders who were forced to work at unpleasant tasks; offenders were punished physically as well.

14 In penal philosophy, the doctrine advocating the removal of harsh, severe, and painful conditions in penal institutions.

DOWN

1 A facility in which the punishment emphasizes assimilation into the community. (4 words, 1 hyphen, 2 spaces)

2 Persons who have committed a criminal offense.

3 Convicted persons whose freedom has been replaced by confinement in a prison, mental ward, or similar institution.

6 Historically the practice of punishing criminals by exiling them to another country, usually far away.

8 In penitentiaries, the historical practice of not allowing offenders to speak with one another. (2 words, 1 space)

9 Legal control over a person or property; physical responsibility for a person or thing.

13 A local, regional, or federal facility used to confine persons awaiting trial, as well as those serving short sentences.

ANSWERS TO WORD SEARCH

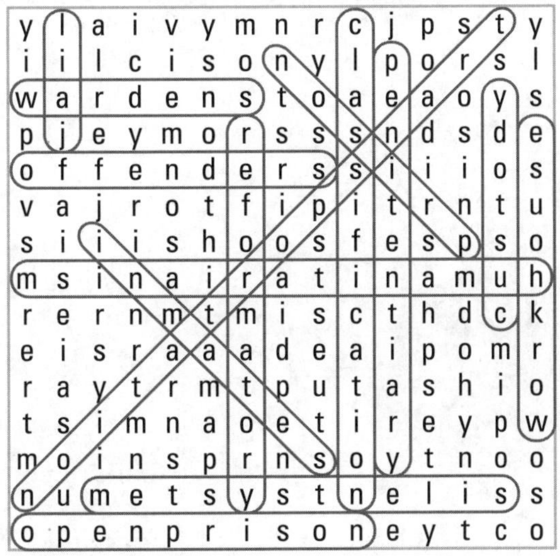

classification
inmates
open prison
reformatory
wardens

custody
jail
penitentiary
silent system
workhouse

humanitarianism
offenders
prison
transportation

E IN PRISON

LEARNING OBJECTIVES

After reading this chapter, students should be able to do the following:

- **Relate the historical to the more recent position of federal courts on the issue of inmates' rights**
- **State the general criteria the U.S. Supreme Court uses to determine whether inmates' rights, such as to be free of cruel and unusual punishment, have been violated**
- **Trace the evolution of prison management styles, and compare them with today's needs**
- **Explain the functions of correctional officers, exploring ways in which they controlled inmates historically and how that has changed recently**
- **Analyze correctional officer recruitment and training**
- **Discuss gender and racial issues concerning correctional administrators**
- **Identify some of the issues that new inmates face, and give a brief overview of inmate prison life**
- **Explain the inmate subculture, discuss its origin, and explore how it affects the adjustment of male and female inmates**
- **Analyze the social control role of the inmate system**
- **Discuss the influence of prison gangs in men's prisons**
- **Analyze the needs of female inmates and of those requiring special care and programs and discuss how those needs are or are not accommodated**
- **Comment on the problems of children whose parents are incarcerated**
- **Discuss the nature and analyze the impact of the Prison Rape Elimination Act of 2003**

Criminal Justice Essentials: Study Guide, Ninth Edition. Shannon Barton-Bellessa.

CHAPTER OUTLINE

KEY TERMS

civil rights
commissary
correctional officer (CO)
deprivation model
hands-off doctrine
importation model
norms
prisonization
social system

CHAPTER SUMMARY

This chapter is the second of three discussing the issues related to the incarceration of offenders. More specifically, this chapter reviews issues related to life in prison. The prison system is a total institution where every facet of an offender's life is regulated, including food, clothing, shelter, medical care, and personal needs. Gresham Sykes referred to the deprivation of liberties experienced by those incarcerated as the "**pains of imprisonment**." As Sykes contends, the moral rejection by society, and the deprivation of goods and services, heterosexual relationships, and security can result in adjustment to the prison environment in a way that encourages manipulation and threats to individual safety. The process of experiencing the pains of imprisonment begins after an offender is sentenced to a term of incarceration. Once sentenced, papers are completed and the individual is turned over to the custody of the state department of corrections or the federal Bureau of Prisons. States differ in the initial administrative processing of offenders. In some states, offenders are sent to diagnostic centers where they receive medical examinations, psychological testing, and orientation. Following a stay at the diagnostic center, the inmates are then sent to the appropriate facility to complete their stay. In other states, they may be sent directly to the facility where they will begin their term of confinement. Regardless, offenders are stripped of their liberties and must now abide by the rules of the institution and the Department of Corrections. As the chapter notes, offenders up until recently were considered "slaves of the state"; therefore, complete deprivation of liberties was determined at the hands of the warden or the state. Once confined, inmates are permitted to purchase goods from the commissary. Unfortunately, if they have no money in their account, they must use only the items provided for them by the state, which in turn adds to the pains of imprisonment. Most prisons do not allow inmates to have money on their person; therefore, if an offender is found with money it is considered to be **contraband**.

The next section of the chapter discusses the legal implications of incarceration. Up until recently (the 1960s), the federal courts observed a **hands-off doctrine** in addressing issues related to inmates and incarceration. It wasn't until 1974 that the U.S. Supreme Court ruled that although incarcerated inmates lose most of their rights, they do not have to surrender all of them. The most serious concerns brought to the attention of the federal courts dealt with the treatment of inmates while incarcerated. Historically, prison officials spoke of the difference between rights and privileges. **Rights** require constitutional protection; **privileges** are there by the grace of prison officials and may be withdrawn at their discretion. A hierarchy of rights, however, does exist. The U.S. Supreme Court has considered violations of the **Eighth Amendment** protections against cruel and unusual punishment to be of the utmost importance. It has ruled that institutions cannot act with **deliberate indifference** in assessing an inmate's needs, such as medical care, safety, and overcrowding. Likewise, they have considered an inmate's **First Amendment** rights to have access to media, including newspapers, magazines, and personal photographs. Unlike many of the upheld Eighth Amendment protections, the U.S. Supreme Court has ruled that inmates can be deprived of access to these items in an effort to encourage better behavior.

The next section of the chapter discusses prison administration. In state prison systems, a director of the department of corrections is responsible for overseeing all institutions and reports to the governor or a corrections board. In the federal system, a director of the U.S. Bureau of Prisons (BOP) reports to the U.S. attorney general's office in the U.S. Department of Justice (DOJ) and also serves as Commissioner of the **Federal Prison Industries** (FPI). **Wardens or superintendents** are responsible for overseeing the day-today operations of the individual prison facilities. Historically, wardens adopted an **authoritarian management approach** to run the prison facility, which essentially ensured total authority. Since the 1970s, significant changes within the institution have taken place that have altered the administration of prisons. First, demographic changes in inmate population resulted in politicalization within prisons. The passage of harsh drug laws increased the number of offenders coming to the institution who were young, poor, minority, and urban. Second, court decisions diminished the authority of the wardens. Finally, prisons continue to face financial problems, which have resulted in difficulties in recruiting, training, and retaining good, qualified personnel. The next level of administration of a facility falls into the hands of **correctional officers** (COs). Correctional officers are critical to the management of an institution because they have the most day-to-day interaction with those confined. To assist with the proper running of a facility, it is imperative that correctional systems encourage professionalism among the staff and provide stress reduction programs for its personnel. Pre-employment requirements for most correctional officers generate concerns for the proper administration of the facility. In most instances, minimum requirements for employment include only the evidence of a high school diploma or its equivalent. In recent years, state departments of corrections and the Bureau of Prisons have increased efforts to hire women and minorities. Evidence has suggested that the presence of women in all-male institutions may have a calming effect on the offender population because of their deprivations of opposite-sex companionship.

The next section of the chapter discusses the inmates' ability to adapt to prison life. The monotony of daily life behind institutional walls can create an environment conducive to violence. Prisons are responsible for ensuring the safety of the community at large and the inmates behind walls. Activities behind institutional walls are limited by the custody level. Gifts from the outside are limited as well as commissary items. In order to cope with the adverse conditions behind bars, inmates encounter and begin to adapt to the prison **subculture** through the process of **prisonization**. The degree to which a prisoner adapts to their environment depends upon their susceptibility and personality; their relationships on the outside; their membership in a primary group; their placement in prison; and the degree to which they accept the dogmas and codes of prison culture. The creation of the inmate subculture has been examined using two models: the **deprivation model** and the **importation model**. According to the deprivation model, the inmate minimizes the pains of imprisonment by adapting to the prison culture. The importation model purports that inmates take patterns of behavior with them to prison; therefore, the activities in which they participated on the outside will continue while they are incarcerated. The inmate social system further serves as a mechanism for **social control** behind institutional walls. The existence and emergence of prison gangs continues to be of the utmost concern to prison administrators, officers, and other inmates.

Female inmates comprise only 7 percent of the total inmate population in 2008. Moreover, the characteristics and roles of the inmate subculture differ for men and women. Research suggests that the motivation for the creation and existence of female subcultures best resembles the traditional roles of women in a free society. The majority of both men and women have children prior to coming to the institution. One significant difference between male and female inmates, however, is that the majority of women are primary caregivers on the outside. Therefore, upon a woman's incarceration, her children tend to live with grandparents or other family members, whereas, when a man is incarcerated, his children tend to live with their mother.

In addition to those already mentioned, there are a variety of other issues pertinent to the prison environment, including: visitation; inmate sexual behavior; AIDS and other medical issues; elderly and physically and mentally challenged inmates; prison education and work programs; and prison violence. Within the context of the prison environment, inmates have limited visitations. The prison system dictates who may visit the offenders, how frequently offenders may receive visits, and how the visits may occur. For some inmates, they are allowed only non-contact visits; for others in less secure environments, they are allowed more contact. Concerns for the security of the institution are at the forefront of any visitation policy. In particular, the institution must ensure that contraband is not smuggled in or out of the facility.

The issue of sex behind prison walls is given attention in this chapter in the context of the AIDS epidemic. Of particular concern are violent sexual encounters. Same-sex relationships among males seldom involve a close relationship; for women, however, same-sex relationships may develop out of mutual interest to alleviate the depersonalization of the prison and to gain status. Sexual contact between correctional personnel and offenders, meanwhile, is prohibited and can result in the firing of employees and the potential for criminal prosecution. Of note in this same context is the increased recognition and handling of AIDS behind institutional walls for both male and female inmates. The importance of this issue is further illustrated by its inclusion as part of the **Prison Rape Elimination Act of 2003**. The most common disease among prison inmates is not AIDS, however, but hepatitis C. Unfortunately, most persons who are infected are not identified, and even when they are, they are not treated. Some states, such as Michigan, have begun testing inmates upon arrival to determine the extent of this very contagious disease so that they can begin treating and minimizing its spread. Another growing concern behind institutional walls is the care for elderly, or physically or mentally challenged. The Ninth Circuit Court of Appeals has ruled that in its administration of treatment programs, prison officials may not discriminate against inmates with disabilities who are "otherwise qualified." A growing concern with handling these populations is the rising costs of treatment for those who require greater medical care and needs at a time when resources are decreasing. Issues of education and work continue to be of central focus in the prison system. It is estimated that 50 to 75 percent of all prison inmates are illiterate. If inmates are to return to society as productive members, they need to have the skills to do so, many of which are gained through formal education. In recent years, however, states in the midst of budgetary crises have begun to eliminate prison education programs. One way to increase the level of adjustment back into society is through work skills. Despite limitations regarding the distribution of prison goods, the prison industries programs continue to thrive and expand providing goods to state-run organizations.

The final issue discussed in the chapter is that of **prison violence**. As noted by the author, prisons are places of violence, manifested in the murders of other inmates or prison officials, escapes, or riots that may result in serious property damage, injuries, or deaths. Attention is given to the role of more recent prison riots such as **Attica** in 1971 and **Santa Fe, New Mexico** in 1980. The result of both of these riots was a change in how administrators respond to violence and hostile environments behind institutional walls. One other area of concern for violence behind institutional walls is self-inflicted violence, sometimes resulting in suicide.

KEY TERMS

civil rights Sometimes called *civil liberties*; all the natural rights guaranteed by the U.S. Constitution (or by individual state constitutions), such as free speech and the right to religious beliefs and practices; also the body of law concerning natural rights.

commissary The prison store as well as the incidental items sold to inmates; also an inmate's account, which is debited when an item is purchased, as inmates are not permitted to have money within correctional facilities.

correctional officer (CO) A corrections employee with supervisory power over a suspect or convicted offender in custody.

deprivation model A model of *prisonization* based on the belief that the prison subculture stems from the way inmates adapt to the severe psychological and physical losses imposed by imprisonment. *See also* **importation model**.

hands-off doctrine A policy that courts use to justify nonintervention in the daily administration of corrections agencies.

importation model A model based on the assumption that the inmate subculture arises not only from internal prison experiences but also from external patterns of behavior that the inmates take into prison. *See also* **deprivation model**.

norms The rules or standards of behavior, shared by members of a social group, that define appropriate behavior.

prisonization The process of an inmate's becoming accustomed to the subculture of prison life.

social system The interrelationship of roles, acts, and statuses of people who make up the social structure; a social group or set of interacting persons or groups considered a unitary whole because it reflects the common values, social norms, and objectives of the individuals whom it comprises, even though the group is considered distinct from those individuals.

STUDY QUESTIONS

These questions are found at the end of your chapter. Your instructor may wish to revisit these or assign them for points. These questions are a good way to integrate the material and to generate your own perspectives during class.

1 What is the *hands-off doctrine*, and to what extent (and why) has it been abandoned?

2 What is meant by a *hierarchy of rights*?

3 What were the characteristics of the authoritarian warden? What do you think should be the characteristics of the ideal warden or prison superintendent?

4 What events have occurred within prisons during the past three decades and forced changes in prison administration?

5 How did early correctional officers control inmates? If permitted, would those techniques be effective today?

6 Discuss recruitment and training issues with regard to correctional officers. Note the issues regarding gender and race.

7 Describe some of the daily aspects of inmate prison life.

8 Define *prisonization* and *subculture*, and explain the development and importance of each in a prison setting. Would the importance be different in prisons for female as compared to male inmates?

9 Distinguish the importation and deprivation models of prisonization, and explain the social control role of inmate social systems.

10 What is the significance of prison gangs? What could be done to lessen their influence?

11 What provisions do you think should be made for incarcerated women who have children at home or for women who give birth during incarceration? What provisions should be made for incarcerated mother and fathers to visit with their children?

12 Do female inmates have special problems other than child care, and if so, how should those problems be handled? Should inmate fathers have the same access to visitation arrangements that inmate mothers have?

13 Explain the Prison Rape Elimination Act of 2003, and discuss what impact you think the statute has on inmate behavior.

14 Distinguish the sexual behavior in prison of gay males from that of lesbians.

15 What has been the impact of AIDS on prisons? How should the problems be handled? What about the spread of other contagious diseases, such as tuberculosis and hepatitis C?

16 Discuss the situations that prison officials face as the result of aging inmate populations. What are the special needs of physically and mentally challenged inmates?

17 If most inmates are relatively poorly educated, why do we not make a greater effort to provide education classes in prisons?

18 Should inmates be required to work within the prisons? If there is a lack of jobs, how should that problem be solved?

19 What policies would you recommend to prison administrators if they were to ask you how to prevent prison riots? What policies might prevent jail or prison suicides?

LEARNING ACTIVITIES

10.1 As noted in this chapter, the 1960s and 1970s were a time of significant change for the correctional system. During this time period the state of Arkansas' entire prison system was ruled unconstitutional by the U.S. Supreme Court. The magnitude of this ruling sent shock waves through the system and even into Hollywood. The movie *Brubaker* was based on the reformation and overhaul of the Arkansas prison system. For this activity, watch the movie on DVD and then answer the following questions:

- a What role did the trustees play in this movie depiction?
- b What were some of the problems associated with the administration of this prison system?
- c What is the tucker telephone? Why were the inmates so afraid when they were told they had received a "telephone call"?

d What were some of the problems associated with how solitary confinement was being used?

e If you were the warden in this movie, how would you have addressed the conditions portrayed? Why should we as a society be concerned with prison conditions such as these?

a ______________________________

b ______________________________

c ______________________________

d ______________________________

e

10.2 Much attention has been given to the issues of the "pains of imprisonment" that offenders confront while they are incarcerated. How do these pains of imprisonment impact on an offender's ability to reintegrate back into society? Given that the majority of offenders have children, what impact do these pains have on their ability to parent? Exploring the department of corrections webpage in your state, what is the mandated policy on visitation of children and persons under the age of majority in your state? Do you agree with this policy? Why or why not?

10.3 According to the author, some research suggests, for example, that more highly educated correctional officers do not have more positive and humane attitudes toward inmates than do less educated officers. Furthermore, the more highly educated officer may be more frustrated in the job. Thus, the appearance of professionalism may be only that, unless adequate prior and on-the-job training programs are implemented to prepare correctional officers for the difficulty they will face. Searching your state's department of corrections webpage, what are the minimum requirements for employment as a corrections officer? What are the training requirements for an entry-level officer? How might the issue of professionalism contribute to misconduct by correctional officers in an institution? How might correctional administrators rectify the problem of an unsatisfied staff, and reduce misconduct while ensuring or increasing the professionalism of staff? What might happen if these institutions fail to recognize some of the competing interests associated with a 24/7 institution?

10.4 A lot of attention has been given to the issue of competing interests of correctional officers' role of ensuring the security and discipline of the facility while instituting treatment. Explore your state's department of correction(s) webpage or speak with a DOC representative to locate a treatment program offered within the correctional system. How might the implementation of this program create conflicts for staff? How might these conflicts be resolved? As David Rothman has suggested, why would the convenience of safety and security always override the conscience and thus the implementation of treatment? Will a department of corrections ever be able to find a compromise between these goals? If no, why not? And if yes, how?

STUDENT STUDY GUIDE PRACTICE QUESTIONS

True or False

10.1 In the 1974 case of *Ruffin v. Commonwealth*, the U.S. Supreme Court held that, although an incarcerated person loses some rights because of institutional needs, "a prisoner is not wholly stripped of constitutional protections when he is imprisoned for crime."

10.2 The commissary is where offenders are allowed to purchase items for personal use such as snacks, soap, etc.

10.3 Governors are responsible for hiring and firing wardens or superintendents within their respective jurisdictions.

10.4 In many jurisdictions, a two-year college degree is required for entry-level officer positions.

10.5 In 1995, a federal court held that the U.S. Constitution does not prohibit the viewing of a male inmate by a female correctional officer.

10.6 Under the authoritarian regime of prison administration and management, inmate cooperation was not necessary to maintain peace within institutions.

10.7 More than 90 percent of all female inmates are mothers, with three-fourths having children under the age of 18.

10.8 The pains of imprisonment, particularly the concept of deprivation, do not differ for men and women.

10.9 The U.S. Supreme Court has ruled that states may create policies that restrict the number and age of visitors an inmate may receive.

10.10 Research suggests that in both prisons and jails the highest rates of inmate rape occurred in overcrowded facilities that were understaffed.

Multiple Choice

10.11 Which of the following generally does not happen during the orientation period in a prison?

- a Inmates are told the rules.
- b Physical exams are given.
- c Inmates are strip searched for drugs and weapons.
- d Inmates have visitors.

10.12 From 1872 until the 1960s, for the most part the federal courts observed a(n) ______ toward inmates and prisons, reasoning that prison administration is a part of the executive, not the judicial, branch of government.

- a reformatory attitude
- b rehabilitation approach
- c hands-off doctrine
- d custody approach

10.13 ______ require constitutional protection; ______ are there by the grace of prison officials and may be withdrawn at their discretion.

- a Rights; duties
- b Rights; privileges
- c Privileges; rights
- d Privileges; concessions

10.14 ______ may be restricted if prison officials can show that the restriction is necessary for security or for other recognized penological purposes, such as discipline and order.

- a Rights
- b Concessions
- c Privileges
- d Duties

10.15 In 1976 in ______, the U.S. Supreme Court stated that allegations of "inadvertent failure to provide adequate medical care" or of a "negligent . . . diagnos[is]" do not establish the requisite state of mind for a violation of the cruel and unusual punishment clause.

- a *Laube v. Campbell*
- b *Hudson v. McMillian*
- c *Farmer v. Brennan*
- d *Estelle v. Gamble*

10.16 In 1992 in _____, the U.S. Supreme Court held that inmates may bring actions for cruel and unusual punishment against prison officials who engage in physical force that results in injuries, even if those injuries are not significant.

a *Laube v. Campbell*
b *Hudson v. McMillian*
c *Farmer v. Brennan*
d *Wilson v. Seiter*

10.17 Which of the following is the most important reform in prison administration?

a Development of research techniques to measure the success of programs
b Standards for criminal justice administration, including correctional administration
c Evaluation strategies for personnel
d Increased attention to professionalism

10.18 What is the primary function of correctional officers?

a Train prisoners for release
b Prepare inmates for work
c Maintain internal security and discipline
d Recreational activities

10.19 Who introduced the concept of prisonization?

a Stanton Wheeler
b Geoffrey Alpert
c Donald Clemmer
d Donald Cressey

10.20 In the case of HIV inmates, two states – _____ and _____ – isolate the inmates from the general population.

a Mississippi; Alabama
b North Carolina; Virginia
c Oregon; Massachusetts
d New Jersey; California

Fill-in-the-Blank

10.21 _____ have the most extensive contact with and perhaps the greatest effect on inmates.

10.22 The new inmate encounters prison subculture through the process of socialization, or_____.

10.23 In his study at the Washington State Reformatory, _____ found that the degree to which inmates became involved in prisonization varied by the length of time the inmate was in prison.

10.24 The traditional approach to an understanding of the inmate subculture, according to John Irwin and Donald R. Cressey, is that inmates take patterns of behavior with them to prison. This constitutes the _____ model.

10.25 When an inmate arrives at prison, both the formal organization and the inmate society compete for his allegiance; these two represent conflicting processes of socialization. Charles W. Thomas calls the efforts of the formal organization _____ and those of the inmate society_____.

10.26 In 1976, the U.S. Supreme Court held that an inmate may bring a successful action against prison officials who deny him or her adequate medical care for a serious medical problem only if it can be shown that the officials acted with _____ to the inmate's needs.

10.27 The most common disease among inmates is _____, with approximately 29 percent of inmates in a study in Maryland testing positive (compared to about 2 percent of the general population).

10.28 In 2004, Congress enacted the _____ Act to divert mentally ill persons to special courts for treatment.

10.29 The 1994 revision of the federal criminal code eliminated _____ that provided college courses in prison.

10.30 Two of the most destructive and highly publicized U.S. prison riots occurred in 1971 in _____ and in 1980 in _____.

CROSSWORD

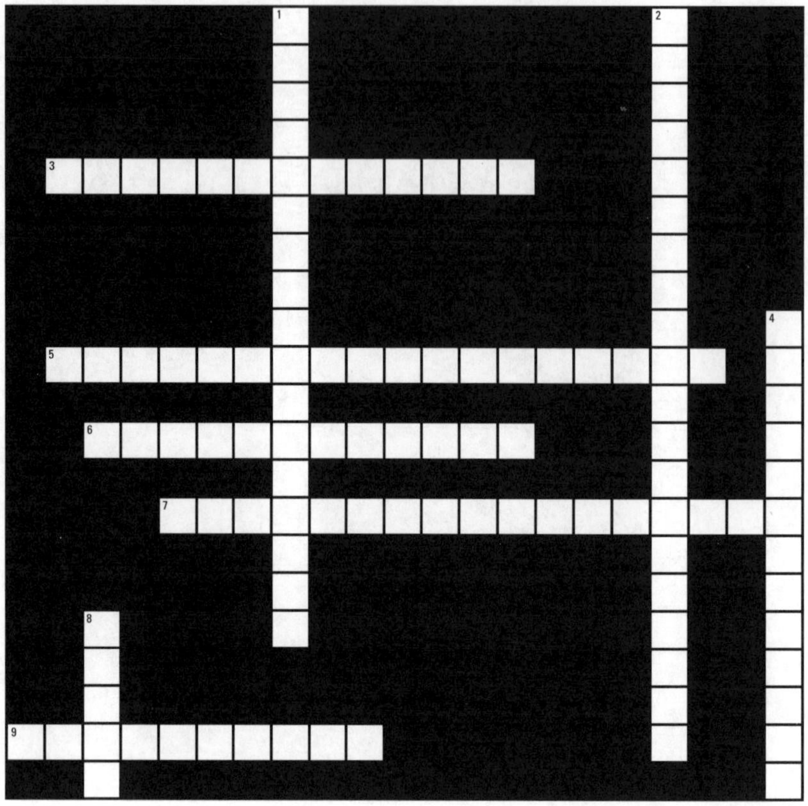

ACROSS

3 The process of an inmate's becoming accustomed to the subculture of prison life.
5 A policy that courts use to justify nonintervention in the daily administration of corrections agencies. (3 words, 1 hyphen, 1 space)
6 All the natural rights guaranteed by the U.S. Constitution, such as free speech and the right to religious beliefs and practices; also the body of law concerning natural rights. (2 words, 1 space)
7 A model based on the assumption that the inmate subculture arises not only from internal prison experiences but also from the external patterns of behavior the inmates take into prison. (2 words, 1 space)
9 The prison store as well as incidental items sold to inmates.

DOWN

1 A model of prisonization based on the belief that the prison subculture stems from the way inmates adapt to the severe psychological and physical losses imposed by imprisonment. (2 words, 1 space)
2 A corrections employee with supervisory power over a suspect or convicted offender in custody. (2 words, 1 space)
4 The interrelationship of roles, acts, and statuses of people who make up the social structure. (2 words, 1 space)
8 The rules or standards of appropriate behavior, shared by members of a social group.

WORD SEARCH

```
h f m o o s i v d r l s v s r i h i i r
d o h a s t t i m e t s y s l a i c o s
t r c a i s m a d l e n d c o a s h q o
j s d c o c o a a m i s j d l s a l t c
a m m s o d o o c n s i r g e n e r l n
m a a e o c c r t i i r i n d s i m m i
d o n n r i t o t m v s m s o d h i t t
i i i i m p o r t a t i o n m o d e l t
a t i a i a s i s u q f l m n r i i s l
o s n n l s p r i y f u l r o t o o i u
n o m d c m f d c d r p i s i i o n u i
m l z m g i o s o v v a i l t g r s u r
t c t o h a p c p o c n s e a o h m c m
o t i f c f t o c v i h m s v i i t r t
a r d c p r i s o n i z a t i o n o s i
o e r i i o e a c s d o a z r m t d i d
o t i n h s s v i m g a n e p o m o r n
o e e l i t e i f a a s o e e c q o a o
s d o s j s r f a n v o i o d s e z c u
r e c i f f o l a n o i t c e r r o c o
```

civil rights
commissary
correctional officer
deprivation model
hands-off doctrine
importation model
norms
prisonization
social system

ANSWERS TO CROSSWORD

ACROSS

3 The process of an inmate's becoming accustomed to the subculture of prison life.

5 A policy that courts use to justify nonintervention in the daily administration of corrections agencies. (3 words, 1 hyphen, 1 space)

6 All the natural rights guaranteed by the U.S. Constitution, such as free speech and the right to religious beliefs and practices; also the body of law concerning natural rights. (2 words, 1 space)

7 A model based on the assumption that the inmate subculture arises not only from internal prison experiences but also from the external patterns of behavior the inmates take into prison. (2 words, 1 space)

9 The prison store as well as incidental items sold to inmates.

DOWN

1 A model of prisonization based on the belief that the prison subculture stems from the way inmates adapt to the severe psychological and physical losses imposed by imprisonment. (2 words, 1 space)

2 A corrections employee with supervisory power over a suspect or convicted offender in custody. (2 words, 1 space)

4 The interrelationship of roles, acts, and statuses of people who make up the social structure. (2 words, 1 space)

8 The rules or standards of appropriate behavior, shared by members of a social group.

ANSWERS TO WORD SEARCH

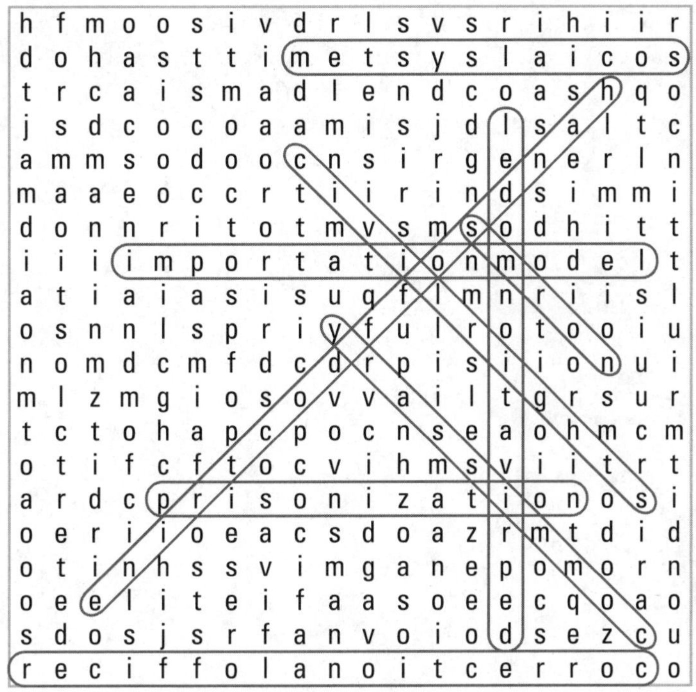

civil rights
deprivation model
norms
commissary
hands-off doctrine
prisonization
correctional officer
importation model
social system

CHAPTER 11 COMMUNITY CORRECTIONS, PROBATION, AND PAROLE

LEARNING OBJECTIVES

After reading this chapter, students should be able to do the following:

- **Explain the meaning of the term *community corrections*, and state the advantages of using this approach**
- **Explore substance abuse and its implications for criminal law**
- **Discuss the development and impact of drug courts and other diversionary programs**
- **Comment on mental health issues regarding community corrections.**
- **Assess the contributions of California to the modern treatment approach toward minor, nonviolent drug offenders**
- **Comment on mental health issues regarding community corrections and evaluate mental health courts**
- **Explain furlough, work release, and prerelease programs**
- **Discuss the nature and importance of the Second Chance Act**
- **Distinguish probation from parole and analyze recent data on each**
- **Explain felony probation, and analyze recent approaches to its use**
- **Analyze the use of electronic monitoring and house arrest**
- **Discuss the legal limitations on probation and parole conditions.**
- **Recognize the advantages and disadvantages of intensive probation supervision (IPS)**
- **Analyze the process of searching and seizing parolees**
- **Identify three organizational models of parole systems**
- **Explain the parole process, with particular attention to due process**
- **Explain the legal controls on parole revocation and probation revocation**
- **Analyze the future of probation and parole**
- **List and discuss the major constitutional issues relating to community corrections, probation, and parole. Note in particular the impact of the Americans with Disabilities Act (ADA)**
- **Discuss the issues surrounding probation revocation or parole revocation.**
- **Assess the practical and constitutional issues involved in today's sex offender registration laws**

Criminal Justice Essentials: Study Guide, Ninth Edition. Shannon Barton-Bellessa.

CHAPTER OUTLINE

Learning Objectives

Supervision of Offenders in the Community

Overview

Diversion of Nonviolent Drug Offenders

Decriminalizing Minor Drug Offenses

Drug Courts

Statutory Provisions for Treatment

Diversion of Mentally Challenged Persons

Problems of Offenders on Release

Furlough and Work Release Programs

Prerelease Programs

Focus on the Second Chance Act

Probation and Parole: An Overview

Probation

Types of Probation

Probation Administration

Probation Conditions

Probation Supervision

Parole

The Organization of Parole Systems

The Parole Process

Eligibility for Parole

The Parole Hearing

Parole Board Discretion

Due Process and the Parole Hearing

Control of Parole Decisions

Parole Conditions

Medical Parole: A New Focus?

Parole Supervision

Constitutional Issues

Search and Seizure

The Americans with Disabilities Act (ADA)

Probation Revocation and Parole Revocation

Sex Offender Registration Laws

Megan's Laws

Adam Walsh Child Protection and Safety Act

Jessica's Laws

Effectiveness Issues

Constitutional Issues

Summary

Key Terms

Study Questions

Notes

KEY TERMS

diversion
furlough
halfway house
house arrest
intensive probation supervision (IPS)
Jessica's Laws
Megan's Laws
parole
parole board
parole officer
parole revocation
probation
probation officer
probation revocation
recidivists
reintegration
work release

CHAPTER SUMMARY

This chapter is the third of three covering the critical area of corrections. The previous two chapters dealt with supervising offenders in an institution. This third chapter covers alternatives to incarceration found in the community. Community-based corrections cover a variety of alternatives to incarceration, ranging from the least restrictive fines to the most restrictive residential placements. **Probation** is probably the most recognizable alternative to imprisonment. This alternative originated in 1840 with the work of **John Augustus**. As a shoemaker in Boston, he would spend afternoons in the county courtroom observing the judicial process. During this time he noticed that many men were appearing in front of the judge for drunkenness. He took it upon himself to volunteer to post bail for the men and provide lodgings for them and employment in his business. His work expanded throughout the course of his lifetime and established the foundation for this community-based alternative. Another variation, the use of **halfway houses**, can be traced back to 1880 in New York City. These facilities permitted inmates a place to stay as they gradually reentered society following incarceration. Although earlier examples exist of community-based alternatives, it wasn't until the mid-1960s, with the passage of the **Federal Prisoner Rehabilitation Act of 1965**, that there was a major impetus for the modern movement toward supervising offenders in the community grew. A report by the President's Commission on Law Enforcement and the Administration of Justice also noted that reintegration was a better alternative for reducing recidivism than confinement.

As the author observes, community-based correctional options are different from diversion – a process of directing the offender away from the criminal (or juvenile) justice systems and into other programs. Diversion typically occurs instead of incarceration and is used most frequently with juvenile offenders. Recent programmatic options, however, have begun to explore using diversionary options for treatment, especially with adult drug offenders. **Drug court programs** serve as a viable option for many offenders. The first drug court, which began in Miami, Florida, in 1989, has now spread to all states. A variation of the drug court program is the **family drug court**. In many states, offenders who successfully complete the drug court treatment program will have the conviction removed from their record. **Mental health courts** represent another variation of diversion. These courts, which began in Broward County, Florida, in 1997, were designed to address the growing concerns and needs of offenders coming to the attention of the courts with mental health problems who had been charged with nonviolent offenses or misdemeanors. In these courts, special judges are appointed with support staff, some of whom are clinically trained.

The next section of the chapter addresses the efforts to assist inmates when they transition back into society. As noted in the chapter, 97 percent of all offenders will reenter society at some point. In 2006, the National Institute of Corrections (NIC) announced its new program, the **Transition from Prison to the Community Initiative**, which was intended to improve the transition processes for offenders from the prison to the community. One of the key components of the program was the mentoring of offenders upon release. Many offenders are released from institutions with as little as $50. This money is to be used as a means for securing housing, employment, transportation, etc. Depending upon the length of time an offender has been incarcerated and upon the ties they have remaining in their respective communities, they may or may not have a placement option available. Mechanisms used by some states to assist with the transition include **furloughs** and/or **work release** programs. Furloughs permit inmates to leave the institution once or occasionally for a specified purpose other than work or study. Work release programs allow inmates to be released for work or study. These programs are normally implemented toward the end of an offender's term of confinement (usually within a year). These programs are important because they provide a mechanism for offenders to reconnect with positive contacts on the outside and to secure employment and housing upon their release. Another program that has been used to assist with offenders transitioning back into the community is the **prerelease center**. These centers were designed to assist with the transition back into society for those who do not have another suitable place to go to.

Next the chapter discusses the recent creation of the **Second Chance Act**. The Second Chance Act was signed into law in 2008 by President George W. Bush. This Act provides $330 million for programs involving reentry, substance abuse, mentoring services, housing, counseling, education, and so on. Additionally, it stresses the importance of involving the offender's family in the treatment process. These efforts include money for drug court programs and diversion/reentry for juvenile drug offenders.

The next section of the chapter provides an overview of probation and parole. **Probation** is a sentence that does not involve confinement but may involve conditions imposed by the court. **Parole** is the release of persons from correctional facilities after they have served part of their sentences. Parole is usually granted by an appointed or elected **parole board**.

Probation may be through a **direct sentence**, usually for less serious infractions, or as part of a **suspended sentence** for either misdemeanor or felony offenders. This alternative as a sentence may be administered as a standalone sanction or in conjunction with others. These programs may include **house arrest** and/or **electronic monitoring**. Other programs such as **shock probation** permit the sending of offenders to prison for a short period of time and then placing them on probation. Probation may also be combined with a jail term, a procedure called **periodic sentencing**.

In most jurisdictions, probation administration is a court function and is administered at the local level and located within the judicial branch. Other jurisdictions have a statewide probation system, which is normally administered at the executive level. Probation departments are usually headed by a **chief probation officer**. In departments that are large enough, there may be an assistant and officers assigned to perform specific tasks such as **presentence investigations**, supervision, programming, etc. In smaller departments, the probation officer will be responsible for ensuring all tasks are completed. Many agencies now require probationers to pay for their supervision. Once an individual is placed on probation, they will meet with their assigned agent and be given **conditions** that they must abide by in order to remain in the community. There are **standard conditions** that all probationers must meet and **special conditions** such as treatment options that can be specified by the crime type. Varying methods for supervising offenders in the community exist, ranging from a weekly phone call to multiple face-to-face contacts per week. Many officers are expected to not only supervise their caseload but also lead treatment groups. In order to ensure the best quality treatment, the NIC has suggested that probation, parole, and community corrections staff need more training to cope with their dual roles of treatment and surveillance.

A final variation of probation, known as **intensive probation supervision** (**IPS**), calls for an increase in the number of contacts between an officer and the probationer. This program was designed as an intermediate sanction used as a tool to keep less serious offenders in the community and out of prison.

Parole is an administrative decision to release an offender after he or she has served time on a sentence to a correctional facility. Some inmates may be released early because they have accumulated credits (**good time**) given for good behavior during incarceration. The amount of time to be reduced is established by statute or legislation. Parole and its use have come under attack, resulting in a movement to abolish the system. In 1984

President Ronald Reagan signed the **Comprehensive Crime Control Act**. That Act abolished early release by parole in the federal system, and over a five-year period phased out the **U.S. Parole Commission**. Under the new statute, inmates in the federal system could receive only a maximum of 15 percent good time credits on their sentences. By January 1999, 15 states had abolished parole boards. Some states have reinstituted them, however, because of overcrowding and the need to process offenders.

As noted in the chapter, the organization of parole is complex. One reason is for the varying structures such as the amount of time off for good behavior. There are three common organizational models: **institutional**, **independent authority**, and **consolidated**. Most parole systems are located in the executive branch of government and are administered at the state level. The process of releasing an offender on parole is very important. Parolees should have a good prerelease plan, including a place for living, working, and treatment upon release. Eligibility differs by state but there are usually statutory provisions. The parole board has almost absolute discretion in determining release. Although there is no constitutional guarantee to parole, the U.S. Supreme Court has held that there are statutes protecting liberty and interests. The conditions of parole are similar to those found in probation. Some states have begun to allow the early release for **medical parole** in instances of age or disease. The section ends with a recommendation that parole officers should have the same qualifications as probation officers.

The next section of the chapter discusses the various constitutional issues governing probation and parole. The U.S. Supreme Court has upheld that exceptions exist to certain fundamental rights, including the Fourth Amendment, for both probationers and parolees. In most instances, probation and parole officers have the right to search a probationer's home with no more than reasonable suspicion. Similarly, the U.S. Supreme Court has ruled that the **revocation** of probation does require the presence of an attorney and that revocation of parole requires that some but not all elements of due process must be followed.

The final section of the chapter addresses the issue of sex offender registration laws. Three laws have been enacted specifically addressing the issues of sexual predators in the community. **Megan's Laws** were created in memory of Megan Kanka, who was sexually assaulted and murdered by a neighbor who had two previous sex offense convictions. These statutes may vary but typically require that residents be notified of the presences of a sex offender in the neighborhood. The **Adam Walsh Child Protection and Safety Act** was passed in 2006 following the kidnapping and murder of Adam Walsh by a pedophile. This Act was instrumental in the establishment of the **National Center for Missing and Exploited Children**. The Act also tightens and broadens sex offender registration requirements. Amended in 2008 with the enactment of the **Keeping the Internet Devoid of Sexual Predators (KIDS) Act**, this law additionally requires sex offenders to register their email and instant messenger addresses with the **National Sex Offender Registry**. Finally, **Jessica's Laws** were named on behalf of Jessica Lunsford, who was raped and murdered by a registered sex offender and neighbor. These laws increased the penalties for convicted sex offenders, including longer sentences and more stringent monitoring requirements for those offenders who are living in the community.

KEY TERMS

diversion The removal of the offender from the criminal proceeding before or after guilt is determined and disposition through other procedures, such as work release, drug treatment, or community service.

furlough In corrections, an authorized, temporary leave from a prison or other penal facility in order to attend a funeral, visit the family, attempt to secure employment, or engage in any other approved activity.

halfway house A place of confinement, such as a prerelease center, used to prepare an inmate for his or her return from confinement to living in free society. A halfway house may also be used to confine convicted offenders rather than send them to prison.

house arrest A form of confinement, usually on probation or parole, in which the offender is permitted to live at home (or some other approved place) but is restricted in his or her movements to and from the area. A curfew may be imposed, and the offender may be subject to unannounced visits from a probation or parole officer. In some cases electronic devices are used to monitor the person's location.

intensive probation supervision (IPS) Close and intensive supervision of probationers by probation officers, presumably with small caseloads.

Jessica's Laws Laws requiring registration and other restrictions placed on sex offenders living in the community; named after Jessica Lunsford, a young Florida victim of a released sex offender living near her home.

Megan's Laws Laws requiring sex offenders released from confinement to register when they move in to a community. In some jurisdictions, the offenders are required only to notify law enforcement officers, but in other jurisdictions, they must notify all residents within a certain distance of their residences. Megan's Laws are named after Megan Kanka, who was raped and murdered by a neighbor across the street, a sex offender who was living there with other sex offenders.

parole The status of an offender who is released before the completion of a prison sentence. Usually the parolee must be supervised in the community by a parole officer.

parole board A panel at the state or federal level that decides whether an inmate is released on parole from a prison before the expiration of his or her sentence. In some jurisdictions the parole board makes recommendations but the governor makes the final decisions.

parole officer A government employee who supervises and counsels inmates paroled to the community.

parole revocation The process of returning a released offender to prison due to violations of parole conditions or for committing a new crime.

probation A type of sentence that places the convicted offender under the supervision of a probation officer within the community instead of in prison. Also the part of the criminal justice system that is in charge of all aspects of probation.

probation officer A government official responsible for writing the presentence reports on offenders; supervising probationers; reporting violations of probation conditions; and providing evidence of those violations.

probation revocation The process of declaring that a sentenced offender violated the terms of probation and that probation will, as a result, be revoked or cancelled. If probation involved a suspended prison or jail sentence, the revocation may mean that the original sentence is invoked and the individual is sent to a prison, jail, or other penal facility.

recidivists Offenders who commit crimes repeatedly.

reintegration A punishment philosophy emphasizing the return of the offender to the community, so that employment, family ties, and education can be restored.

work release The release of an inmate to attend school or to work outside the institution but requiring that person to return to the institution at specified times, such as at night.

STUDY QUESTIONS

These questions are found at the end of your chapter. Your instructor may wish to revisit these or assign them for points. These questions are a good way to integrate the material and to generate your own perspectives during class.

1 Define *community-based corrections,* and give reasons why some argue that this approach is preferred over incarceration of offenders.

2 Evaluate the role of drug courts and other diversionary processing and treatment of nonviolent drug offenders.

3 Do we need mental health courts? Why or why not?

4 What problems do offenders face when they return to the community from incarceration? What is being done to assist them in coping with those problems? Evaluate furlough, work release, and prerelease programs.

5 Explain the meaning and importance of the Second Chance Act.

6 What is the difference between probation and parole? Which is used more frequently and why? What are the trends in the use of probation and parole?

7 What are the arguments for and against the use of house arrest?

8 What is electronic monitoring? What are global positioning systems?

9 Discuss and evaluate shock probation.

10 What typical restrictions or conditions are placed on probationers? What should be the guidelines, legally or practically, for such restrictions?

11 What is meant by *intensive probation supervision*? How does it compare in effectiveness with traditional methods of supervision?

12 Describe and analyze recent trends in parole systems.

13 What effect do due process requirements have on parole granting or on parole revocation?

14 What are the search and seizure issues in probation and parole, and how have they been resolved?

15 Explain and discuss the practical and legal implications of sex offender registration laws. Distinguish the types of laws.

LEARNING ACTIVITIES

11.1 For this activity think about the use of drug courts as an alternative to traditional processing of drug- or alcohol-involved offenders through the system. Using your state, describe the drug court program that is being used. How is the program administered? How are the accused or convicted referred to the program? Who is eligible for participating in the program? What is the length of the program? What constitutes success or failure from the program? What happens if a person fails? How many offenders are processed annually through the program? Do you think this program should be continued in your state?

11.2 Imagine you are an individual who was convicted of aggravated assault (second offense) and you have served 10 years in prison. You are scheduled to be released into your community under the supervision of a parole officer, for a term of no more than two years. You have been given $200 and ordered to remain in a halfway house for up to six months or until you obtain gainful employment, whichever comes first. What are some of the barriers you will face upon release into society? How has society changed since you were incarcerated 10 years prior (e.g., cost of living, clothes, telephones, television, computers, etc.)? What might a society's criminal justice system do to assist someone in this predicament so that they will not choose to commit crime once released?

11.3 Offenders who have served time in a correctional facility are released in a number of ways, including through the use of parole. Parole, however, is administered according to the state sentencing structure (determinate or indeterminate) and organizational model (institutional, independent authority, and consolidated). This being said, not all states use a parole board to determine early release from an institution (determinate sentence), while other states use the parole board to make early release decisions (indeterminate). For this activity, locate one state using a determinate sentencing structure and one state using an indeterminate sentencing structure. For each of the states answer the following questions:

a How is parole administered in this state?
b What are the terms for parole in this state?
c Can offenders be released early from parole?
d What organizational model does this state use for releasing offenders?
e Are good time credits allowed? How are they administered (e.g., one day off for one day of good behavior, etc.)?

a

b

c

d

e

11.4 In 2003, Brady Drakenheimer, age 32, was convicted of his second drunk driving offense in just over five years. After he pleaded guilty, the trial court judge sentenced Mr. Drakenheimer to four days in jail, a six-month suspended driver's license, and one year of probation. You have been assigned to be Mr. Drakenheimer's probation officer. A review of his pre-sentence investigation report reveals the following information: Mr. Drakenheimer is divorced with two children. He is in arrears for six months' child support. He has demonstrated an inability to maintain full-time employment over the past two years. His BAC (blood alcohol content) was .24 at the time of his arrest. He has a full-time residence in low-income housing, where he is responsible for paying $350 per month in rent. He has a high school diploma. He previously completed a mandated alcohol treatment program on his first drunk driving charge.

As a probation officer, you are required to develop Mr. Drakenheimer's Conditions of Probation. Before writing these, you must first find the standard conditions for your state. What conditions, if any, do you think should be added to these standard conditions? What do you think might increase Mr. Drakenheimer's likelihood for success? Do you think Mr. Drakenheimer is likely to recidivate? Why or why not? What conditions in this individual's background might make you alter your decision regarding conditions of probation?

STUDENT STUDY GUIDE PRACTICE QUESTIONS

True or False

11.1 According to the National Institute of Corrections, 85 percent of all offenders will be released back into the community.

11.2 There are no problems associated with finding employment for offenders on work release in their community.

11.3 According to the research reported in the Second Chance Act, within three years after their release, two-thirds of the offenders will be arrested for additional offenses.

11.4 John Augustus is considered the father of probation in the United States.

11.5 GPS technology has been used with electronic monitoring as a mechanism for reducing overcrowding in jails.

11.6 Electronic monitoring as an alternative to incarceration has successfully been used with violent offenders, including sexual predators.

11.7 The purpose of probation is to provide another mechanism for punishment in the community.

11.8 The aging prison population, along with the expense of incarcerating older inmates, especially those with medical problems, and overcrowded prisons, has led some jurisdictions to provide for medical parole for inmates who are frail, who have life-threatening diseases, or, for other reasons, are near death.

11.9 Probation and parole revocation require all of the due process rights of a criminal trial.

11.10 Aside from the practical problems of whether sex offender registration laws are effective are the legal issues. Some courts have ruled that the registration statutes (or portions of them) are unconstitutional, while other courts have upheld all or a portion of challenged statutes.

Multiple Choice

11.11 In which of the following facilities does the offender live in a supervised environment, but may leave that facility during the day to work or to participate in vocational, treatment, or educational programs?

a Detention centers
b Open prisons
c Halfway houses
d Custody facilities

11.12 Which state had the first drug court?

a Texas
b Florida
c Mississippi
d Connecticut

11.13 A variation of the drug court is the family drug court, such as the one cited in ______.

a Kentucky
b Miami
c Atlanta
d Tallahassee

11.14 Under the ______ system, once a drug offender completes the treatment program successfully, that person's conviction is removed from the records.
- a Florida
- b Pennsylvania
- c Texas
- d California

11.15 Work release is also referred to as ______.
- a day parole
- b outmate program
- c None of the above
- d Both a and b

11.16 Identify the term that denotes a sentence that does not involve confinement but may involve conditions imposed by the court, usually under supervision.
- a Prerelease
- b Furlough
- c Parole
- d Probation

11.17 Probation may be combined with a jail term, a procedure called ______.
- a shock probation
- b intermittent probation
- c periodic sentencing
- d adaptation

11.18 According to a suggestion by the National Institute of Corrections, probation officers should be trained to recognize and respond appropriately to the escalation of violence, a process called ______.
- a continuum training
- b reference training
- c critical training
- d escalation training

11.19 Probation supervisors should meet with probationers in the probationers' homes at all hours – not just regular probation office hours – a process the Reinventing Probation Council panel called ______.
- a shock probation
- b fortress probation
- c periodic probation
- d alert probation

11.20 What are the main reasons for parole in the United States?
- a Reform, cost, prison overcrowding
- b Rehabilitation, justice, prison overcrowding
- c Rehabilitation, reform, prison overcrowding
- d Rehabilitation, cost, prison overcrowding

Fill-in-the-Blank

11.21 Community-based corrections should be distinguished from ______, a process of directing the offender away from the adult criminal (or juvenile) systems and into other programs.

11.22 A(n) _____ involves permitting the inmate to leave the institution once or occasionally for a specified purpose other than work or study.

11.23 Some statutes permit sending offenders to prison for a short period and then placing them on probation. This process is called _____.

11.24 Probation is granted by the_____.

11.25 Under the _____ model, found mainly in the juvenile field, the decision to release is made by the correctional staff.

11.26 Individuals who have been convicted of an offense and sentenced who commit an additional crime following their release are known as _____.

11.27 Name the three common organizational models of parole: _____, _____, and _____.

11.28 _____ Laws require community notification for all sex offenders. The notification statutes vary in their provisions, but many require that residents be notified of the presence of a sex offender the neighborhood.

11.29 Before release, all inmates should have the opportunity to participate in a _____ program.

11.30 The inmate's ability to convey an improved self-image and to demonstrate an ability to work with others and stick with a job may influence the board's decision in _____.

CROSSWORD

ACROSS

3 The removal of the offender from the criminal proceeding before or after guilt is determined and disposition through other procedures, such as work release, drug treatment, or community service.

4 A type of sentence that places the convicted offender under the supervision of a probation officer within the community instead of in prison.

5 An authorized, temporary leave from a prison or other penal facility in order to attend a funeral, visit the family, attempt to secure employment, or engage in any other approved activity.

8 A government employee who supervises and counsels inmates paroled to the community. (2 words, 1 space)

10 The process of declaring that a sentenced offender violated the terms of probation. (2 words, 1 space)

12 A panel at the state or federal level that decides whether an inmate is released on parole from a correctional institution before the expiration of his or her sentence. (2 words, 1 space)

13 A form of confinement, usually on probation, in which the offender is permitted to live at home but is restricted in his or her movements to and from the area. (2 words, 1 space)

14 Laws requiring community notification on sex offenders released from prison. (2 words, 1 space)

15 Strict sex offender laws requiring longer sentences for convicted sex offenders and more stringent monitoring requirements for those offenders who are living in the community. (2 words, 1 space)

DOWN

1 With small caseloads, probation officers provide more careful supervision than they could provide with larger caseloads. (3 words, 2 spaces)

2 A punishment philosophy emphasizing the return of the offender to the community, so that employment, family ties, and education can be restored.

4 The process of returning a released offender to an institution for technical violations of parole conditions or for committing a new crime. (2 words, 1 space)

6 Those who commit crimes repeatedly.

7 A government official responsible for supervising persons on probation and for writing the presentence reports on offenders. (2 words, 1 space)

9 A place for offenders nearing the end of their terms to live during a period of gradual reentry into society. (2 words, 1 space)

11 The release of an inmate to attend school or to work outside the institution but requiring that person to return to the institution at specified times. (2 words, 1 space)

12 The status of an offender who is released before the completion of a prison sentence.

WORD SEARCH

```
e l a s s s l a o h t n a e s t o i p w a e t a h i i f r
r r w w b i f r t s e t b p c e o t o o w b t t i r h p e
a f r a r a a e e t c s k r r o s s s c s o e p p d i b c
h t s l n n s e v r o r a o t e d o i u p i w h e a o s i
r i p s w d e t t l o v o e r l s r c r o f r i o k e p f
o o s a t l a o s n e f u r l o u g h t t r e o s i o o f
e f n c r v a o d e r a a p i e o s c f a e e b o c s f o
w h e i n o i t a r g e t n i e r e e n u d o a s e r h n
t i n s i d l i i p s a c o e i l k i i a i r a n e r s o
n o i s i v r e p u s n o i t a b o r p e v i s n e t n i
o r a e b t b a o l s n v t f r n r r o e e r w c c o a t
e a o j t d n h o f e u l a s f d t s a w r r i s s c s a
e s n f r a r o o b f l r c v e o o g l p s d i l i w a b
s p r o b a t i o n e i s o n e o n l i e i i e b a n o o
e i l a a i r e p c n l c v a a r s o l v o a a l t t i r
p i i e t e i n r a e a o e s o v a a i e n g s t s c r p
e e e l l e o o t t a p a r r r r a s c t c n i c k w i o
r q o e e o n w u c a t a n a a i t v r e a o n c o v s n
e w c n p i a r b e r o o o o p s w b f g a b n c l u w e
p e p r r p f p b e e n o i t a c o v e r e l o r a p r d
e i b c t a r s a a r l g t u o e o m h w i r h r r u f s
e n o s w o r n i i t r a a i s t r t r o t f n e p v l n
a e f n i a o u i e s n a b t s a t a o n e s e o v h i o
s e u f h r a a p l r o o o d l n t r r a c o o r i u o o
u r o i a c o r e o a g u r b o a a i n g o v i a e a i r
o t o a v c s o p o p g g p u v o r o m p a a r r s t l o
e s u o h y a w f l a h s r n o s a v y r e p n p c s l o
b g a i b a r u h e g p o a r u o a e l t t o r w c e e a
v e l o o o e u s a e e a i r n o e d e o f s r n r d a b
```

diversion
house arrest
Megan's Laws
parole officer
probation officer
reintegration

furlough
intensive probation supervision
parole
parole revocation
probation revocation
work release

halfway house
Jessica's Laws
parole board
probation
recidivists

ANSWERS TO CROSSWORD

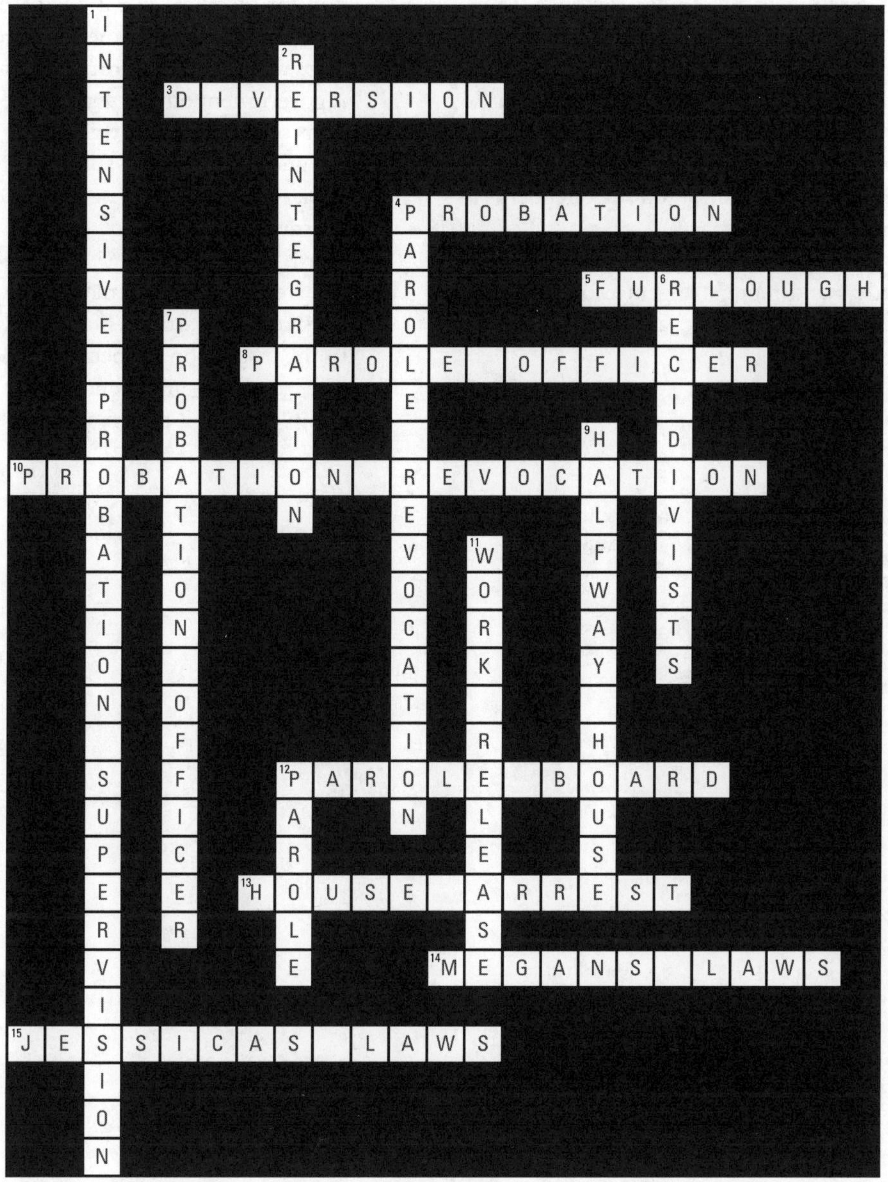

ACROSS

3 The removal of the offender from the criminal proceeding before or after guilt is determined and disposition through other procedures, such as work release, drug treatment, or community service.

4 A type of sentence that places the convicted offender under the supervision of a probation officer within the community instead of in prison.

5 An authorized, temporary leave from a prison or other penal facility in order to attend a funeral, visit the family, attempt to secure employment, or engage in any other approved activity.

8 A government employee who supervises and counsels inmates paroled to the community. (2 words, 1 space)

10 The process of declaring that a sentenced offender violated the terms of probation. (2 words, 1 space)

12 A panel at the state or federal level that decides whether an inmate is released on parole from a correctional institution before the expiration of his or her sentence. (2 words, 1 space)

13 A form of confinement, usually on probation, in which the offender is permitted to live at home but is restricted in his or her movements to and from the area. (2 words, 1 space)

14 Laws requiring community notification on sex offenders released from prison. (2 words, 1 space)

15 Strict sex offender laws requiring longer sentences for convicted sex offenders and more stringent monitoring requirements for those offenders who are living in the community. (2 words, 1 space)

DOWN

1 With small caseloads, probation officers provide more careful supervision than they could provide with larger caseloads. (3 words, 2 spaces)

2 A punishment philosophy emphasizing the return of the offender to the community, so that employment, family ties, and education can be restored.

4 The process of returning a released offender to an institution for technical violations of parole conditions or for committing a new crime. (2 words, 1 space)

6 Those who commit crimes repeatedly.

7 A government official responsible for supervising persons on probation and for writing the presentence reports on offenders. (2 words, 1 space)

9 A place for offenders nearing the end of their terms to live during a period of gradual reentry into society. (2 words, 1 space)

11 The release of an inmate to attend school or to work outside the institution but requiring that person to return to the institution at specified times. (2 words, 1 space)

12 The status of an offender who is released before the completion of a prison sentence.

ANSWERS TO WORD SEARCH

e l a s s s l a o h t n a e s t o i p w a e t a h i i f r
r r w w b i f r t s e t b p c e o t o o w b t t i r h p e
a f r a r a a e e t c s k r r o s s s c s o e p p d i b c
h t s l n n s e v r o r a o t e d o i u p i w h e a o s i
r i p s w d e t t l o v o e r l s r c r o f r i o k e p f
o o s a t l a o s n e f u r l o u g h t t r e o s i o o f
e f n c r v a o d e r a a p i e o s c f a e e b o c s f o
w h e i n o i t a r g e t n i e r e e n u d o a s e r h n
t i n s i d l i i p s a c o e i l k i i a i r a n e r s o
n o i s i v r e p u s n o i t a b o r p e v i s n e t n i
o r a e b t b a o l s n v t f r n r r o e e r w c c o a t
e a o j t d n h o f e u l a s f d t s a w r r i s s c s a
e s n f r a r o o b f l r c v e o o g l p s d i l i w a b
s p r o b a t i o n e i s o n e o n l i e i i e b a n o o
e i l a a i r e p c n l c v a a r s o l v o a a l t t i r
p i i e t e i n r a e a o e s o v a a i e n g s t s c r p
e e e l l e o o t t a p a r r r r a s c t c n i c k w i o
r q o e e o n w u c a t a n a a i t v r e a o n c o v s n
e w c n p i a r b e r o o o o p s w b f g a b n c l u w e
p e p r r p f p b e e n o i t a c o v e r e l o r a p r d
e i b c t a r s a a r l g t u o e o m h w i r h r r u f s
e n o s w o r n i i t r a a i s t r t r o t f n e p v l n
a e f n i a o u i e s n a b t s a t a o n e s e o v h i o
s e u f h r a a p l r o o o d l n t r r a c o o r i u o o
u r o i a c o r e o a g u r b o a a i n g o v i a e a i r
o t o a v c s o p o p g g p u v o r o m p a a r r s t l o
e s u o h y a w f l a h s r n o s a v y r e p n p c s l o
b g a i b a r u h e g p o a r u o a e l t t o r w c e e a
v e l o o o e u s a e e a i r n o e d e o f s r n r d a b

diversion
house arrest
Megan's Laws
parole officer
probation officer
reintegration

furlough
intensive probation supervision
parole
parole revocation
probation revocation
work release

halfway house
Jessica's Laws
parole board
probation
recidivists

VENILE JUSTICE:
SPECIAL CASE

A TER 12

J VENILE JUSTICE S STEMS

LEARNING OBJECTIVES

After reading this chapter, students should be able to do the following:

- **List and explain the basic procedural and philosophical differences between juvenile and criminal courts historically and currently**
- **Discuss current data on delinquency, especially data on violent crimes**
- **Analyze the impact of youth gangs on our society**
- **List and explain the major U.S. Supreme Court cases regarding juveniles' constitutional rights, and assess the impact of the right to counsel**
- **State the standard of proof in juvenile proceedings**
- **Explain how the following apply to juvenile proceedings: the right not to be tried twice for the same offense; the right to a jury trial; the right to a probable cause hearing; and the application of harsher penalties through a juvenile court than would be assessed a juvenile in an adult criminal court**
- **Enumerate and explain the purpose and practice of juvenile curfews and discuss the legal issues involved**
- **Explore the racial, ethnic, and gender issues of juvenile justice systems**
- **Discuss the general procedures of juvenile courts**
- **Analyze the role of attorneys in juvenile courts**
- **Explain the processing of juvenile offenders in adult criminal courts, and relate your discussion to persistently violent juvenile offenders**
- **Assess the wisdom of sentencing juveniles to life without parole**
- **Analyze the practice of confining juveniles in adult jails and prisons**
- **Discuss the application of sex registration laws to juveniles**
- **Analyze substance abuse among juveniles**
- **Assess the importance of drug courts to juvenile justice systems, and compare them to those in adult criminal court systems**
- **Summarize recent changes in juvenile corrections**
- **Discuss deinstitutionalization and the wisdom of supervising juveniles within the community rather than in institutions**
- **Evaluate the recent legal status of the capital punishment of juveniles**
- **Comment on the future of juvenile court systems**

Criminal Justice Essentials: Study Guide, Ninth Edition. Shannon Barton-Bellessa.

CHAPTER OUTLINE

Learning Objectives

Juvenile Justice Systems: An Overview

Juvenile Delinquency Data

Youth Gangs

The Nature and Extent of Gangs

Female Gang Members

The Constitutional Rights of Juveniles

U.S. Supreme Court Cases

Juvenile Curfews

Race and Ethnicity Issues

Gender Issues

Juvenile Courts

Court Organization and Procedures

The Role of Attorneys

Juveniles in Adult Criminal Courts

Procedural Requirements for Waivers

Evaluation of Waivers

Sentencing

Life without Parole (LWOP)

Juveniles in Adult Jails and Prisons

Sex Registration Laws and Juveniles

Juveniles and Substance Abuse

Recent Data

Drug Courts

Juveniles in Correctional Facilities

Historical Background

Recent Data on Offenders and Facilities

Types of Institutions for Juveniles

Legal Issues in Juvenile Facilities

Treatment and Juvenile Corrections

Deinstitutionalization

Juveniles in the Community

Juveniles and Capital Punishment

Juvenile and Adult Criminal Justice Systems: A Brief Assessment

Summary

Key Terms

Study Questions

Notes

KEY TERMS

adjudication
aftercare
certification
delinquency
detention
detention centers
disposition
intake decision
juvenile
juvenile court
juvenile delinquent
parens patriae
petition
status offense
training school

CHAPTER SUMMARY

Chapter 12 is the final chapter of the text. This chapter focuses exclusively on the role of the system in handling juvenile offenders. The concept of childhood and delinquency is a relatively new phenomenon, although the first discussion of juvenile problems dates back 4,000 years to the Code of Hammurabi. The treatment of juveniles in the United States can be traced back to the English system. As noted in the chapter, it wasn't until the 11th and 12th centuries that children began to be treated differently. At this time, a child under the age of 7 was considered incapable of forming the intent required for criminal prosecutions, and a child over the age of 14 was treated as an adult. Because children were treated separately, the English criminal justice system was informed by the belief that the king could exercise the power of a parent over children and others, a concept called ***parens patriae***. The doctrine of *parens patriae* applied only to children who were in need of supervision or help because of the actions of their parents or guardians, not to children who were delinquent. These children were categorized as **children in need of supervision (CHINS), persons in need of supervision (PINS)**, and **dependent or neglected**. These concepts were later extended to the creation of the **juvenile court** in Cook County, Illinois, in 1899.

The purpose of the juvenile court was to prevent children from becoming criminals. In doing so, it was the belief that the court should create a separate vocabulary to deal with juveniles through the process so as not to stigmatize them and cause greater harm. It was also believed, and continues to be the case, that the juvenile court should have jurisdiction over **status offenses** or those behaviors that would not be deemed criminal if committed by an adult, i.e., running away, truancy, etc. The distinction in vocabulary covered every facet of the system, including the following: **apprehension** (arrest), **petition** (indictment), **detention** (jail), **adjudication** (finding/ruling), and **disposition** (sentence). Rules of evidence were not applied to juvenile cases. The burden of proof was analogous to that found in civil cases (preponderance of evidence). The belief was that the state, acting as the benevolent parent, was helping the youth rather than punishing them. Despite the original intent of the court, an ongoing debate exists among scholars who argue that the juvenile court system does not in fact function as a benevolent parent but rather diminishes the civil rights and privacy of youth. Although the system itself has evolved, the public still indicates a preference for handling youth differently in the system.

The next section of the chapter reviews juvenile delinquency data. Data reviewed usually relate to persons under the age of 18. Methods for collecting data, however, differ from the adult system. In most instances, juvenile records are confidential. In 2009, persons under the age of 18 accounted for 14.1 percent of all arrests, 14.9 percent of arrests for violent crimes, and 24.9 percent of all arrests for property crimes.

Gang membership is a factor that leads to juvenile crime. The next section of the chapter covers gang membership and efforts to combat crime. The **National Youth Gang Center (NYGC)** reported in 2008 that there were an estimated 774,000 gang members active and 27,900 gangs. Although the majority of gang members are adults, juvenile gang membership still occurs frequently enough to constitute an issue worth studying. Research suggests, for example, that youths join gangs because of poverty, unstable living conditions, availability of drugs and alcohol, parental tolerance of violence, failing or falling behind in school, and delinquent peer associations. Although gang members tend to be male, there is a growing trend for female associations. Research suggests that girls join gangs for the same reasons as boys, primarily a sense of belonging.

Next, the chapter discusses the constitutional rights of juveniles. With the evolution of the juvenile court and the recognition of the concept of *parens patriae*, this meant the limiting of constitutional rights for juveniles. Between 1899 and 1966, juveniles essentially had no protections. With the passage of ***Kent v. the United States*** (1966), the U.S. Supreme Court first acknowledged that juveniles had some due process protections when being transferred to the adult court system. The first case to be heard from a state was ***In re Gault*** (1967). This case extended the due process rights at trial, including notice of charges, right to counsel, right to confrontation and cross-examination, privilege against self-incrimination, right to a transcript, and right to appellate review. The issue of burden of proof was considered in ***In re Winship*** (1970). In this case the U.S. Supreme Court ruled that juvenile court proceedings require the same standard of proof as do adult criminal courts. The U.S. Supreme Court in ***Breed v. Jones*** (1975), upheld the constitutional provisions that defendants may not be tried twice for the same offense. Additionally, the U.S. Supreme Court upheld the legality of preventively detaining youth for their own safety or the safety of the community in ***Schall v. Martin*** (1984). The constitutionality of curfews has also been questioned. In this case the court has upheld that curfews are legal as long as they are tailored to further the city's compelling interest in reducing and preventing juvenile crime and victimization. Essentially, juveniles have been afforded all of the rights of the adult court system except the right to a jury trial (***McKeiver v. Pennsylvania***, 1971). Issues of race, ethnicity, and gender continue to permeate the system as well. The **National Council on Crime and Delinquency (NCCD)** reported that race and ethnicity are factors at every stage of the system. Recent attention has also been given to the differing needs of girls when they enter the system, ranging from types of offenses committed to treatment once adjudicated.

The next section of the chapter covers the juvenile court system. As noted previously, the process for juveniles differs in vocabulary but not necessarily in treatment. Law enforcement officers upon **detention** of a juvenile delinquent or status offender typically have more discretion at their disposal with how to handle juvenile offenders. Should the juvenile reside in a home that the officer believes will address minor infractions, they may choose to reprimand and release them into the custody of the parents. Should more official attention be required, the youth may be detained and formally processed. Once a juvenile is detained, they will be interviewed by the **intake officer** (who may also be a probation officer) and that person will decide whether or not to file a **petition** to bring formal charges. Once the petition is filed, a preliminary inquiry or hearing is held. As in the adult system, the juvenile will admit or deny guilt. Some jurisdictions allow youth the right to the process of **discovery**. Following either an admission of guilt or being found guilty (**adjudication**), the juvenile will receive a **disposition** (sentence). Dispositions may include **nominal dispositions** (warnings and reprimands); **conditional dispositions** (work assignments, restitution, fines, etc.); or placement in a **secure or nonsecure facility**. Attorneys play a role in these processes but are different from the adult system. Representation inherently implies an adversarial system. Both prosecutors and defense, however, must work in the best interests of the child.

Next, the chapter discusses the role of the juvenile transferred to the adult court system. Many juvenile cases tried in adult criminal courts go through a process of **waiver**. A waiver, also called a **transfer or certification**, means that the juvenile court waives jurisdiction. In 2005, less than 1 percent of all cases were judicially waived to adult criminal courts. When a juvenile is waived to the adult court system, they must go through the same process as adults. Some jurisdictions give the right to the adult court system for specific crimes but transfer the case back to the juvenile court through a process known as **reverse certification**. Once a juvenile is found guilty in the adult court system, multiple sentencing options exist, such as life without parole (LWOP); sending the juvenile to an adult facility; or sending them to a juvenile facility until the age of majority. Each of these options is controversial in its own right.

The next section of the chapter addresses the use of **sex offender registries** for juveniles. Because of the confidential nature of handling juvenile offenders, the U.S. Supreme Court has ruled that it is permissible to maintain juvenile names on a sex offender registry. However, states must maintain separate registries for those over the age of majority (public) and those under the majority (private, made available only to law enforcement, schools, courts, etc.).

Similar to the focus with adult offenders, the issue of substance abuse is a growing concern for juveniles. Recent legislation makes a commitment to increasing the response by the government to reducing the use of substances. **Drug courts** are one such initiative. Three key differences exist between juvenile and adult drug courts: (1) juveniles typically are not addicted to substances and, therefore, they may best be served by treatment; (2) juvenile drug courts focus on the family; and (3) juvenile drug courts must involve schools.

As noted in the chapter, placing juveniles in correctional facilities is a relatively new practice. Historically, the family, church, and other social institutions were responsible for handling delinquents. It was not until the 1850s that there was a recognition that the institutions used to house delinquent juveniles offered little more than custody. The result of this acknowledgement was the creation of **training schools**. Training schools were built around the **cottage system**, where parents were supposed to oversee the work of the youth housed in the facility and to gain reformation through hard work and discipline. It was not until the late 1980s that the use of this type of facility was brought into question. A survey of their purpose and standards revealed that most failed examination. More recently, efforts to address these concerns have resulted in institutions that are less crowded, offering more educational opportunities, and treatment facilities. Today the types of institutions that house juveniles range from detention centers and shelters, to training schools and **boot camps**, to the least restrictive option, the **group home**.

The detaining of juveniles, particularly in more secure environments, has raised a number of questions regarding issues of religion, access to education, treatment, discipline, and safety. Whatever the institution, they must not force youth to participate in religious activities, they must provide educational opportunities and treatment, and they must ensure that discipline does not violate the **Eighth Amendment** protections against cruel and unusual punishment. As mentioned in the text, *parens partriae* is the key concept underlying the creation and continuation of a separate juvenile justice system. Unfortunately, many facilities fail to adequately diagnose confined youth, therefore resulting in their mistreatment in the system. One way to address these concerns has been through the **deinstitutionalization movement**. Key to this movement is to keep youth out of confined settings and to make greater use of **diversionary alternatives** and community-based corrections. In the community, juveniles may be placed in **aftercare programs** that begin prior to being released. These programs can be specialized to meet the need of the youth, which includes variations in length. Juveniles may also be diverted from the system completely and placed on **probation**, where supervision is similar to that found in the adult system, although it may be formal or informal. Another form of community care is **respite care**. With respite care, children who have run away from home or who have difficulty living with their parents may be removed from the environment so that both parties are given a break from one another.

The chapter next discusses the use of **capital punishment** with juveniles. The subject of capital punishment is controversial at best. The U.S. Supreme Court has wavered in its decision to uphold the constitutionality of the death penalty for capital crimes committed by persons prior to the age of majority. Most recently the Supreme Court held that juveniles who were the age of 16 or 17 when they committed a capital offense could be executed. Finally, the chapter and text concludes with a discussion on the future of the juvenile justice system, including the evolution of the system and the need for its existence at all.

KEY TERMS

adjudication The process of decision making by a court; normally used to refer to juvenile proceedings. The term is also used to refer to rule enforcement by administrative agencies.

aftercare The continued supervision of juveniles after they are released from a correctional facility; similar to the term *parole* in adult criminal court systems.

certification The process used to remove juveniles from the jurisdiction of the juvenile court to that of the adult criminal court; also called *transfer* or *waiver*.

delinquency *See* **juvenile delinquent**.

detention *See* **pretrial detention**

detention centers Facilities for the temporary confinement of juveniles in custody who are awaiting court disposition.

disposition The final decision of a court in a criminal proceeding to accept a plea, to find the defendant guilty or not guilty, or to terminate the proceedings against the defendant.

intake decision In prosecution, the first review of a case by an official in the prosecutor's office. Weak cases may be weeded out at this stage; in juvenile courts the reception of a juvenile against whom complaints have been made. The decision to dismiss or proceed with a case is made at this stage.

juvenile A young person under age for certain privileges, such as voting or drinking alcoholic beverages. If accused of a criminal or juvenile offense, usually a juvenile is not tried by an adult criminal court but is processed in the juvenile court, although when serious crimes are alleged, in many jurisdictions, juveniles may be transferred to adult criminal courts for trial. Some jurisdictions have statutory requirements that juveniles must be tried in adult criminal courts if they are accused of serious specified crimes (e.g., murder, burglary).

juvenile court The court having jurisdiction over juveniles who are accused of delinquent acts or offenses or criminal acts or who are in need of supervision because they are being neglected or mistreated by their parents or guardians.

juvenile delinquent A person under legal age (the maximum age varies among the states from 16 to 21, but 18 is the most common) whom a juvenile court has determined to be incorrigible or in violation of a criminal statute.

parens patriae: Literally, "parent of the country"; the doctrine from English common law that was the basis for allowing the state to take over guardianship of a child. In the United States the doctrine forms the basis for juvenile court jurisdiction. The doctrine presumes that the state acts in the best interests of the child.

petition A formal document for filing an action in juvenile court, in contrast to a grand jury indictment or prosecutor's presentment in the criminal court.

status offense A class of crime that does not consist of proscribed action or inaction but, rather, of the personal condition or characteristic of the accused – for example, being a vagrant. In juvenile law, a variety of acts that would not be considered criminal if committed by an adult – for example, being insubordinate, truant, or running away from home.

training school A secure corrections facility for juveniles who are confined by court order.

STUDY QUESTIONS

These questions are found at the end of your chapter. Your instructor may wish to revisit these or assign them for points. These questions are a good way to integrate the material and to generate your own perspectives during class.

1. How were juvenile offenders processed historically?
2. What events led to the emergence of juvenile courts in the United States?
3. What are the basic ways in which juvenile courts and adult criminal courts differ?
4. Analyze current data on juvenile offenders.
5. Discuss the nature and impact of juvenile gangs. What is the gender issue?
6. Briefly describe what the Supreme Court held in each of the following cases: *Kent, Gault, Winship, McKeiver, Breed, Schall,* and *R.L.C.*
7. What are the legal issues involved in juvenile curfews? What are the practical implications of curfews?
8. What is the burden of proof standard in juvenile court proceedings?
9. Do juveniles have a federal constitutional right to a trial by jury in juvenile court proceedings?
10. Can juveniles be processed twice in juvenile courts for the same offense?
11. Evaluate pretrial detention of juveniles.
12. How does a probable cause hearing apply to juvenile courts?
13. What are the major race, ethnicity, and gender issues regarding juvenile offenders?
14. What is the relationship of the police to juvenile offenders?
15. Define and discuss intake proceedings in juvenile systems.
16. Describe the role of the prosecutor and of the defense attorney in juvenile proceedings.
17. Discuss the disposition of a juvenile case and the appeals process.
18. Why are some juveniles tried in adult criminal courts, and how is this accomplished? Evaluate this policy.

19 Discuss and evaluate sentencing juveniles to life without parole (LWOP).

20 What are the results of confining juveniles in adult facilities?

21 Should sex offender registration laws be applied to juveniles? Why or why not? What do the courts hold?

22 Discuss the nature and extent of juvenile substance abuse.

23 Should drug courts be extended to juvenile offenders? Why or why not?

24 Why did separate institutions for juveniles develop? Are they successful? Should they be continued? What is meant by deinstitutionalization?

25 Discuss some of the recent findings about juvenile institutions.

26 What is the current legal status of the capital punishment of juveniles?

LEARNING ACTIVITIES

12.1 The processing of youth through a different system from adults has a short and controversial history. The decision of how the system should process youth generates a large amount of debate. Using the following scenarios, answer the questions below:

On Tuesday morning, Phillip Smokesalot (17) and his two friends, Coco Hogan (16) and Darin Deerslayer (17), decided to skip school, drink beer, smoke marijuana, listen to music, and play video games at Phillip's house. Phillip lived with his mother Susan, and younger brother Joey (12). Every Monday through Friday, Susan leaves the Smokesalot household at approximately 6:30 a.m. to go to work at the local factory. She returns each night at approximately 6:00 p.m. The Smokesalot family neighbor Betty Boop noticed on this particular day that Susan was gone and yet the music was blaring loudly from the house. Being concerned, she went to the door and noticed a sweet-smelling odor coming from the home. She immediately called the police, who responded with a visit to the house.

a Using your state, what is the minimum and maximum age that a youth can be handled by the juvenile court system?

b Given the above scenario(s), how and where should the case be handled?

c What should happen to Phillip, Coco, and Darin?

d Would your recommendation for the handling of the youth change if you were told they were 14, 13, and 15 years of age? If yes, how? If no, why not?

a ____

____

____

____

____

____

____

b

c

d

12.2 Using the same scenario presented in activity question 12.1, how might your response to the case change if you had known that the boys had earlier in the day secured a pistol from Phillip's mother's nightstand and had robbed a local convenience store?

12.3 Using your state, how is the juvenile justice system administered? How are juveniles processed in your county? How does this processing differ from your state to the next?

12.4 As noted in the text, there are a growing number of juveniles participating in gangs or pseudo-gangs in communities. Using your community, are there any indicators of gang or pseudo-gang involvement? Describe. What efforts are members of the local community making to reduce the appeal of gang membership or participation? To answer this question, you may need to interview a local law enforcement officer, someone from the juvenile probation department, or other juvenile court personnel.

STUDENT STUDY GUIDE PRACTICE QUESTIONS

True or False

12.1 Female juveniles typically participate in gangs for the same reasons as their male counterparts, i.e., a sense of belonging.

12.2 Juveniles have all the same constitutional rights guaranteed to adults.

12.3 The U.S. Supreme Court has ruled that courts do not have the right to preventively detain juveniles for the safety of themselves and society.

12.4 Studies demonstrate that minorities are disproportionately represented in the juvenile justice system.

12.5 In 2005, 10 percent of all juvenile cases were waived to the adult court system.

12.6 The Illinois Sex Offender Registration Act outlines the legal guidelines providing for sex offender registries for juveniles.

12.7 The purpose of the cottage system for juvenile offenders was to ensure that youth resided in a location where education would be the key focal point of reformation.

12.8 The least physically secure facilities are known as training schools.

12.9 Between 1969 and 1973, Jerome G. Miller closed down the state of Missouri's juvenile institutions, placing juveniles in community-based facilities.

12.10 The U.S. Supreme Court has ruled it unconstitutional to execute any person under the age of 18.

Multiple Choice

12.11 In England the _____ courts were established for the purpose of avoiding the harshness of the strict technicalities of the English common law.

a trial
b appellate
c justice
d equity

12.12 _____ was interpreted in England to mean that the sovereign had the responsibility to oversee any children in the kingdom who might be neglected or abused.

a Juvenile law
b Royal obligation
c *Parens patriae*
d Juvenile delinquency

12.13 Which of the following cities is considered to be the murder capital of the United States?

a Chicago
b Los Angeles
c Miami
d Las Vegas

12.14 _____, decided in 1966, is important because it signaled the beginning of the movement to infuse juvenile court proceedings with some due process elements.

a *In re Gault*
b *In re Winship*
c *McKeiver v. Pennsylvania*
d *Kent v. United States*

12.15 Identify the first juvenile case from a state court to be heard by the U.S. Supreme Court.

a *In re Gault*
b *In re Winship*
c *McKeiver v. Pennsylvania*
d *Kent v. United States*

12.16 In 1975 in ______, the U.S. Supreme Court held that the constitutional provision that defendants may not be tried twice for the same offense applies to juveniles.

a *In re Gault*
b *Breed v. Jones*
c *McKeiver v. Pennsylvania*
d *Kent v. United States*

12.17 In 1993, the U.S. Court of Appeals for the Fifth Circuit upheld the ______, emphasizing that the ordinance was narrowly tailored to further the city's compelling interest in reducing and preventing juvenile crime and victimization.

a San Diego ordinance
b Sumner curfew
c Dallas ordinance
d Charlottesville curfew

12.18 ______ means that the juvenile court waives jurisdiction; the case is transferred from the juvenile court to the adult criminal court; or the juvenile court certifies that the juvenile should be tried as an adult.

a Diversion
b Waiver
c Certification
d Deinstitutionalization

12.19 Identify the program designed for runaways and their families.

a Probation
b Respite care
c Aftercare
d Confinement

12.20 Which movement began with an emphasis on probation, foster homes, and community treatment centers for juveniles?

a Diversion
b Community corrections
c Deinstitutionalization
d Certification

Fill-in-the-Blank

12.21 The processing of juveniles through the juvenile court system differs not only in purpose but in vocabulary. For example, instead of finding a youth guilty in juvenile court they are ______.

12.22 Theoretically, ______ does not refer to children processed through juvenile courts because they are in need of supervision, because they are dependent or neglected, or because they are abused.

12.23 If a decision is made to detain a juvenile, that individual is taken to ______.

12.24 Warnings and reprimands are examples of ______.

12.25 ______ in juvenile courts are similar to those in adult criminal courts: restitution, fine, community service, suspended disposition, or community supervision.

12.26 A(n) ______, also called ______, means that the juvenile court waives jurisdiction, the case is transferred from the juvenile court to the adult criminal court, or the juvenile court certifies that the juvenile should be tried as an adult.

12.27 A variation of the adult drug courts used for juveniles is known as a(n) ______.

12.28 The process of diverting youth out of institutions and into community-based correctional alternatives is known as ______.

12.29 When juveniles in custody are released from institutions and placed on parole, this is usually called ______.

12.30 ______ care is designed for runaways and their families to give them an opportunity to get a break from one another.

CROSSWORD

ACROSS

3 The court having jurisdiction over juveniles who are accused of delinquent acts or offenses or criminal acts or who are in need of supervision because they are being neglected or mistreated by their parents or guardians. (2 words, 1 space)

4 Facilities for the temporary confinement of juveniles in custody who are awaiting court disposition. (2 words, 1 space)

7 Literally, "parent of the country." (2 words, 1 space)

9 A formal document for filing an action in juvenile court, in contrast to a grand jury indictment or prosecutor's presentment in the criminal court.

11 The final decision of a court in a criminal proceeding to accept a guilty plea, to find the defendant guilty or not guilty, or to terminate the proceedings against the defendant.

12 In prosecution, the first review of a case by an official in the prosecutor's office. (2 words, 1 space)

13 The process of decision making by a court; normally used to refer to juvenile proceedings.

14 A young person under age for certain privileges, such as voting or drinking alcoholic beverages.

DOWN

1 The continued supervision of juveniles after they are released from a correctional facility.

2 A person under legal age whom a juvenile court has determined to be incorrigible or in violation of a criminal statute. (2 words, 1 space)

5 A class of crime that does not consist of proscribed action or inaction but, rather, of the personal condition or characteristic of the accused – for example, being a vagrant. (2 words, 1 space)

6 A secure corrections facility to which juveniles are confined by court order. (2 words, 1 space)

8 The process used to remove juveniles from the jurisdiction of the juvenile court to that of the adult criminal court; also called transfer or waiver.

10 Antisocial or illegal behavior (especially of juveniles).

WORD SEARCH

```
o t t e e n e u n v e s i y i p a s
n e s t e n n d a e t s n t n o d i
e s l c t r p e t i t i o n d e j j
t n e u q n i l e d e l i n e v u j
e e j u v e n i l e c o u r t v d q
a f o i a a o n o p i f t s e i i s
i f o d e a i q c i r s l n n e c s
r o n n e h t u h s v e i a t t a s
t s v v i i a e s i r l f d i l t o
a u s e e q c n c d e t i t o j i o
p t n o i s i c e d e k a t n i o c
s a p a p c f y q r j t i i c s n e
n t i i o l i i c s c u e d e v g i
e s s o n l t a n n i e u n n v i n
r e u l a o r d i s p o s i t i o n
a o u c u e e a i i t p a n e i l d
p i l o o h c s g n i n i a r t o t
e p i u o j i n i a t c u e s r c n
```

adjudication
delinquency
disposition
juvenile court
petition

aftercare
detention
intake decision
juvenile delinquent
status offense

certification
detention centers
juvenile
parens patriae
training school

ANSWERS TO CROSSWORD

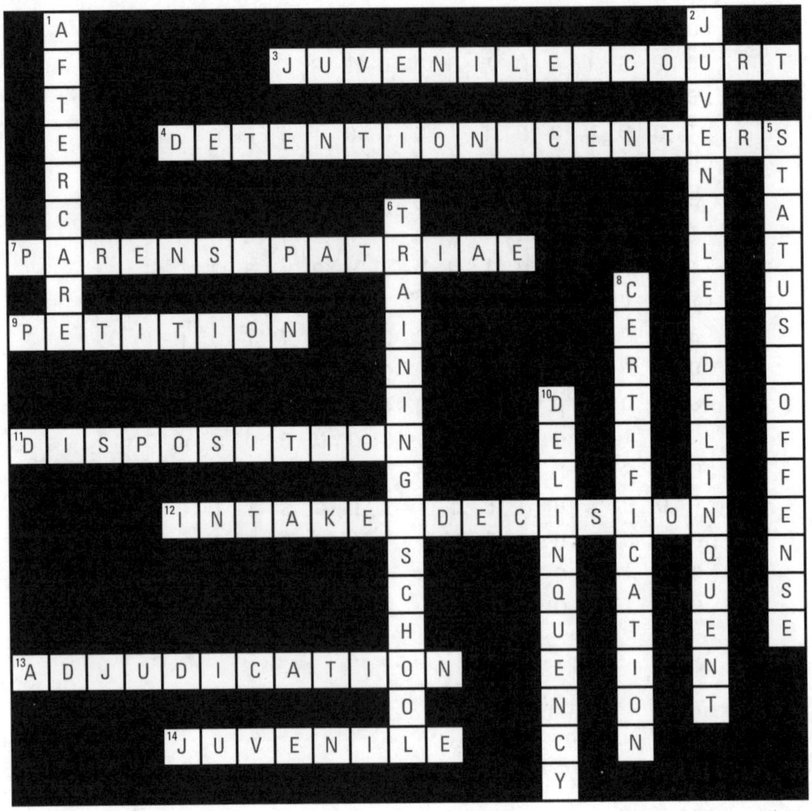

ACROSS

3 The court having jurisdiction over juveniles who are accused of delinquent acts or offenses or criminal acts or who are in need of supervision because they are being neglected or mistreated by their parents or guardians. (2 words, 1 space)
4 Facilities for the temporary confinement of juveniles in custody who are awaiting court disposition. (2 words, 1 space)
7 Literally, "parent of the country." (2 words, 1 space)
9 A formal document for filing an action in juvenile court, in contrast to a grand jury indictment or prosecutor's presentment in the criminal court.
11 The final decision of a court in a criminal proceeding to accept a guilty plea, to find the defendant guilty or not guilty, or to terminate the proceedings against the defendant.
12 In prosecution, the first review of a case by an official in the prosecutor's office. (2 words, 1 space)
13 The process of decision making by a court; normally used to refer to juvenile proceedings.
14 A young person under age for certain privileges, such as voting or drinking alcoholic beverages.

DOWN

1 The continued supervision of juveniles after they are released from a correctional facility.
2 A person under legal age whom a juvenile court has determined to be incorrigible or in violation of a criminal statute. (2 words, 1 space)
5 A class of crime that does not consist of proscribed action or inaction but, rather, of the personal condition or characteristic of the accused – for example, being a vagrant. (2 words, 1 space)
6 A secure corrections facility to which juveniles are confined by court order. (2 words, 1 space)
8 The process used to remove juveniles from the jurisdiction of the juvenile court to that of the adult criminal court; also called transfer or waiver.
10 Antisocial or illegal behavior (especially of juveniles).

ANSWERS TO WORD SEARCH

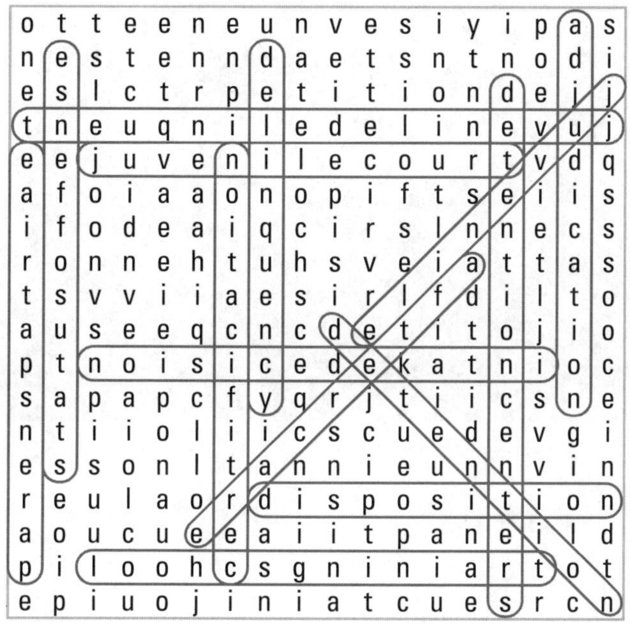

adjudication
delinquency
disposition
juvenile court
petition

aftercare
detention
intake decision
juvenile delinquent
status offense

certification
detention centers
juvenile
parens patriae
training school

A SWERS TO THE Q ESTIONS

CHAPTER 1

True or False

1.1 True – *Rationale*: The criminal justice system was designed to prevent people from violating its rules and to sanction, or impose legal punishment on, those who do.
The Nature and Philosophical Bases of Punishment (p. 5)

1.2 True – *Rationale*: General deterrence is one variation of deterrence. The premise is to punish an individual as a mechanism for preventing future criminal acts by the general public by using the individual as an example.
The Nature and Philosophical Bases of Punishment (p. 9)

1.3 False – *Rationale*: Similar to general deterrence, this form of punishment seeks only to prevent future criminal acts of the individual.
The Nature and Philosophical Bases of Punishment (p. 9)

1.4 True – *Rationale*: A case enters the system either upon being reported to the police or when police observe behavior that appears to be criminal.
Components of Criminal Justice Systems (p. 11)

1.5 True – *Rationale*: If a suspect pleads guilty to an offense, they go directly to the sentencing phase of the criminal justice process.
Components of Criminal Justice Systems (p. 12)

1.6 False – *Rationale*: Any attempted activity or behavior that could be classified as criminal constitutes a crime.
The Concept of Crime (p. 17)

1.7 False – *Rationale*: The Communications Decency Act was passed in 1996.
The Reach of Criminal Law (p. 23)

Criminal Justice Essentials: Study Guide, Ninth Edition. Shannon Barton-Bellessa.

1.8 False – *Rationale*: Due process rights are found in the Fourteenth Amendment to the U.S. Constitution.
Criminal Law: An Overview (p. 14)

1.9 True – *Rationale*: The equal protection clause of the Fourteenth Amendment does mean that, in general, the government may not infringe on the rights of persons solely because of characteristics such as race, age, national origin, ethnicity, religion, or gender.
Criminal Law: An Overview (pp. 14–15)

1.10 False – *Rationale*: Procedural laws define the procedures that are appropriate for law enforcement. Substantive laws define the elements that are necessary for an act to constitute a violation of the civil or criminal law.
Sources of Criminal Law (p. 16)

Multiple Choice

1.11 a Rehabilitation
Rationale: Rehabilitation, also known as the rehabilitative ideal, is based on the premise that human behavior is the result of antecedent causes that may be known by objective analysis and that permit scientific control.
The Nature and Philosophical Bases of Punishment (p. 8)

1.12 b Deterrence
Rationale: The philosophy of deterrence assumes that offenders are free-will thinkers and therefore have the ability to weigh the costs of the crime with the benefits gained from its commission. Therefore, violations of the stated law and its requisite punishment are based upon the offense and the harm caused to society rather than the motivation of the offender.
The Nature and Philosophical Bases of Punishment (p. 9)

1.13 b Discretion
Rationale: The process of using your own judgment is the definition of discretion.
The Role of Discretion in Punishment (p. 10)

1.14 d All of the above
Rationale: All actors in the criminal justice system are allowed to use discretion in their roles within the process. The amount of discretion may be determined and controlled by law but will never be eliminated.
The Role of Discretion in Punishment (p. 10)

1.15 c A legal process that provides the basis for the actions that take place in the criminal justice systems
Rationale: Criminal law is defined as a legal process that provides the basis for the actions that take place in the criminal justice system.
Criminal Law: An Overview (p. 12)

1.16 a Procedural law
Rationale: Statutes define the procedures that are appropriate for law enforcement. These are called procedural laws.
Sources of Criminal Law (p. 16)

1.17 **b** *Mala prohibita*
Rationale: *Mala prohibita* refers to acts that are not universally regarded as criminal; they are criminal because the legislature has designated them as crime. Violations of laws regulating the private, consensual sexual conduct of adults, the use of some drugs, and the use of alcohol by certain age groups are examples of *mala prohibita* crimes.
The Concept of Crime (**p. 17**)

1.18 **c** Adversary
Rationale: The adversary approach assumes that the accused are innocent.
Criminal Law: An Overview (**pp. 13–14**)

1.19 **a** Inquisitory
Rationale: The inquisitory approach focuses on the conviction rather than on the process by which that conviction is secured.
Criminal Law: An Overview (**p. 14**)

1.20 **b** legal duty
Rationale: Failure to act may also constitute a crime but only when a person has a legal duty to act.
The Concept of Crime (**p. 17**)

Fill-in-the-Blank

1.21 Crime

1.22 Misdemeanors

1.23 Felonies

1.24 *Mala in se*

1.25 *Mala prohibita*

1.26 euthanasia

1.27 just deserts

1.28 attendant circumstances

1.29 agreement

1.30 act; intent

CHAPTER 2

True or False

2.1 True – *Rationale*: The FBI data revealed that both violent and property crimes had continued to decrease.
Crime, Offenders, and Victims Introduction (**p. 32**)

2.2 True – *Rationale*: The *Uniform Crime Reports* are crimes reported to the police and the National Crime Victimization Surveys are surveys conducted of 50,000

households in the United States asking for reported victimizations of persons occupying the home.
Sources of Crime Data (p. 33)

2.3 False – *Rationale*: The *Uniform Crime Reports* consist of data collected by the Federal Bureau of Investigation (FBI).
Sources of Crime Data (p. 34)

2.4 False – *Rationale*: Violent crimes are more likely to be cleared by arrest than property crimes.
Sources of Crime Data (p. 35)

2.5 True – *Rationale*: In 2009, 69.1 percent of arrestees were white, 74.7 percent were male, and 85.9 percent were over the age of 18.
Crime and Offenders (pp. 44–5)

2.6 True – *Rationale*: There were 4.3 million violent and 15.6 million property crime victimizations reported in 2009.
Crime Victims (p. 49)

2.7 False – *Rationale*: In June 2010, the Kentucky Supreme Court held that it was unconstitutional under that state's law to prosecute a pregnant woman for wanton endangerment in the first degree because she ingested drugs during her pregnancy.
Crime Victims (p. 50)

2.8 False – *Rationale* Persons from lower-income households suffer more property crimes than those in higher-income households.
Crime Victims (p. 52)

2.9 True – *Rationale*: Women on college campuses are more likely to become victims of rape relative to women in the general population, therefore increasing their levels of fear of personal violence more so than others.
Fear of Crime and Citizens' Reactions (p. 54)

2.10 True – *Rationale*: This was the largest terrorist attack to that date in the U.S. This has since been exceeded by the attacks of September 11, 2011, which killed approximately 3,000.
Special Focus on Specific Crimes (p. 59)

Multiple Choice

2.11 d The FBI requires that only senior officer arrests can be included in the *UCR* data.
Rationale: The department may choose which offenses meet the criteria for inclusion but these decisions are not based upon seniority of the officers.
Sources of Crime Data (p. 36)

2.12 b Arson
Rationale: Arson was added to the Uniform Crime Reporting system in 1979 and referred to the crime index as the modified crime index.
Sources of Crime Data (p. 41)

2.13 d 46
Rationale: The NIBRS system collects information on 46 different offenses, including the characteristics of victims and offenders, the circumstances in which the alleged

offenses were committed, and the consequences that the alleged crime had for the victim(s).
Sources of Crime Data (p. 37)

2.14 **c** Burglary
Rationale: Burglary is a property crime. Aggravated assault is the fourth violent crime.
Crime and Offenders (pp. 39–40)

2.15 **a** The dark figure of crime
Rationale: The dark figure of crime refers to crimes that are unreported to the police.
Sources of Crime Data (p. 37)

2.16 **d** All are criticisms of self-report studies
Rationale: Self-report studies typically ask respondents to report minor offenses; are conducted on school-aged youth who may not be able to correctly define delinquent/criminal behavior; and often do not include a good representation of minority respondents.
Sources of Crime Data (p. 37)

2.17 **b** 12- to 19-year-olds
Rationale: 12- to 19-year-olds are most likely to be victims of crime, while persons aged 50 and older are least likely to be victims of crime.
Crime Victims (p. 50)

2.18 **c** South Carolina
Rationale: Fifteen states have considered legislation on the issue of charging a pregnant woman with child endangerment after she and her child test positive for drugs, but only South Carolina has enacted a statute that provides for a charge of homicide by child abuse against a pregnant woman whose act or omission causes the death of a fetus.
Crime Victims (p. 50)

2.19 **b** fear of violent crime by strangers
Rationale: The fear of violent crime by strangers, who often pick their victims randomly, led U.S. Supreme Court Chief Justice Warren E. Burger to refer in 1981 to the "reign of terror in American cities."
Fear of Crime and Citizens' Reactions (p. 53)

2.20 **a** Larceny-theft
Rationale: Larceny-theft is classified as a Part I Index Offense and not as a white-collar crime.
Special Focus on Specific Crimes (p. 58)

Fill-in-the-Blank

2.21 Clearance rate

2.22 The dark figure of crime

2.23 Cybercrime

2.24 Stalking

2.25 victim precipitation

2.26 Victims of Crime Act (VOCA)

2.27 Victim compensation programs

2.28 Fetal abuse

2.29 Baby Moses

2.30 white-collar

CHAPTER 3

True or False

3.1 False – *Rationale*: The watch system was the immediate forerunner of modern police systems.
The History of Policing (p. 73)

3.2 True – *Rationale*: The first modern police force, the Metropolitan Police, was founded in London by Sir Robert Peel in 1829.
The History of Policing (p. 74)

3.3 False – *Rationale*: The United States did develop a decentralized form of policing, but this was different from European countries, whose systems tended to be centralized.
The History of Policing (p. 74)

3.4 True – *Rationale*: The majority of law enforcement in the United States is done at the local level. The majority of these agencies are located in small towns, villages, or boroughs.
Decentralized Policing: U.S. Systems (p. 77)

3.5 False – *Rationale*: Most sheriffs are elected officials.
Decentralized Policing: U.S. Systems (p. 79)

3.6 False – *Rationale*: The United States Constitution does not provide for a central police agency.
Decentralized Policing: U.S. Systems (p. 81)

3.7 False – *Rationale*: The FBI is the primary governmental agency charged with enforcing all federal laws not assigned to other special agencies.
Decentralized Policing: U.S. Systems (p. 82)

3.8 True – *Rationale*: The Department of Homeland Security is a presidential cabinet level agency that combines 22 former federal agencies.
Decentralized Policing: U.S. Systems (p. 86)

3.9 False – *Rationale*: During the 2004/5 school year, almost 93 percent of public colleges and universities had sworn officers, compared to only 42 percent of private campuses.
Decentralized Policing: U.S. Systems (p. 91)

3.10 True – *Rationale*: The use of private security forces has increased substantially worldwide. One form of private security is the proprietary system, in which organizations or individuals have their own private investigators and security personnel.
Private Police and Security Forces (p. 92)

Multiple Choice

3.11 b The appointment of a constable
Rationale: An unpaid constable was appointed during the 12th century to take care of the weapons and the equipment of the hundred, as well as for keeping the peace by enforcing laws.
The History of Policing (p. 72)

3.12 a The Bow Street Runners were constables who were given police investigation and arrest powers.
Rationale: Bow Street Runners were constables hired by John and Henry Fielding to investigate crimes and arrest perpetrators. The Bow Street Runners were paid a portion of the fine upon successful prosecution.
The History of Policing (p. 73)

3.13 c Territories, and they reported to a central government.
Rationale: Sir Robert Peel founded the first full-time police officers known as the Peelers or Bobbies after their founder. They were organized by territories, and they reported to a central government.
The History of Policing (p. 74)

3.14 a First state-supported police organization in the United States
Rationale: The Texas Rangers became the first state-supported police organization in the United States in 1835.
Decentralized Policing: U.S. Systems (p. 80)

3.15 d All of the above
Rationale: The U.S. Department of Justice is responsible for overseeing the U.S. Marshals, the ATF, the DEA, and the Federal Bureau of Investigation (FBI).
Decentralized Policing: U.S. Systems (pp. 81–2)

3.16 a August Vollmer
Rationale: August Vollmer is often regarded as the father of modern policing.
The Organization, Administration, and Management of Police Systems (p. 94)

3.17 b Professional policing model
Rationale: The professional model of policing emphasizes a hierarchical structure with the police chief as the central authority and all subordinates in each unit reporting directly to their division heads, who report to the police chief.
The Organization, Administration, and Management of Police Systems (p. 95)

3.18 c Problem-oriented policing
Rationale: In problem-oriented policing the emphasis is on solving problems. Power comes from the ability of employees to succeed in that goal, not from the titles of their positions. The focus of this model is on problems not on incidents.
The Organization, Administration, and Management of Police Systems (p. 96)

3.19 c broken windows thesis
Rationale: The broken windows thesis embodies the belief that minor offenders who disrupt the quality of life should be controlled, thus making neighborhoods safer, resulting in a reduction of fear and of crime.
The Organization, Administration, and Management of Police Systems (p. 97)

3.20 a Community policing model
Rationale: Community policing is a form of problem-oriented policing that emphasizes the sharing of information, enhancement of community safety, and the reduction in crime through the use of foot patrols.
The Organization, Administration, and Management of Police Systems (p. 98)

Fill-in-the-Blank

3.21 frankpledge

3.22 sheriff

3.23 posse

3.24 J. Edgar Hoover

3.25 INTERPOL

3.26 professional

3.27 authoritarian

3.28 Problem-oriented policing

3.29 foot patrol

3.30 COMPSTAT

CHAPTER 4

True or False

4.1 True – *Rationale:* Good policing does require intelligence and the ability to think independently, to perform different roles and functions, to comprehend and accept other cultures and subcultures, and to understand the importance of freedom and the dangers of abusing authority.
Preparing for Policing (p. 106)

4.2 False – *Rationale*: The success of efforts to recruit persons with high moral and ethical standards into policing and to encourage them to maintain those standards may be analyzed in terms of the subsequent behavior of recruits.
Preparing for Policing (p. 107)

4.3 False – *Rationale*: In 2007, the Bureau of Justice Statistics reported that 16 percent of officers were employed by departments that required some college education, and only 9 percent were in departments that required a two-year degree for recruits.
Preparing for Policing (p. 109)

4.4 False – *Rationale*: A 2007 publication by the RAND Corporation concluded that most police stops in New York City the previous year did not constitute widespread evidence of racial profiling, despite the fact that nonwhites were disproportionately stopped and frisked.
Law Enforcement (p. 122)

4.5 True – *Rationale*: Officers are able to conduct some searches and seizures without a warrant subsequent to arrest: when a person is booked into jail; routine searches at the border; fixed checkpoints for drugs and/or alcohol; and exigent circumstances.
Law Enforcement (p. 129)

4.6 False – *Rationale*: Persons arrested without a warrant are entitled to prompt judicial determination of whether probable cause existed. The U.S. Supreme Court has interpreted prompt to mean 48 hours under most circumstances.
Law Enforcement (p. 130)

4.7 True – *Rationale*: In the 2009 case of *Arizona v. Gant* the U.S. Supreme Court retracted its position regarding a warrantless vehicle search incident to an arrest stating that the 1981 case too broadly defined search incident to arrest.
Law Enforcement (p. 135)

4.8 False – *Rationale*: In the case of *Illinois v. Caballes*, the U.S. Supreme Court ruled that a well-trained narcotics-detection dog used to sniff only the outside of the vehicle during a legitimate traffic stop is permitted by the Fourth Amendment.
Law Enforcement (p. 137)

4.9 True – *Rationale*: In the 1949 U.S. Supreme Court case of *Rochin v. California*, the concept of shocking the conscience was introduced. This term has since been revised and now the U.S. Supreme Court uses the objective test based on the Fourth Amendment to determine whether body cavity searches are legal.
Law Enforcement (p. 137)

4.10 True – *Rationale*: *Miranda* warnings apply only to custodial interrogations.
Law Enforcement (p. 144)

Multiple Choice

4.11 d All are criticisms of requiring higher education for law enforcement officers.
Rationale: Those who do not favor college education for police cite four reasons: raising educational requirements might discriminate against minority applicants; the applicant pool may be too small; unions are opposed to higher educational requirements; and criminal justice programs that place too much emphasis on technical skills at the expense of a broad educational background have come under attack.
Preparing for Policing (p. 109)

4.12 b It is not permissible to use ethnicity as a fact in deciding whether to stop an individual suspected of a crime.
Rationale: In 2000 case of *United States v. Montero-Camargo*, the Ninth Circuit Court of Appeals upheld that it is not permissible to use ethnicity as a fact in deciding whether to stop an individual suspected of a crime. The U.S. Supreme Court refused to hear the case so it was permitted to stand.
Law Enforcement (p. 123)

4.13 c Police may not use a vague statute for purposes of stopping, questioning, and otherwise harassing individuals but they may stop and question individuals.
Rationale: The U.S. Supreme Court ruled that police may not use a vague statute for purposes of stopping, questioning, and otherwise harassing individuals but that they may stop and question individuals.
Law Enforcement (p. 124)

4.14 **d** It is constitutional for the police to establish "information-seeking checkpoints" in their efforts to combat crime.
Rationale: In 2003, the U.S. Supreme Court ruled in *Illinois v. Lidster* that it is constitutional for the police to establish "information-seeking checkpoints" in their efforts to combat crime.
Law Enforcement (p. 121)

4.15 **a** The "totality of circumstances" gives legal permission to officers to stop and frisk an individual based upon experience and safety of the community.
Rationale: In *Terry v. Ohio*, the U.S. Supreme Court emphasized that even brief detention of a person without probable cause for an arrest is a seizure of that person. Further, the U.S. Supreme Court looked at the totality of the circumstances, holding that if, during the pat down search, the police feel an object that might be a weapon, they may continue the search until they are satisfied that it is not a weapon.
Law Enforcement (p. 125)

4.16 **c** First, the initial stop must be lawful and, second, to conduct a frisk, the officer must have reason to believe that the suspect is armed and dangerous.
Rationale: In the 2009 decision of *Arizona v. Johnson*, the U.S. Supreme Court upheld the pat down search based on *Terry v. Ohio* stating that two conditions must occur before such searches do not constitute an unreasonable search and seizure. First, the initial stop must be lawful and, second, to conduct a frisk, the officer must have reason to believe that the suspect is armed and dangerous.
Law Enforcement (pp. 126–7)

4.17 **b** Fourth Amendment
Rationale: The Fourth Amendment to the U.S. Constitution prohibits unreasonable search and seizure.
Law Enforcement (p. 127)

4.18 **a** Extended the use of the exclusionary rule to all 50 states, ensuring that individuals were guaranteed the Fourth Amendment protections against flagrant abuse and that individuals did have the right to privacy free from unreasonable state intrusion.
Rationale: In *Mapp v. Ohio* (1961) the U.S. Supreme Court extended the use of the exclusionary rule to all 50 states ensuring that individuals were guaranteed the Fourth Amendment protections again flagrant abuse and that individuals did have the right to privacy free from unreasonable state intrusion.
Law Enforcement (p. 131)

4.19 **d** An individual does have the right to be advised by his lawyer of his privilege against self-incrimination.
Rationale: In 1964, the U.S. Supreme Court in *Escobedo v. Illinois* ruled that an individual has a right to be advised by his lawyer of his privilege against self-incrimination.
Law Enforcement (p. 138)

4.20 **c** A suspect has this right prior to custodial interrogation.
Rationale: In 1966, the U.S. Supreme Court ruled in *Miranda v. Arizona* that prior to custodial interrogation a suspect has the right to have their Fifth Amendment rights read to them and to voluntarily and knowingly not speak to authorities without the presence of an attorney.
Law Enforcement (p. 142)

Fill-in-the-Blank

4.21 Extralegal

4.22 driving while black

4.23 frisk

4.24 plain feel doctrine

4.25 Probable cause

4.26 anticipatory search warrant

4.27 plain view doctrine

4.28 Alimentary canal smuggling

4.29 Fingerprinting

4.30 DNA genetic fingerprinting

CHAPTER 5

True or False

5.1 False – *Rationale*: In a classic 1966 study conducted by James Q. Wilson, he found that the majority of calls to law enforcement officers were for service-related functions.
Dilemmas in Policing (p. 157)

5.2 False – *Rationale*: The wide discretion police have in law enforcement may create political problems.
Dilemmas in Policing (p. 157)

5.3 False – *Rationale*: Most police work is reactive not proactive.
Dilemmas in Policing (p. 159)

5.4 True – *Rationale*: Evidence suggests that law enforcement officers in communities with mandatory arrest policies are more likely to arrest and detain females than males.
Dilemmas in Policing (p. 161)

5.5 True – *Rationale*: A little over a month after the 9/11 terrorist attacks, officials expressed concern that the diversion of FBI agents to counterterrorism task forces and a de-emphasis on drug-related offenses and bank robberies placed increasing pressure on local departments to provide law enforcement in these areas.
Dilemmas in Policing (p. 165)

5.6 True – *Rationale*: The Mollen Commission coined a new word, *testilying*, to characterize the pervasive falsifications they found by police in New York City..
Police Misconduct (p. 168)

5.7 False – *Rationale*: Law enforcement officers are at a higher risk of workplace violence than other types of employee.
Violence and the Police (p. 177)

5.8 True – *Rationale*: Police departments should enforce their written policies actively and fairly. If officers believe that they will not be reprimanded for violating departmental policies, those policies may be ineffective in curbing police abuse of discretion.
The Control of Policing (pp. 177–8)

5.9 True – *Rationale*: These lower court decisions are permitted because they result in enlarging, not reducing defendants' rights.
The Control of Policing (p. 180)

5.10 True – *Rationale*: In 1989 the U.S. Supreme Court ruled in the case of *City of Canton, Ohio v. Harris* that inadequate police training may result in civil liability of the municipality under which the police department operates.
The Control of Policing (p. 183)

Multiple Choice

5.11 d When officers made an arrest, subsequent calls for domestic violence were reduced.
Rationale: In the Minneapolis Domestic Violence Experiment, investigators concluded that arrest was the most effective of three standard methods police use to reduce domestic violence. This study is considered one of the most notable on domestic violence response by officers.
Dilemmas in Policing (p. 160)

5.12 a Empathetic
Rationale: Earlier studies suggested that police were a homogeneous group who formed subcultures and manifested a distinct personality. They were said to be authoritarian, cynical, punitive, rigid, physically aggressive, assertive, and impulsive risk takers.
The Police Subculture (p. 166)

5.13 a Watchman style
Rationale: According to Wilson, most police corruption is found in department characterized by the watchman style of policing, in which police are expected to maintain order, not regulate conduct.
Police Misconduct (p. 167)

5.14 d Widespread evidence that officers participated in organized crime, payoffs or traffic citations, and acceptance of money for overlooking violations of licensing ordinance.
Rationale: In 1970, in response to allegations of corruption in New York City, Mayor John V. Lindsay issued an executive order establishing the Knapp Commission to study corruption.
Police Misconduct (p. 168)

5.15 a This rule articulates when it is lawful for an officer to use deadly force to apprehend a suspect.
Rationale: In *Tennessee v. Garner*, the U.S. Supreme Court emphasized that, to be lawful, police use of deadly force must be reasonable.
Violence and the Police (p. 173)

5.16 c 56
Rationale: Preliminary data from 2010 reveal that 56 law enforcement officers were killed in the line of duty, with these specifics accounting for most of the deaths: 15 deaths were by ambush; 8 while investigating suspicious circumstances of persons; 7 during traffic pursuits/stops; 6 responding to disturbance calls (4 of which involved domestic violence); 6 while investigating or interrupting robberies; 3 while investigating burglaries or pursuing burglars; and 3 during tactical situations (e.g. hostage taking).
Violence and the Police (p. 177)

5.17 b Exclusionary rule
Rationale: According to the exclusionary rule, if police seize evidence illegally or secure confessions improperly, the evidence may be excluded from trial.
The Control of Policing (p. 179)

5.18 c Good faith exception
Rationale: The good faith exception allows for illegally obtained evidence to be presented at trial if it can be shown that police had a reasonable belief that they were acting in accordance with the law.
The Control of Policing (p. 179)

5.19 a Inevitable discovery
Rationale: Illegally seized evidence can be admitted at trial if it can be shown that, eventually, the evidence would have been discovered by legal methods.
The Control of Policing (p. 180)

5.20 d 11.8% (women); 25.3% (racial and ethnic minorities)
Rationale: In the latest available published data by the BJS, women represented 11.8 percent of all local officers, while racial and ethnic minorities accounted for 25.3 percent.
Affirmative Action Recruitment and Hiring (p. 187)

Fill-in-the-Blank

5.21 domestic violence

5.22 mandatory arrest

5.23 stress reduction

5.24 subculture

5.25 blue code of silence

5.26 deadly force

5.27 fleeing felon

5.28 early warning system

5.29 harmful error

5.30 1983 actions

CHAPTER 6

True or False

6.1 False – *Rationale*: Trial courts try the facts of the case, and appellate courts are concerned only with law.
The Judicial Branch of Government (p. 200)

6.2 True – *Rationale*: The decision of one federal court of appeals is not binding on another federal appellate court. If federal circuit courts decide similar cases differently, the resulting conflict may be resolved only by the U.S. Supreme Court, the final appellate court in the federal system, which may or may not choose to resolve the issues.
The Dual Court System (p. 205)

6.3 False – *Rationale*: The U.S. Supreme Court is the only specific court established by the federal Constitution, which designates a few cases in which the Supreme Court has original jurisdiction.
The Dual Court System (p. 205)

6.4 True – *Rationale*: At trial, judges do essentially serve as the referees. Theoretically, they are neither for nor against a particular position or issue, but, rather, are committed to the fair implementation of the rules of evidence and law.
Judges in Criminal Court Systems (p. 209)

6.5 False – *Rationale*: It is the responsibility of the trial court judge to determine whether the offered expert is qualified to testify about that evidence and whether the proposed evidence is acceptable.
Judges in Criminal Court Systems (p. 209)

6.6 False – *Rationale*: In an effort to avoid public pressure on judicial decision making, federal judges, along with U.S. Supreme Court Justices, are appointed.
Judges in Criminal Court Systems (p. 214)

6.7 True – *Rationale*: Most U.S. jurisdictions do not have required formal training for judges, but we are making progress in providing training programs for newly appointed or elected judges.
Judges in Criminal Court Systems (p. 214)

6.8 True – *Rationale*: According to a study published in 2009 entitled "A Disturbing Trend in Law School Admission," minority representation in law schools has diminished since 1993. The proportion of African Americans in 2008 entering classes for law schools across the nation was 7.5 percent less than in 1993; the proportion of Mexican Americans was 11.7 percent lower.
Judges in Criminal Court Systems (p. 216)

6.9 False – *Rationale*: Research on diversity in criminal court cases suggests that women judges vote more conservatively in criminal procedure cases and more liberally in civil rights and liberties cases than their male counterparts.
Judges in Criminal Court Systems (pp. 217–18)

6.10 True – *Rationale*: It is not easy to unseat judges, even after they have been convicted of a crime. Usually, they are asked to resign their seats but it may take months or even years to go through appropriate channels to unseat them.
Judges in Criminal Court Systems (p. 219)

Multiple Choice

6.11 **b** Original
Rationale: Original jurisdiction refers to the jurisdiction of the court that may hear a case first – that is, the court that may try the facts.
The Judicial Branch of Government (p. 199)

6.12 **d** Concurrent
Rationale: When more than one court may hear a case, those courts have concurrent jurisdiction.
The Judicial Branch of Government (p. 199)

6.13 **a** Exclusive
Rationale: When only one court may hear a case, that court has exclusive jurisdiction.
The Judicial Branch of Government (p. 199)

6.14 **c** Appellate
Rationale: Appellate jurisdiction refers to the jurisdiction of the court that may hear the case on appeal.
The Judicial Branch of Government (p. 199)

6.15 **c** 9
Rationale: Nine justices (one chief justice and 8 associate justices) sit on the U.S. Supreme Court.
The Dual Court System (p. 206)

6.16 **c** election
Rationale: Today most states use the election process for some of their judges.
Judges in Criminal Court Systems (p. 213)

6.17 **d** All are true.
Rationale: Chief Justice John Roberts of the U.S. Supreme Court made statements referencing the difficulty in a judge's tenure being eroded if the compensation were not sufficient and that the Framers' goal of an independent judiciary would be in jeopardy if there were high rates of turnover. As evidenced by the diminished salaries of judges compared to other federal employees, private practice compensation is much more lucrative.
Judges in Criminal Court Systems (pp. 214–15)

6.18 **a** The Judicial Councils Reform and Judicial Conduct and Disability Act of 1980
Rationale: At the federal level, the Judicial Councils Reform and Judicial Conduct and Disability Act of 1980 provides several sanctions: certify disability, request the judge to retire, strip the judge of his or her caseload "on a temporary basis," and censure or reprimand privately or publicly.
Judges in Criminal Court Systems (p. 219)

6.19 **d** All are problems associated with budget shortfalls
Rationale: By November 2008, 31 states faced budget shortfalls in the justice system because of shifting a number of federal cases to the state courts. Budget shortfalls lead to overcrowded jails, an increase in the backlog of cases, and an increase in court congestion.
Crisis in the Courts (pp. 221–2)

6.20 **d** Shift court cases back to federal jurisdiction
Rationale: The only option not discussed is shifting cases back to the federal level. Discussions of expanding alternatives such as pretrial continue to be considered as well.
Crisis in the Courts (p. 222)

Fill-in-the-Blank

6.21 Jurisdiction

6.22 writ of *certiorari*

6.23 recusal

6.24 acquittal

6.25 sentencing

6.26 Missouri; Missouri Plan

6.27 Merit selection

6.28 stress

6.29 California

6.30 Continuances

CHAPTER 7

True or False

7.1 False – *Rationale*: During the 17th century, the American colonies operated under a legal system without lawyers. Lawyers were so distrusted and scorned that most people handled their own cases.
Lawyers and the Legal Profession (p. 228)

7.2 True – *Rationale*: Between 1830 and 1870, Michigan and Indiana permitted any male voter of good moral character to practice law.
Lawyers and the Legal Profession (p. 228)

7.3 True – *Rationale*: Most local and state prosecutors are elected officials, although the elected prosecutor may appoint other attorneys to serve as deputy (or assistant) prosecutors within the office.
Prosecution (p. 230)

7.4 True – *Rationale*: According to the American Bar Association, the duty of the prosecuting attorney is to "seek justice, not merely to convict".
Prosecution (p. 235)

7.5 True – *Rationale*: The prosecutor in most jurisdictions has extensive discretion in deciding whether to bring formal charges against the accused. Statutes vary, but generally they have been interpreted to mean that prosecutions must be brought by prosecutors or their assistants and not that prosecutors must file charges in all crimes brought to their attention.
Prosecution (p. 235)

7.6 True – *Rationale*: The primary job of a defense attorney is to protect the defendant's legal rights and thereby preserve the adversary system.
Defense (p. 243)

7.7 False – *Rationale*: Approximately 80 percent of jail inmates and 75 percent of prison inmates are represented by court-appointed attorneys.
Defense (p. 251)

7.8 False – *Rationale*: The initial appearance is held for the purpose of having the court determine whether there is probable cause to charge the suspect with the crime.
Pretrial Procedures (p. 256)

7.9 False – *Rationale*: In theory, the grand jury serves as a check on prosecutorial discretion.
Pretrial Procedures (p. 257)

7.10 True – *Rationale*: The U.S. Constitution does not guarantee a legal right to a plea bargain. The Fifth and Fourteenth Amendments to the U.S. Constitution outline the requirements of due process. It has been interpreted by the U.S. Supreme Court that the due process clause is "not a code of ethics for prosecutors" but, rather, is concerned "with the manner in which persons are deprived of their liberty".
Pretrial Procedures (p. 264)

Multiple Choice

7.11 d Prosecution at the federal level
Rationale: The Judiciary Act of 1789 provided for prosecution at the federal level.
Prosecution (p. 231)

7.12 c Most cases go to trial.
Rationale: In rural areas, the advantages to having a rural prosecution system are numerous. Case processing tends to be more informal; caseloads are lighter; cases are handled individually; and most cases are settled by guilty pleas.
Prosecution (p. 230)

7.13 c Judicial review
Rationale: One way to control prosecutorial discretion is by the exercise of judicial review.
Prosecution (p. 241)

7.14 **a** Crime displacement
Rationale: The prosecutor's office has three primary goals in charging an individual: crime reduction; efficient use of resources in the prosecutor's office; and rehabilitation of the defendant.
Prosecution (pp. 240–1)

7.15 **d** Sixth
Rationale: The Sixth Amendment to the U.S. Constitution states that "in all criminal prosecutions, the accused shall enjoy the right…to have the Assistance of Counsel for his defense".
Defense (p. 245)

7.16 **b** Interview the client and obtain as many facts as possible.
Rationale: The first responsibility of the defense attorney is to interview the client and obtain as many facts as possible.
Defense (p. 243)

7.17 **b** *Gideon v. Wainwright*
Rationale: In 1962, the U.S. Supreme Court ruled in *Gideon v. Wainwright* that "in our adversary system of criminal justice, any person haled into court, who is too poor to hire a lawyer, cannot be assured a fair trial unless counsel is provided for him." This ruling applied the right to counsel in state felony cases.
Defense (p. 246)

7.18 **c** *Argersinger v. Hamlin*
Rationale: In the 1972 case of *Argersinger v. Hamlin*, the U.S. Supreme Court extended the right to counsel for indigent defendants to misdemeanor offenses for which a conviction might result in the "actual deprivation of a person's liberty", e.g., imprisonment.
Defense (p. 247)

7.19 **d** Eighth
Rationale: The Eighth Amendment to the U.S. Constitution prohibits requiring excessive bail. It does not guarantee the right to bail just protections against excessive bail.
Pretrial Procedures (p. 259)

7.20 **a** *United States v. Salerno*
Rationale: In the 1987 case of *United States v. Salerno*, the U.S. Supreme Court upheld the Bail Reform Act's provision of preventive detention pretrial.
Pretrial Procedures (p. 260)

Fill-in-the-Blank

7.21 prosecution

7.22 Community prosecution

7.23 information

7.24 engaged in misconduct; a criminal act

7.25 Overcharging

7.26 waiver

7.27 true bill

7.28 discovery

7.29 venue

7.30 Pretrial conferences or status conferences

CHAPTER 8

True or False

8.1 False – *Rationale*: The 1974 Speedy Trial Act applies only to federal court cases, providing that an indictment or an information charging the suspect must be filed within 30 days of the arrest or of the time when the suspect is served with a summons on the charge. That period may be extended for 30 days in a felony charge if the grand jury was not in session during that time.
Constitutional Issues at Trial (p. 276)

8.2 True – *Rationale*: The Sixth Amendment guarantees the right to a public trial, but that does not mean that the defendant may be tried by the media.
Constitutional Issues at Trial (p. 277)

8.3 False – *Rationale*: The U.S. Constitution does not specify how many jurors must be present for the defendant's right to a jury trial to be legal. Although 12 is the usual number of petit jurors, the U.S. Supreme Court has upheld the use of smaller juries in some cases.
Constitutional Issues at Trial (p. 279)

8.4 False – *Rationale*: Presentence investigations (PSIs) are conducted after a verdict of guilty is given. These documents take an inordinate amount of time to complete. Information collected is based on interviews with the defendant, family, friends, employers, or others who might have information pertinent to a sentencing decision.
Sentencing (p. 296)

8.5 True – *Rationale*: In civil cases, the standard of proof is the preponderance of evidence, e.g., 51 percent sure the defendant committed the violation. In criminal cases, the standard of proof is beyond a reasonable doubt, e.g., 99 percent sure the defendant committed the offense.
Sentencing (p. 296)

8.6 True – *Rationale*: In this case the U.S. Supreme Court overturned the *Booth v. Maryland* decision and said that Victim Impact Statements could be used in capital murder cases.
Sentencing (p. 299)

8.7 False – *Rationale*: Probation is used nearly three times as often as incarceration.
Sentencing (p. 300)

8.8 False – *Rationale*: Although not required, the federal government created a grant opportunity under the Violent Offender Incarceration and Truth in Sentencing Incentive Grants Act of 1995 that offered states grants for prison construction and

operation if they required violent offenders to serve 85 percent of their sentences before release.
Sentencing (p. 309)

8.9 True – *Rationale*: Writs of *habeas corpus*, which means "you have the body," are oftentimes used by inmates who are questioning the legality of their confinement.
Appeals and Writs (p. 310)

8.10 False – *Rationale:* The ultimate wrongful conviction is the execution of an innocent person. According to the author, 138 persons on death row have been exonerated.
Wrongful Convictions (p. 311)

Multiple Choice

8.11 c Sixth
Rationale: The right to a speedy trial is embodied in the Sixth Amendment to the U.S. Constitution.
Constitutional Issues at Trial (p. 276)

8.12 b The Speedy Trial Act applies to prosecutions in federal and state courts.
Rationale: The Speedy Trial Act applies only to prosecutions in federal courts, but most states have constitutional provisions for the right to a speedy trial.
Constitutional Issues at Trial (p. 276)

8.13 c Peremptory challenge
Rationale: A peremptory challenge is a challenge that does not require the attorney to state a reason.
Constitutional Issues at Trial (p. 280)

8.14 b Juries must be representative of the community.
Rationale: Juries must be representative of the community, but that does not mean that juries must mirror the community and reflect the various distinctive groups in the population.
Constitutional Issues at Trial (p. 280)

8.15 b Demonstrative
Rationale: Demonstrative evidence is real to the senses, in contrast to evidence presented by the testimony of other people.
The Trial Process (p. 288)

8.16 b Victim-witness
Rationale: The testimony of a victim-witness is a preferred type of testimonial evidence.
The Trial Process (p. 288)

8.17 c Hearsay evidence
Rationale: Hearsay evidence is not admissible because there is no opportunity to cross-examine the source of the information.
The Trial Process (p. 288)

8.18 b circumstantial evidence
Rationale: Much evidence is not direct; rather, it is inferred from a fact or series of facts and is called circumstantial evidence.
The Trial Process (p. 289)

8.19 a redirect
Rationale: After the defense cross-examines a prosecution witness, the prosecutor may follow with additional questions, in a process called redirect examination.
The Trial Process (**p. 289**)

8.20 d presumptive
Rationale: In presumptive sentencing the normal sentence is specified for each offense, but judges are permitted to deviate from that norm.
Sentencing (**p. 294**)

Fill-in-the-Blank

8.21 mandatory

8.22 indeterminate

8.23 Restitution

8.24 petit jury

8.25 *voir dire*

8.26 for cause; peremptory challenges

8.27 direct; circumstantial

8.28 presumption of innocence

8.29 aggravating; mitigating

8.30 concurrent; consecutive

CHAPTER 9

True or False

9.1 False – *Rationale*: The first formal prison institution in the United States codifying the principle of solitary confinement was opened in 1790 and known as the Walnut Street Jail.
The Emergence of Prisons for Punishment (**p. 324**)

9.2 True – *Rationale*: During the 1800s there were two types of prison systems that developed: the Pennsylvania, or separate, system, based on solitary confinement; and the New York, or Auburn, system, known as the silent system.
The Emergence of Prisons for Punishment (**p. 325**)

9.3 False – *Rationale*: The Auburn system of punishment was also known as the congregate system, whereby inmates worked during the day with an enforced silent system and were housed in their individual cells at night.
The Emergence of Prisons for Punishment (**p. 326**)

9.4 False – *Rationale*: The works of Captain Alexander Maconochie and Sir Walter Crofton were credited for the beginnings of a reformatory movement.
The Emergence of Prisons for Punishment (**p. 327**)

9.5 True – *Rationale*: The National Prison Association drafted 37 principles calling for changes in the correctional system that included such things as indeterminate sentences and cultivation of inmates' self-respect, inmate classification, and advancement of the philosophy of reformation rather than punishment.
The Emergence of Prisons for Punishment (p. 328)

9.6 False – *Rationale*: Although the terms "jail" and "prison" are used interchangeably and the two types of institutions have many common characteristics, they can be distinguished by their purposes. Jails and detention centers confine persons awaiting trial and are used for the short-term detention of persons in need of care when no other facilities are available immediately. Prisons are used for the incarceration of offenders who have been convicted of serious offenses, usually felonies, and who have been sentenced to lengthy terms (usually over a year) or to capital punishment.
Confinement Institutions (p. 329)

9.7 True – *Rationale*: Prison security levels are typically divided into three main categories: maximum, medium, and minimum custody. The federal government and most states have all three types.
Confinement Institutions (p. 330)

9.8 True – *Rationale*: Alcatraz Island serves as a good example of an open prison. Open prisons make use of th natural environment for security.
Confinement Institutions (p. 331)

9.9 False – *Rationale*: In 1873, the first separate prison for women, the Indiana Women's Prison was opened.
Confinement Institutions (p. 334)

9.10 True – *Rationale*: On 14 May, 1930, President Herbert Hoover signed the law that created the federal Bureau of Prisons (BOP).
Federal and State Prisons (p. 337)

Multiple Choice

9.11 c John Howard
Rationale: John Howard, an Englishman, was credited with the beginning of the penitentiary system.
The Emergence of Prisons for Punishment (p. 323)

9.12 d The Walnut Street Jail
Rationale: The Walnut Street Jail is often cited as the first U.S. prison.
The Emergence of Prisons for Punishment (p. 324)

9.13 d Uniforms for inmates
Rationale: The Walnut Street Jail and other early prisons faced serious problems. Despite the thick walls and high security, inmates escaped. To combat that problem, some wardens required inmates to wear uniforms.
The Emergence of Prisons for Punishment (p. 324)

9.14 d Work was provided for inmates in their cells.
Rationale: The Eastern Penitentiary (Pennsylvania system) was the first large-scale attempt at implementing the philosophy of solitary confinement at all times, with work provided for inmates in their cells.
The Emergence of Prisons for Punishment (p. 325)

9.15 a To restrict the sale of prison goods
Rationale: In 1929, the Hawes–Cooper Act was passed, followed in 1935 by the Ashurst–Summers Act to restrict the sale of prison goods.
The Emergence of Prisons for Punishment (p. 328)

9.16 d All of the above
Rationale: The Irish system was recognized for its emphasis on the following: (1) a reward system, (2) individual influence of the prison administrators on the inmates, (3) gradual release from restrictions, and (4) a parole system.
The Emergence of Prisons for Punishment (p. 327)

9.17 c retribution
Rationale: Rehabilitation has been replaced by an emphasis on deterrence and retribution.
Modern Prisons: An Overview (p. 329)

9.18 b Alcatraz Island
Rationale: Open prisons make use of the natural environment for security. An example is Alcatraz Island, located in San Francisco Bay.
Confinement Institutions (p. 331)

9.19 b director
Rationale: All states have correctional systems; most are centralized and headed by a director, who reports to the governor.
Federal and State Prisons (p. 338)

9.20 d Administration of punishment
Rationale: The involvement of the private sector in corrections exists in three main areas: (1) prison work programs, (2) the financing of construction, and (3) the management of facilities.
Private Correctional Facilities (p. 343)

Fill-in-the-Blank

9.21 imprisonment

9.22 silent

9.23 custody

9.24 Prisons

9.25 negative

9.26 Western Penitentiary

9.27 (1) a reward system for good behavior; (2) a small prison administrator/inmate ratio; (3) gradual release from restrictions prior to release from prison; (4) supervised parole after release and revocation and reincarceration for those who violated the strict regulations imposed on releasees

9.28 Hawes–Cooper; Ashurst–Summers

9.29 Bridewell

9.30 (1) prison work programs; (2) the financing of constructions; (3) the management of facilities

CHAPTER 10

True or False

10.1 False – *Rationale*: In the 1974 case of *Wolff v. McDonald*, the U.S. Supreme Court held that, although an incarcerated person loses some rights because of institutional needs, "a prisoner is not wholly stripped of constitutional protections when he is imprisoned for crime".
Legal Implications of Incarceration (p. 356)

10.2 True – *Rationale*: The commissary is where offenders are allowed to purchase items for personal use such a snacks, soap, etc..
The Incarceration of Offenders (p. 355)

10.3 False – *Rationale*: Prison directors are responsible for hiring and firing wardens or superintendents within their respective jurisdictions.
Prison Administration (p. 359)

10.4 False – *Rationale*: In many jurisdictions, a high-school diploma is required for entry-level officer positions.
Prison Administration (p. 365)

10.5 True – *Rationale*: In 1995, a federal court held that the U.S. Constitution does not prohibit the viewing of a male inmate by a female correctional officer.
Prison Administration (p. 365)

10.6 False – *Rationale*: Under the authoritarian regime of prison administration and management, inmate cooperation was necessary to maintain peace within institutions.
Adaptation to Prison Life (p. 369)

10.7 False – *Rationale*: More than three-fourths of all female inmates are mothers, with two-thirds having children under the age of 18.
Female Inmates (p. 371)

10.8 False – *Rationale*: For men the loss of security is the greatest problem the male inmate faces. For women, the loss of liberty and autonomy, as well as the loss of goods and services to which they are accustomed, is the major deprivation.
Female Inmates (p. 372)

10.9 True – *Rationale*: The U.S. Supreme Court in *Overton v. Bazzetta* (2003) ruled that Michigan corrections policies that limit the number of visitors inmates may receive is constitutional.
Prison Issues (p. 376)

10.10 True – *Rationale*: Research suggests that in both prisons and jails the highest rates of inmate rape occurred in overcrowded facilities that were understaffed.
Prison Issues (p. 379)

Multiple Choice

10.11 d Inmates have visitors
Rationale: Generally, inmates are not permitted to have visitors during the orientation period.
The Incarceration of Offenders (p. 355)

10.12 c hands-off doctrine
Rationale: From 1872 until the 1960s, for the most part the federal courts observed a hands-off doctrine towards inmates and prisons, reasoning that prison administration is a part of the executive, not the judicial, branch of government.
Legal Implications of Incarceration (p. 356)

10.13 b Rights; privileges
Rationale: Rights require constitutional protection; privileges are there by the grace of prison officials and may be withdrawn at their discretion.
Legal Implications of Incarceration (p. 357)

10.14 a Rights
Rationale: Rights may be restricted if prison officials can show that the restriction is necessary for security or for other recognized penological purposes, such as discipline and order.
Legal Implications of Incarceration (p. 357)

10.15 d *Estelle v. Gamble*
Rationale: In 1976 in *Estelle v. Gamble* the Court stated that allegations of "inadvertent failure to provide adequate medical care" or of a "negligent . . . diagnos[is]" do not establish the requisite state of mind for a violation of the cruel and unusual punishment clause.
Legal Implications of Incarceration (p. 357)

10.16 b *Hudson v. McMillian*
Rationale: In 1992 in *Hudson v. McMillian*, the U.S. Supreme Court held that inmates may bring actions for cruel and unusual punishment against prison officials who engage in physical force that results in injuries, even if those injuries are not significant.
Legal Implications of Incarceration (p. 359)

10.17 d Increased attention to professionalism
Rationale: The most important reform in prison administration is the increased attention to professionalism.
Prison Administration (p. 362)

10.18 c Maintain internal security and discipline
Rationale: The primary function of correctional officers is to maintain internal security and discipline.
Prison Administration (p. 362)

10.19 c Donald Clemmer
Rationale: Many of the more recent studies of prisons have been conducted as tests of Donald Clemmer's theories, the most important of which was his concept of prisonization.
Adaptation to Prison Life (p. 367)

10.20 a Mississippi; Alabama
Rationale: In the case of HIV inmates, two states – Mississippi and Alabama – isolate the infected inmates from the general population, which means those inmates are unable to participate in most prison programs.
Prison Issues (p. 382)

Fill-in-the-Blank

10.21 Correctional officers

10.22 prisonization

10.23 Stanton Wheeler

10.24 importation

10.25 resocialization; prisonization

10.26 deliberate indifference

10.27 hepatitis C

10.28 Mentally Ill Offender Treatment and Crime Reduction

10.29 grants

10.30 Attica, New York; Santa Fe, New Mexico

CHAPTER 11

True or False

11.1 False – *Rationale*: According to the National Institute of Corrections, 97 percent of all offenders will be released back into the community.
Problems of Offenders on Release (p. 408)

11.2 False – *Rationale*: Problems with work release involve the process of selecting the participants, finding sufficient jobs for them, gaining community acceptance, and ensuring that inmates do not commit crimes while they are on release.
Problems of Offenders on Release (p. 410)

11.3 True – *Rationale*: According to the research reported in the Second Chance Act, within three years after their release, two-thirds of the offenders will be arrested for additional offenses.
Focus on the Second Chance Act (p. 411)

11.4 True – *Rationale*: John Augustus is considered the father of probation in the United States.
Probation (p. 413)

11.5 True – *Rationale*: GPS was proposed in 2005 in Hillsborough County (Florida) to alleviate jail overcrowding. The sheriff estimated that the use of electronic monitoring would save about $2 million a year.
Probation (p. 416)

11.6 True – *Rationale*: Electronic monitoring as an alternative to incarceration has successfully been used with violent offenders, including sexual predators.
Probation (p. 416)

11.7 False – *Rationale*: The purpose of probation is to assist offenders in making social adjustments and in reintegrating into society as law-abiding citizens without compromising public safety.
Probation (p. 418)

11.8 True – *Rationale*: The aging prison population, along with the expense of incarcerating older inmates, especially those with medical problems, and overcrowded prisons, have led some jurisdictions to provide for medical parole for inmates who are frail, who have life threatening diseases, or, for other reasons, are near death.
Parole (p. 429)

11.9 False – *Rationale*: Although probation and parole revocation proceedings do require some of the due process rights of a criminal trial, they are not all required.
Constitutional Issues (p. 434)

11.10 True – *Rationale:* Aside from the practical problems of whether sex offender registration laws are effective are the legal issues. Some courts have ruled that the registration statutes (or portions of them) are unconstitutional, while other courts have upheld all or a portion of challenge statutes.
Sex Offender Registration Laws (p. 440)

Multiple Choice

11.11 c Halfway houses
Rationale: Halfway houses: The offender lives in a supervised environment but may leave that facility during the day to work or to participate in vocational, treatment, or educational programs.
Supervision of Offenders in the Community (p. 403)

11.12 b Florida
Rationale: Drug courts began in Miami, Florida, in 1989 and have spread to all states.
Supervision of Offenders in the Community (p. 406)

11.13 a Kentucky
Rationale: A variation of the drug court is the family drug court in Kentucky.
Supervision of Offenders in the Community (p. 406)

11.14 d California
Rationale: Under the California system, once a drug offender completes the treatment program successfully, that person's conviction is removed from the records.
Supervision of Offenders in the Community (p. 407)

11.15 d Both a and b
Rationale: Work release is referred to by other names as well: day parole, outmate program, day work, daylight parole, free labor, intermittent jailing, and work furlough.
Problems of Offenders on Release (p. 409)

11.16 d Probation
Rationale: Probation is a sentence that does not involve confinement but may involve conditions imposed by the court, usually under supervision.
Probation and Parole: An Overview (p. 412)

11.17 c periodic sentencing
Rationale: Probation may be combined with a jail term, a procedure called periodic sentencing.
Probation (p. 417)

11.18 a continuum training
Rationale: According to a suggestion by the National Institute of Corrections, officers should be trained to recognize and respond appropriately to the escalation of violence, or what the report called continuum training.
Probation (p. 422)

11.19 b fortress probation
Rationale: Probation supervisors should meet with probationers in the probationers' homes at all hours – not just regular probation office hours – a process the Reinventing Probation Council panel called fortress probation.
Probation (p. 422)

11.20 d Rehabilitation, justice, prison overcrowding.
Rationale: These are the main reasons for parole in the United States.
Parole (p. 423)

Fill-in-the-Blank

11.21 diversion

11.22 furlough

11.23 shock probation

11.24 judge

11.25 institutional

11.26 recidivists

11.27 institutional; independent authority; consolidated

11.28 Megan's

11.29 prerelease

11.30 parole

CHAPTER 12

True or False

12.1 True – *Rationale*: Female juveniles typically participate in gangs for the same reasons as male counterparts, i.e., a sense of belonging.
Youth Gangs (p. 459)

12.2 False – *Rationale*: Juveniles do not have all the same constitutional rights guaranteed to adults. They do not have the constitutional right to a trial by jury.
The Constitutional Rights of Juveniles (pp. 460–1)

12.3 False – *Rationale*: The U.S. Supreme Court ruled in *Schall v. Martin* (1984) that courts do have the right to preventively detain juveniles for the safety of themselves and society.
The Constitutional Rights of Juveniles (p. 463)

12.4 True – *Rationale*: Studies demonstrate that minorities are disproportionately represented in the juvenile justice system.
The Constitutional Rights of Juveniles (p. 466)

12.5 False – *Rationale*: In 2005, less than 1 percent of all juvenile cases were waived to the adult court system.
Juveniles in Adult Criminal Courts (p. 472)

12.6 True – *Rationale*: The Illinois Sex Offender Registration Act outlines the legal guidelines providing for sex offender registries for juveniles. Two registries exist: one for those over the age of majority (public) and one for those under the age of majority (private).
Sex Registration Laws and Juveniles (p. 477)

12.7 False – *Rationale*: The purpose of the cottage system for juvenile offenders was to ensure that youth resided in a location where hard work, especially farm work, was the key focal point of reformation.
Juveniles in Correctional Facilities (p. 480)

12.8 False – *Rationale*: The least physically secure facilities are known as group homes.
Juveniles in Correctional Facilities (p. 483)

12.9 False – *Rationale*: Between 1969 and 1973, Jerome G. Miller closed down the state of Massachusetts' juvenile institutions, placing juveniles in community-based facilities.
Juveniles in Correctional Facilities (p. 486)

12.10 False – *Rationale* The U.S. Supreme Court has ruled it is constitutional to execute persons aged 16 and 17 convicted of a capital crime.
Juveniles and Capital Punishment (p. 489)

Multiple Choice

12.11 d equity
Rationale: In England, the chancery, or equity, courts were established for the purpose of avoiding the harshness of the strict technicalities of the English common law.
Juvenile Justice Systems: An Overview (p. 451)

12.12 c *Parens patriae*
Rationale: *Parens patriae* was interpreted in England to mean that the sovereign had the responsibility to oversee any children in the kingdom who might be neglected or abused.
Juvenile Justice Systems: An Overview (p. 451)

12.13 b Los Angeles
Rationale: Los Angeles is considered the murder capital of the United States, a position in which gang murders have played a significant role.
Youth Gangs (p. 458)

12.14 d *Kent v. United States*
Rationale: *Kent v. United States*, decided in 1966, is important because it signaled the beginning of the movement to infuse juvenile court proceedings with some due process elements.
The Constitutional Rights of Juveniles (p. 461)

12.15 a *In re Gault*
Rationale: The first juvenile case from a state court to be heard by the U.S. Supreme Court was *In re Gault* (1967).
The Constitutional Rights of Juveniles (p. 461)

12.16 b *Breed v. Jones*
Rationale: In 1975 in *Breed v. Jones*, the U.S. Supreme Court held that the constitutional provision that defendants may not be tried twice for the same offense applies to juveniles.
The Constitutional Rights of Juveniles (p. 463)

12.17 c Dallas ordinance
Rationale: In 1993, the U.S. Court of Appeals for the Fifth Circuit upheld the Dallas ordinance, emphasizing that the ordinance was narrowly tailored to further the city's compelling interest in reducing and preventing juvenile crime and victimization.
The Constitutional Rights of Juveniles (p. 464)

12.18 c Certification
Rationale: Transfer or certification means that the juvenile court waives jurisdiction; the case is transferred from the juvenile court to the adult criminal court; or the juvenile court certifies that the juvenile should be tried as an adult.
Juveniles in Adult Criminal Courts (p. 472)

12.19 b Respite care
Rationale: These programs, which exist in various jurisdictions throughout the country, are designed for runaways and their families.
Juveniles in the Community (p. 488)

12.20 c Deinstitutionalization
Rationale: The deinstitutionalization movement began with an emphasis on probation, foster homes, and community treatment centers for juveniles.
Juveniles in Correctional Facilities (p. 486)

Fill-in-the-Blank

12.21 adjudicated

12.22 delinquency

12.23 intake screening

12.24 nominal dispositions

12.25 Conditional dispositions

12.26 waiver; transfer or certification

12.27 juvenile drug court

12.28 deinstitutionalization

12.29 aftercare

12.30 Respite